Memorable Quotations of
Franklin D. Roosevelt

Memorable Quotations of

Franklin D. Roosevelt

———•◦⤫◦•———

Compiled by

E. Taylor Parks

&

Lois F. Parks

Thomas Y. Crowell Company

New York / Established 1834

Foreword

No one-volume compilation of excerpts from the speeches and public papers of Franklin D. Roosevelt can pretend to be exhaustive. The limited aim of this work is twofold: (1) to give the flavor of the man and his philosophy, and (2) to provide a ready reference to the best expressions of his views and programs in the various fields of public interest—largely for the period from 1928 to 1945.

There has been no effort to select all that Mr. Roosevelt said or wrote on any one subject, nor have we consciously attempted to point up either consistencies or inconsistencies in his views or policies. We have sought to choose quotations concerned with the vital problems of his era and those that possess the most enduring qualities.

In general, the arrangement of the excerpts is chronological under topics which were selected after a wide sampling of Mr. Roosevelt's speeches. The few departures from this arrangement within categories seemed desirable as a means of bringing close together items relating to a particular aspect of a larger topic. The final choice and order of topics were the result of the adoption of a framework for the excerpts that would be most useful for the reader.

The very nature of a compilation makes necessary the tearing of sentences and paragraphs from their original context. In regrouping these under subject headings, extreme care has been exercised to prevent distortion of their intent or meaning. Omissions within the texts and editorial insertions have been indicated in accordance with standard practices.

Excerpts that might logically fall under more than one category have been placed according to their chief emphasis and, in general, not repeated. The grouping of related topics in the text and the alphabetical subject headings in the index should be adequate aids for finding special items or all the material included on a particular subject. The quotations have been taken from official sources, either government publications or original White House releases. No attempt has been made to achieve uniformity of capitalization or punctuation in the official texts.

We have found Judge Samuel I. Rosenman's compilation *The Public Papers and Addresses of Franklin D. Roosevelt* (Volumes I–V, Random House; VI–IX, The Macmillan Company; X–XIII, Harper and Brothers, 1938–1950) most useful in checking the texts of the quotations, and the dates, places, and occasions for the delivery of many of the speeches. For assistance in the early stages of the preparation of this volume, we are greatly indebted to Mrs. Sylvia C. Levy.

E. TAYLOR PARKS
LOIS F. PARKS

Arlington, Virginia

Contents

Part II
The United States in an Interdependent World

From Unreasoning Fear to Active Faith

. . . the only thing we have to fear is fear itself—nameless, unreasoning, unjustified terror which paralyzes needed efforts to convert retreat into advance.

First Inaugural Address, March 4, 1933

We have always held to the hope, the belief, the conviction, that there is a better life, a better world, beyond the horizon.

Address at Dayton, Ohio, Oct. 12, 1940

The only limit to our realization of tomorrow will be our doubts of today. Let us move forward with strong and active faith.

Final Message, April 11, 1945

Memorable Quotations of
Franklin D. Roosevelt

Part I

The American
Way of Life

I

Constitutional Democracy

1 / The safety of the system of representative government is in the last analysis based on two essentials: first, that at frequent periods the voters must choose a new Congress and a new President; and second, that this choice must be made freely, that is to say without any undue force against, or influence over, the voter in the expression of his personal and sincere opinion.

That, after all, is the greatest difference between what we know as democracy, and those other forms of government which, though they seem new to us, are essentially old—for they revert to those systems of concentrated self-perpetuating power against which the representatives of the democratic system were successfully striving many centuries ago.

Today, with many other democracies, the United States will give no encouragement to the belief that our processes are outworn, or that we will approvingly watch the return of forms of government which for two thousand years have proved their tyranny and their instability alike.

With the direct control of the free choosing of public servants by a free electorate, our Constitution has proved that our type of government cannot long remain in the hands of any who seek personal aggrandisement for selfish ends, whether they act as individuals, as classes, or as groups.

It is therefore in the spirit of our system that our elections are positive in their mandate, rather than passive in their acquiescence. Many other nations envy us the enthusiasm, the attacks, the wild overstatements, the falsehood gaily intermingled with the truth that mark our general elections. Yes, they envy us because all of these things are promptly followed by acquiescence in the result and a return to calmer waters as soon as the ballots are counted.

We celebrate today the completion of the building of the constitutional house. But one essential was lacking—for the house had to be made habitable. And even in the period of the building, those who put stone upon stone, those who voted to accept it from the hands of the builders knew that life within the house needed other things for its inhabitants. Without those things, indeed, they could never be secure in their tenure, happy in their toil or in their rest.

And so there came about that tacit understanding that to the Constitution would be added a Bill of Rights. Well and truly did the first Congress of the United States fulfill that first unwritten pledge; and the personal guarantees thus given to our individual citizens have established, we trust for all time, what has become as ingrained in our American natures as the free elective choice of our representatives itself.

In that Bill of Rights lies another vast chasm between our representative democracy and those reversions to personal rule which have characterized these recent years.

Jury trial: do the people of our own land ever stop to compare that blessed right of ours with some processes of trial and punishment which of late have reincarnated the so-called "justice" of the dark ages?

The taking of private property without due compensation: would we willingly abandon our security against that in the face of the events of recent years?

The right to be safe against unwarrantable searches and seizures: read your newspapers and rejoice that our firesides and our households are still safe.

Freedom to assemble and petition the Congress for a redress of grievances: the mail and the telegraph bring daily proof to every Senator and every Representative that that right is at the height of an unrestrained popularity.

Freedom of speech: yes, that, too, is unchecked for never in all history has there been so much of it on every side of every subject. It is indeed a freedom which, because of the mildness of our laws of libel and slander, goes unchecked except by the good sense of the American people. Any person is constitutionally entitled to criticize and call to account the highest and the lowest in the land—save only in one exception. For be it noted that the Constitution of the United States itself protects Senators and Representatives and provides that "for any speech or debate in either House they shall not be questioned in any other place." And that immunity is most carefully not extended to either the Chief Justice of the United States or the President.

Freedom of the press: I take it that no sensible man or woman believes that it has been curtailed or threatened or that it should be. The influence of the printed word will always depend on its veracity; and the nation can safely rely on the wise discrimination of a reading public which with the increase in the general education is well able to sort truth from fiction. Representative democracy will never tolerate suppression of true news at the behest of government.

Freedom of religion: that essential of the rights of mankind everywhere goes back also to the origins of representative government. Where democracy is snuffed out, where it is curtailed, there, too, the right to worship God in one's own way is circumscribed or abrogated. Shall we by our passiveness, by our silence, by assuming the attitude of the Levite who pulled his skirts together and passed by on the other side, lend encouragement to those who today persecute religion or deny it?

The answer to that is "no" today, just as in the days of the first Congress of the United States it was "no."

Not for freedom of religion alone does this nation contend by every peaceful means. We believe in the other freedoms of the Bill of Rights, the other freedoms that are inherent in the right of free choice by free men and women. That means democracy to us under the Constitution, not democracy by direct action of the mob; but democracy exercised by representatives chosen by the people themselves.

Address on the 150th anniversary of Congress, Washington, D.C., March 4, 1939

2 / The United States Constitution has proved itself the most marvelously elastic compilation of rules of government ever written. Drawn up at a time when the population of this country was practically confined to a fringe along our Atlantic coast, combining into one nation for the first time scattered and feeble states, newly released from the autocratic control of the English government, its preparation involved innumerable compromises between the different commonwealths. Fortunately for the stability of our nation, it was already apparent that the vastness of our territory presented geographical and climatic differences which gave to the states wide differences in the nature of their industry, their agriculture and their commerce. Already the New England states had turned toward shipping and manufacturing, while the South was devoting itself almost exclusively to the easier agriculture which a milder climate permitted. Thus, it was clear to the framers of our Constitution that the greatest possible liberty of self-government must be given to each state, and that any national administration attempting to make all laws for the whole nation, such as was wholly practical in Great Britain, would inevitably result at some future time in a dissolution of the Union itself.

Radio address on the proper relationship between federal and state governments, March 2, 1930

3 / The task of statesmanship has always been the redefinition of these rights [of the individual] in terms of a changing and growing social order. New conditions impose new requirements upon goverment and those who conduct government. . . .

Every man [in the United States] has a right to life; and this means that he has also a right to make a comfortable living. He may by sloth or crime decline to exercise that right; but it may not be denied him. We have no actual famine or dearth; our industrial and agricultural mechanism can produce enough and to spare. Our government, formal and informal, political and economic, owes to everyone an avenue to possess himself of a portion of that plenty sufficient for his needs, through his own work.

Every man has a right to his own property; which means a right to be assured, to the fullest extent attainable, in the safety of his savings. By no other means can men carry the burdens of those parts of life which, in the nature of things, afford no chance of labor; childhood, sickness, old age. In all thought of property, this right is paramount; all other property rights must yield to it. If, in accord with this principle, we must restrict the operations of the speculator, the manipulator, even the financier, I believe we must accept the restriction as needful, not to hamper individualism but to protect it. . . .

We know that individual liberty and individual happiness mean nothing unless both are ordered in the sense that one man's meat is not another man's poison. We know that the old "rights of personal competency," the right to read, to think, to speak, to choose and live a mode of life, must be respected at all hazards. We know that liberty to do anything which deprives others of those elemental rights is outside the protection of any compact; and that government in this regard is the maintenance of a balance, within which every individual may have a place if he will take it; in which every individual may find safety if he wishes it; in which every individual may attain such power as his ability permits, consistent with his assuming the accompanying responsibility.

Campaign address, San Francisco, Calif., Sept. 23, 1932

4 / Our Constitution is so simple and practical that it is possible always to meet extraordinary needs by changes in emphasis and arrangement without loss of essential form. That is why our constitutional system has proved itself the most superbly enduring political mechanism the modern world has produced. It has met every stress of vast expansion of territory, of foreign wars, of bitter internal strife, of world relations.

First Inaugural Address, March 4, 1933

5 / We have undertaken a new order of things; yet we progress to it under the framework and in the spirit and intent of the American Constitution. . . . We seek it through tested liberal traditions, through processes which retain all of the deep essentials of that republican form of representative government first given to a troubled world by the United States.

State of the Union Message, Jan. 4, 1935

6 / I believe that democratic government in this country can do all the things which common-sense people, seeing that picture as a whole, have the right to expect. I believe that these things can be done under the Constitution, without the surrender of a single one of the civil and religious liberties it was intended to safeguard.

And I am determined that under the Constitution these things *shall* be done. . . .

Let me put the real situation in the simplest terms. The present government of the United States has never taken away and never will take away any liberty from any minority, unless it be a minority which so abuses its liberty as to do positive and definite harm to its neighbors constituting the majority. But the government of the United States refuses to forget that the Bill of Rights was put into the Constitution not only to protect minorities against intolerance of majorities, but to protect majorities against the enthronement of minorities.

Nothing would so surely destroy the substance of what the Bill of Rights protects than its perversion to prevent social progress. The surest protection of the individual and of minorities is that fundamental tolerance and feeling for fair play which the Bill of Rights assumes. But tolerance and fair play would disappear here as it has in some other lands if the great mass of people were denied confidence in their justice, their security and their self-respect. Desperate people in other lands surrendered their liberties when freedom came merely to mean humiliation and starvation. The crisis of 1933 should make us understand that.

On this solemn anniversary I ask that the American people rejoice in the wisdom of their Constitution.

I ask that they guarantee the effectiveness of each of its parts by living by the Constitution as a *whole*.

I ask that they have faith in its ultimate capacity to work out the problems of democracy, but that they justify that faith by making it work now rather than twenty years from now.

I ask that they give their fealty to the Constitution *itself* and not to its misinterpreters.

I ask that they exalt the glorious simplicity of its purposes rather than a century of complicated legalism.

I ask that majorities and minorities subordinate intolerance and power alike to the common good of all.

For us the Constitution is a common bond, without bitterness, for those who see America as Lincoln saw it, "the last, best hope of earth."

So we revere it—not because it is old but because it is ever new—not in the worship of its past alone but in the faith of the living who keep it young, now and in the years to come.

Radio address on the 150th anniversary of the Constitution, Washington, D.C., Sept. 17, 1937

7 / In the framework of government which had been devised, and in the early years of its administration, it is of enormous significance to us today that those early leaders successfully planned for such use of the Constitution as would fit it to a constantly expanding nation. That the original framework was capable of expansion from its application to thirteen states with less than 4,000,000 people to . . . forty-eight states with more than 130,000,000 people, is the best tribute to the vision of the Fathers. In this it stands unique in the whole history of the world, for no other form of government has remained unchanged so long and seen, at the same time, any comparable expansion of population or of area.

Address at the opening of the New York World's Fair, April 30, 1939

8 / Once the Constitution was ratified it presented the outline of a form of government. To become a workable instrument of government its words needed men in every succeeding generation to administer it, as great as the men who wrote it.

And the greatest of them have been the men who have sought to make the Constitution workable in the face of the new problems and conditions that have faced the American nation from year to year.

Radio address on Constitution Day, Sept. 17, 1938

9 / What is the State? It is the duly constituted representative of an organized society of human beings, created by them for their mutual protection and well-being. "The State" or "the Government" is but the machinery through which such mutual aid and protection are achieved. The cave man fought for existence unaided or even opposed by his fellow man, but today the humblest citizen of our state stands protected by all the power and strength of his government. Our government is not the master but the creature of the people. The duty of the state toward the citizens is the duty

of the servant to its master. The people have created it; the people, by common consent, permit its continual existence.

> Message to the N.Y. State Legislature on government as the servant of the people,
> Aug. 28, 1931

10 / We cannot call ourselves either wise or patriotic if we seek to escape
the responsibility of remolding government to make it more serviceable to
all the people and more responsive to modern needs.

> Address on the finances and responsibilities of local government, University of
> Virginia, Charlottesville, July 6, 1931

11 / The object of government is the welfare of the people. The liberty of
people to carry on their business should not be abridged unless the larger
interests of the many are concerned. When the interests of the many are
concerned, the interests of the few must yield. It is the purpose of the
government to see not only that the legitimate interests of the few are
protected but that the welfare and rights of the many are conserved. These
are the principles which we must remember in any consideration of this
question. This, I take it, is sound government—not politics. Those are the
essential basic conditions under which government can be of service.

> Campaign address, Portland, Ore., Sept. 21, 1932

12 / The task of government is that of application and encouragement. A
wise government seeks to provide the opportunity through which the best
of individual achievement can be obtained, while at the same time it seeks to
remove such obstruction, such unfairness as springs from selfish human motives. Our common life under our various agencies of government, our laws
and our basic Constitution, exist primarily to protect the individual, to
cherish his rights and to make clear his just principles.

> Address, San Diego Exposition, San Diego, Calif., Oct. 2, 1935

13 / Government has become one of the most important instruments for
the prevention and cure of . . . evils of society. . . . Its concern at the
moment is unabated. It conceives of itself as an instrument through which
social justice may prevail more greatly among men. In the determination of
the standards that make up social justice, the widest discussion is necessary.
In the last analysis, government can be no more than the collective wisdom
of its citizens.

> Message to the Fifth Annual Women's Conference on Current Problems, Oct. 17,
> 1935

14 / The deeper purpose of democratic government is to assist as many of its citizens as possible, especially those who need it most, to improve their conditions of life, to retain all personal liberty which does not adversely affect their neighbors, and to pursue the happiness which comes with security and an opportunity for recreation and culture.

State of the Union Message, Jan. 6, 1937

15 / As intricacies of human relationships increase, so power to govern them also must increase—power to stop evil; power to do good. The essential democracy of our nation and the safety of our people depend not upon the absence of power, but upon lodging it with those whom the people can change or continue at stated intervals through an honest and free system of elections.

Second Inaugural Address, Jan. 20, 1937

16 / Majority rule must be preserved as the safeguard of both liberty and civilization. Under it property can be secure; under it abuses can end; under it order can be maintained—and all of this for the simple, cogent reason that to the average of our citizenship can be brought a life of greater opportunity, of greater security, of greater happiness.

Address on traditional American democracy, Roanoke Island, N.C., Aug. 18, 1937

17 / [Americans] do not look on government as an interloper in their affairs. On the contrary, they regard it as the most effective form of organized self-help.

Radio address (Fireside Chat) announcing a call for a special session of Congress, Oct. 12, 1937

18 / History proves that dictatorships do not grow out of strong and successful governments, but out of weak and helpless ones. If by democratic methods people get a government strong enough to protect them from fear and starvation, their democracy succeeds; but if they do not, they grow impatient. Therefore, the only sure bulwark of continuing liberty is a government strong enough to protect the interests of the people, and a people strong enough and well enough informed to maintain its sovereign control over its government.

Radio address (Fireside Chat) on the economic situation, April 14, 1938

19 / The efficiency of our system of government is not as great as that of the corporate state, because there are delays and compromises which are

inherent in any democracy. The Executive, properly, cannot pass laws; these have to be worked out in conjunction with the Legislature, called the Congress. And in working them out, it takes a long time for them to pass, sometimes, at the least, several months and, at the most, a good many years.

And then after that has been done and your legislation, through the process of compromise, has been passed, you still have another place to go— and that is the courts. . . .

The delay is because of the compromise necessary in working things out constitutionally among the three different agencies. There are a lot of people in this country who object to that time lag and, unthinkingly, play into the hands of the people who advocate the corporate state.

Press conference, Hyde Park, N.Y., July 5, 1940

20 / The democratic form of government works slowly. There always exists in a democratic society a large group which, quite naturally, champs at the bit over the slowness of democracy; and that is why it is right for us who believe in democracy to keep the democratic processes progressive— in other words, moving forward with the advances in civilization. That is why it is dangerous for democracy to stop moving forward because any period of stagnation increases the numbers of those who demand action and action now.

There are, therefore, two distinct dangers to democracy. There is the peril from those who seek the fulfillment of fine ideals at a pace that is too fast for the machinery of the modern body politic to function—people who by insistence on too great speed foster an oligarchic form of government such as communism, or naziism, or fascism.

The other group, which presents an equal danger, is composed of that small minority which complains that the democratic processes are inefficient as well as being too slow, people who would have the whole of government put into the hands of a little group of those who have proved their efficiency in lines of specialized science or specialized private business, but who do not see the picture as a whole. They equally, and in most cases unconsciously too, are in effect advocating the oligarchic form of government—communism, or naziism, or fascism.

Radio address to the New York *Herald Tribune* Forum, Oct. 26, 1939

21 / The American form of government [is] a three horse team provided by the Constitution to the American people so that their field might be plowed. The three horses are, of course, the three branches of government —the Congress, the Executive and the Courts. Two of the horses are pulling in unison today; the third is not. Those who have intimated that the President of the United States is trying to drive that team overlook the simple

fact that the President, as Chief Executive, is himself one of the three horses.

It is the American people themselves who are in the driver's seat.

It is the American people themselves who want the furrow plowed.

It is the American people themselves who expect the third horse to pull in unison with the other two.

Radio address (Fireside Chat) on reorganization of the judiciary, March 9, 1937

22 / We are, fortunately, building a strong and permanent tie between the Legislative and Executive branches of the government. The letter of the Constitution wisely declared a separation, but the impulse of common purpose declares a union. In this spirit we join once more in serving the American people.

State of the Union Message, Jan. 3, 1934

23 / The Presidency carries with it, for the time being, the leadership of a political party as well. But the Presidency carries with it a far higher obligation than this—the duty of analyzing and setting forth national needs and ideals which transcend and cut across all lines of party affiliation.

Radio message to the Young Democratic Clubs of America, Aug. 24, 1935

24 / Many unthinking people have inveighed against the Congress in every generation of our republic, little realizing that they are striking at the very fabric of our Constitution. If they would but think for a moment, they would realize that if we were to eliminate the Congress of the United States, we would automatically cease to be a republic.

The real purpose of the Constitution was based on the rightful assumption that the President and the Congress would be sufficiently right-minded, sufficiently practical and sufficiently patriotic to make every effort to cooperate the one with the other.

Campaign address, New York City, Nov. 3, 1932

25 / The function of Congress is to decide what has to be done and to select the appropriate agency to carry out its will. To this policy it has strictly adhered. The only thing that has been happening has been to designate the President as the agency to carry out certain of the purposes of the Congress. This was constitutional and in keeping with the past American tradition.

Radio address (Fireside Chat) on achievements and plans of the new administration, May 7, 1933

26 / It would be a great deal better for the government as a whole if Congress could keep in very close touch with the operations of the administrative branch of the government right straight through the year. The custom in the past has been for Congress, every once in so often, to conduct an investigation which goes back two or three or four or five years. It doesn't do anybody any particular good, because, if the Administration is doing anything it should not do, it would be a great deal better to have it known right away.

Press conference, Dec. 29, 1933

27 / It is the duty of the President to propose and it is the privilege of the Congress to dispose.

Ibid., July 23, 1937

28 / Modern complexities call also for a constant infusion of new blood in the courts, just as it is needed in executive functions of the government and in private business. A lowered mental or physical vigor leads men to avoid an examination of complicated and changed conditions. Little by little, new facts become blurred through old glasses fitted, as it were, for the needs of another generation; older men, assuming that the scene is the same as it was in the past, cease to explore or inquire into the present or the future.

We have recognized this truth in the civil service of the nation and of many states by compelling retirement on pay at the age of seventy. We have recognized it in the Army and Navy by retiring officers at the age of sixty-four. A number of states have recognized it by providing in their constitutions for compulsory retirement of aged judges.

Life tenure of judges, assured by the Constitution, was designed to place the courts beyond temptations or influences which might impair their judgments: it was not intended to create a static judiciary. A constant and systematic addition of younger blood will vitalize the courts and better equip them to recognize and apply the essential concepts of justice in the light of the needs and the facts of an ever-changing world.

It is obvious, therefore, from both reason and experience, that some provision must be adopted, which will operate automatically to supplement the work of older judges and accelerate the work of the court.

Message to Congress recommending the reorganization of the judicial branch of government, Feb. 5, 1937

29 / I want—as all Americans want—an independent judiciary as proposed by the framers of the Constitution. That means a Supreme Court that will

enforce the Constitution as written—that will refuse to amend the Constitution by the arbitrary exercise of judicial power—amendment by judicial say-so. It does not mean a judiciary so independent that it can deny the existence of facts universally recognized. . . .

If by that phrase "packing the Court" it is charged that I wish to place on the bench spineless puppets who would disregard the law and would decide specific cases as I wished them to be decided, I make this answer: that no President fit for his office would appoint, and no Senate of honorable men fit for their office would confirm, that kind of appointees to the Supreme Court.

But if by that phrase the charge is made that I would appoint and the Senate would confirm Justices worthy to sit beside present members of the Court who understand those modern conditions, that I will appoint Justices who will not undertake to over-ride the judgment of the Congress on legislative policy, that I will appoint Justices who will act as Justices and not as legislators—if the appointment of such Justices can be called "packing the Courts," then I say that I and with me the vast majority of the American people favor doing just that thing—now. . . .

This plan of mine is no attack on the Court; it seeks to restore the Court to its rightful and historic place in our system of constitutional government and to have it resume its high task of building anew on the Constitution "a system of living law." The Court itself can best undo what the Court has done.

> Radio address (Fireside Chat) on reorganization of the judiciary, March 9, 1937

30 / The attitude of the Supreme Court toward constitutional questions is entirely changed. Its recent decisions are eloquent testimony of a willingness to collaborate with the two other branches of government to make democracy work.

> Radio address (Fireside Chat) reporting on achievements of his administration, June 24, 1938

31 / Let us never forget that government is *ourselves* and not an alien power over us. The ultimate rulers of our democracy are not a President and senators and congressmen and government officials but the voters of this country.

> Address on popular government, Marietta, Ohio, July 8, 1938

32 / It matters not what political party is in power by the elective will of the people. The government functions for all. And there can be no question

of greater moment or broader effect than the maintenance, strengthening and extension of the merit system established in the competitive principles of the Civil Service Act.

Letter to the National League of Women Voters, St. Louis, Mo., Jan. 16, 1936

33 / Government business, of course, should be performed with the highest economy and efficiency in order that the public may have the best service for which it pays; and the public also is entitled to untrammeled opportunity for employment in the transaction of government business. The merit system has been most effective in this connection, and I would, therefore, urge upon the Congress that all but policy-forming positions be placed within its provisions.

Letter to the Speaker of the House of Representatives recommending extension of the merit system, June 2, 1937

34 / Government servants are more concerned with the public good, and more unselfish in the work they do, than ever before. That is due in large part to the fact that the public as a whole—the rank and file of American citizenship, men and women—are taking more interest in their government than ever before.

Extemporaneous remarks on solving current problems through democratic processes, Casper, Wyo., Sept. 24, 1937

35 / If a government is to be prudent its taxes must produce ample revenues without discouraging enterprise; and if it is to be just it must distribute the burden of taxes equitably. . . .

Wealth in the modern world does not come merely from individual effort; it results from a combination of individual effort and of the manifold uses to which the community puts that effort. . . .

Message to Congress on tax methods and policies, June 19, 1935

36 / Taxes, after all, are the dues that we pay for the privileges of membership in an organized society.

As society becomes more civilized, government—national, state and local government—is called on to assume more obligations to its citizens. The privileges of membership in a civilized society have vastly increased in modern times.

Campaign address, Worcester, Mass., Oct. 21, 1936

37 / The accumulation of surplus in corporations controlled by taxpayers with large incomes is encouraged by the present freedom of undistributed corporate income from surtaxes. Since stockholders are the beneficial owners of both distributed and undistributed corporate income, the aim, as a matter of fundamental equity, should be to seek equality of tax burden on all corporate income whether distributed or withheld from the beneficial owners. As the law now stands our corporate taxes dip too deeply into the shares of corporate earnings going to stockholders who need the disbursement of dividends; while the shares of stockholders who can afford to leave earnings undistributed escape current surtaxes altogether.

This method of evading existing surtaxes constitutes a problem as old as the income tax law itself. Repeated attempts by the Congress to prevent this form of evasion have not been successful. The evil has been a growing one. It has now reached disturbing proportions from the standpoint of the inequality it represents and of its serious effect on the federal revenue. Thus the Treasury estimates that, during the calendar year 1936, over four and one-half billion dollars of corporate income will be withheld from stockholders. If this undistributed income were distributed, it would be added to the income of stockholders and there taxed as is other personal income. But, as matters now stand, it will be withheld from stockholders by those in control of these corporations. In one year alone, the government will be deprived of revenues amounting to over one billion, three hundred million dollars.

Message to Congress emphasizing the effect of tax evasion on federal revenue, March 3, 1936

38 / It is human nature to argue that this or that tax is responsible for every ill. It is human nature on the part of those who pay graduated taxes to attack all taxes based on the principle of ability to pay. These are the same complainants who for a generation blocked the imposition of a graduated income tax. They are the same complainants who would impose the type of flat sales tax which places the burden of government more on those least able to pay and less on those most able to pay.

Our conclusion must be that while proven hardships should be corrected, they should not be corrected in such a way as to restore abuses already terminated or to shift a greater burden to the less fortunate.

State of the Union Message, Jan. 3, 1938

39 / You cannot borrow your way out of debt: but you can invest your way into a sounder future.

Address, Atlanta, Ga., Nov. 29, 1935

40 / Let us talk about the debt in businessmen's terms.

In the first place, a nation's debt, like the deposit liability of a bank, must be considered in relation to its assets.

A large part of the government debt is offset by debts owed to the government—loans of many kinds made on a business basis by the R.F.C. and the Farm Credit Administration, for instance, and now being repaid on schedule. These assets are just as sound as the loans made by the bankers of the country.

Another portion of the debt is invested in federally owned enterprises, like Boulder Dam, which . . . will pay out, principal and interest, over a period of years.

A third part of the debt has been invested in works like flood control dams and levees, to save us from heavy future losses. They will pay for themselves in a very few years by eliminating annual property damage which each year has run into hundreds of millions—pay by the saving of taxable values which otherwise would have floated off down stream.

The next thing to remember about the debt is that Government, like businessmen, is investing in order to create a higher volume of business income and, therefore, a bigger net yield for government. National income will be greater tomorrow than it is today because Government has had the courage to borrow idle capital and put idle labor to work. . . .

Our national debt after all is an internal debt owed not only *by* the nation but *to* the nation. If our children have to pay interest on it they will pay that interest to *themselves*. A reasonable internal debt will not impoverish our children. . . .

Address before the American Retail Federation, Washington, D.C., May 22, 1939

41 / It should be borne in mind that our national debt results from wars and the economic upheavals following war. These conditions are not of our own making. They have been forced upon us. The national debt of almost all nations would be far lower today if competitive armaments had not existed during the past quarter of a century. If this war should be followed, as I hope it will, by peace in a world of good neighbors, then the complete elimination of competitive armaments will become possible. Only in such a world can economic stability be restored.

Annual budget message to Congress, Jan. 3, 1941

2

Traditions and Ideals

1 / The most precious of our heritage—high ideals, noble character, devotion to causes for communal betterment and enrichment of its intellectual and spiritual life—grow richer with age and contemplation.

Letter to the Society of the Genessee on its 35th annual reunion, Jan. 19, 1934

2 / We in this country are upholders of the ideal of democracy in the government of man. We believe with heart and soul that in the long struggle of the human race to attain an orderly society the democratic form of government is the highest achievement. All of our hopes have their basis in the democratic ideal.

Letter to the Eighth National Eucharistic Congress, New Orleans, La., Oct. 1, 1938

3 / It is a good thing to demand liberty for ourselves and for those who agree with us, but it is a better thing and rarer thing to give liberty to others who do not agree with us.

Radio address on tercentenary of the founding of Maryland, Nov. 22, 1933

4 / I am not for a return to that definition of liberty under which for many years a free people were being gradually regimented into the service of the privileged few. I prefer . . . that broader definition of liberty under which we are moving forward to greater freedom, to greater security for the average man than he has ever known before in the history of America.

Radio address (Fireside Chat) on the record of his administration, Sept. 30, 1934

13 / To recognize national unity, to hold it above all else, seeing that upon it depends our common welfare, is just another way to say that we have patriotism. . . .

National unity is as essential in time of peace as in time of war. If this country is worth living in, if this flag of ours is worth living under, if our social order means anything to us, then this country of ours is worth defending every day and every year of the life of every individual one of us.

Address before the American Legion convention, Chicago, Ill., Oct. 2, 1933

14 / I sometimes think that the saving grace of America lies in the fact that the overwhelming majority of Americans are possessed of two great qualities—a sense of humor and a sense of proportion.

Address on the bicentennial celebration of the founding of Georgia, Savannah, Nov. 18, 1933

15 / Self-help and self-control are the essence of the American tradition.

State of the Union Message, Jan. 3, 1934

16 / We are starting something absolutely new, something in which we have very little experience to fall back on, something that has to be developed through what I call evolution. When people talk to you about the word "revolution" in this country, you tell them that they have one letter too many in the word.

Informal speech at the Subsistence Homes Exhibition, Washington, D.C., April 24, 1934

17 / We . . . have come to a realization of the pregnant fact that the accustomed order of our formerly established lives does not suffice to meet the perils and the problems which we are compelled to face. Again, mere survival calls for new pioneering on our part.

Some portion of the blood of the Colonists and the blood of the pioneers who worked their way, through the generations, across the mountains and across the plains and again across the mountains until they came to the Pacific—that blood is present in very large part in the veins of millions of our people. More than that, the example and the spirit of these earlier Americans is present in the mind and the heart of all our population.

Address at the George Rogers Clark celebration, Harrodsburg, Ky., Nov. 16, 1934

18 / I, for one, do not believe that the era of the pioneer is at an end; I only believe that the area for pioneering has changed. The period of geographical pioneering is largely finished. But, my friends, the period of social

pioneering is only at its beginning. And make no mistake about it—the same qualities of heroism and faith and vision that were required to bring the forces of nature into subjection will be required—in even greater measure —to bring under proper control the forces of modern society. There is a task which, for importance and for magnitude, calls for the best that you and I have to offer.

Address to the Young Democratic Club, Baltimore, Md., April 13, 1936

19 / We shall ever find inspiration and guidance in the achievement of the American pioneers, not merely those who founded the nation but those who extended its boundaries from ocean to ocean. . . . The frontier . . . has forever passed; but it has left a permanent imprint upon our political life and our social outlook. . . . We still find inspiration for the work before us, in the old spirit which meant achievement through self-reliance; a willingness to lend a hand to the fellow down in his luck through no fault of his own. Upon those principles our democracy was reborn a century ago; upon those principles alone will it endure.

Address on the centennial of Arkansas's admission into the Union, Little Rock, June 10, 1936

20 / Human personality is something sacred. It enjoys the light of reason and liberty. It grows by rising above material things and wedding itself to spiritual ideals. Our social order is worthy of human beings only in so far as it recognizes the inherent value of human personality. Our cities, our states and our nations exist not for themselves but for men and women. We cannot be satisfied with any form of society in which human personality is submerged.

Letter to the National Conference of Social Work, Atlantic City, N.J., May 23, 1936

21 / We know that equality of individual ability has never existed and never will, but we do insist that equality of opportunity still must be sought. We know that equality of local justice is, alas, not yet an established fact; this also is a goal we must and do seek.

Address on the centennial of Arkansas's admission into the Union, Little Rock, June 10, 1936

22 / The freedoms that we must and will protect in the United States are the freedoms which will make the individual paramount in a true democracy.

Letter to the Economics Club of New York, New York City, Dec. 2, 1940

23 / The only rule we have ever put up with is the rule of the majority. That is the only rule we ever will put up with. Spelled with a small "d" we are all democrats.

In some places in the world the tides are running against democracy. But our faith has not been unsettled. We believe in democracy because of our traditions. But we believe in it even more because of our experience.

Here in the United States we have been a long time at the business of self-government. The longer we are at it the more certain we become that we can continue to govern ourselves, that progress is on the side of the majority rule, that if mistakes are to be made we prefer to make them ourselves and to do our own correcting.

Final campaign radio address, Nov. 2, 1936

24 / Cooperation . . . means discipline, not meticulous though unthinking obedience to guardroom technique, nor blind mass cooperation of a Macedonian phalanx or the close-order attack. Discipline is the well-tempered working together of many minds and will, each preserving independent judgment, but all prepared to sink individual differences and egotisms to attain an objective which is accepted and understood. When men are taken far apart by mechanics and specialization, teamwork is far more essential than when they are close together; for it must be teamwork of the mind as well as of the body.

Commencement address, U.S. Military Academy, West Point, N.Y., June 12, 1939

25 / Democracy can thrive only when it enlists the devotion of those whom Lincoln called the common people. Democracy can hold that devotion only when it adequately respects their dignity by so ordering society as to assure to the masses of men and women reasonable security and hope for themselves and for their children.

Acceptance speech, Democratic National Convention, Chicago, Ill., July 19, 1940

26 / The family still remains the basis of society as we know it, and it must be preserved as an institution if our democracy is to be perpetuated. If we lose the home we are in grave risk of undermining all those other elements of stability and strength which contribute to the well-being of our national life.

Radio address on Mobilization for Human Needs, Washington, D.C., Oct. 9, 1939

27 / We have been extending to our national life the old principle of home community—that no individual, no family, has a right to do things which

hurt the neighbors. Many centuries ago that was a tenet of the old English common law and its development has been constant and consistent. It is unfair to our neighbors if we allow our cattle to roam on their land. It is unfair to our neighbors if we maintain a pigsty on Main Street. It became unfair to our neighbors if we sought to make unreasonable profit from a monopoly in a service such as electricity or gas or railroad tickets which they had to use. It became unfair to our neighbors if we tried to hire their children at starvation wages and long hours of work.

Many years ago we went even further in saying that the government would place increasing taxes on increasing profits because very large profits were, of course, made at the expense of the neighbors and should, to some extent at least, be used for the benefit of the neighbors.

The extension of the idea of not hurting the neighbors is recognized today as no infringement on the guarantee of personal liberty to the individual because, for example, it is no more a restriction to tell a man that he must pay adequate wages than it is to tell a man that he must not hire child labor, or that he must not maintain a nuisance.

Address, Vassar College, Poughkeepsie, N.Y., Aug. 26, 1933

28 / We still believe in the community; and things are going to advance in this country exactly in proportion to the community effort. This is not regimentation—it is community rugged individualism. It means no longer the kind of rugged individualism that allows an individual to do this, that or the other thing that will hurt his neighbors. He is forbidden to do that from now on—and it is a mighty good thing. But he is going to be encouraged in every known way from the National Capitol and the state capitol and the county seat to use his individualism in cooperation with his neighbor's individualism so that he and his neighbors may improve their lot in life.

Informal speech on development of the Tennessee Valley, Tupelo, Miss., Nov. 18, 1934

29 / The good neighbor is not just the man who lives next door to you. The objective includes the relationship not between you and him alone, but it includes the relationship between your family and his; it extends to all the people who live in the same block; it spreads to all the people who live in the same city and the same county and the same state; and most important of all for the future of our nation, it must and shall extend to all your neighbors, to your fellow citizens in all the states and in all the regions that make up the nation.

Address on receiving an honorary degree, Rollins College, Winter Park, Fla., March 23, 1936

3

Political Processes

1 / Long before Jackson became President, the two-party system of government had become firmly entrenched as a basic principle of American political life. It had shown its value as a method of obtaining free and open discussion of public issues, formulating new policies to meet new conditions, and fixing responsibility in affairs of government as an indispensable part of our conception of free elections.

The dictators cannot seem to realize that here in America our people can maintain two parties, and at the same time maintain an inviolate and indivisible nation. The totalitarian mentality is too narrow to comprehend the greatness of a people who can be divided in party allegiance at *election* time, but remain united in devotion to their country and to the ideals of democracy at *all* times.

In dictatorships there can be no party divisions. For all men must think as they are told, speak as they are told, write as they are told, live— and die—as they are told. In those countries the nation is not above the party, as with us; the party is above the nation; the party *is* the nation.

Every common man and woman is forced to walk the straight and narrow path of the party line, as drawn by the dictator himself.

In our country, disagreements among us are expressed in the polling place. In the dictatorships, disagreements are suppressed in the concentration camp.

Radio address to Jackson Day dinners, from Fort Lauderdale, Fla., March 29, 1941

2 / We Americans have found party organizations to be useful, and indeed necessary, in the crystallization of opinion and in the demarcation of issues. It is true that I have received many honors at the hands of one

of our great parties. It is nevertheless true that in the grave questions that confront the United States at this hour, I, as President of the United States, must and will consider our common problems first, foremost and pre-eminently from the American point of view.

Address, Jackson Day dinner, Washington, D.C., Jan. 8, 1936

3 / The genius of America is stronger than any candidate or any party. . . . The fate of America cannot depend on any one man. The greatness of America is grounded in principles and not on any single personality. I, for one, shall remember that, even as President. Unless by victory we can accomplish a greater unity toward liberal effort, we shall have done little indeed. . . . You vote according to your common sense and your calm judgment after hearing each party set forth its program. To you I say that the strength of this independent thought is the great contribution of the American political system.

Campaign address, New York City, Nov. 5, 1932

4 / The Democratic party of itself cannot elect a President. The Republican party is in the same fix. This is fortunate for all of us, for it means that no party can continue in power unless its policies are such as to add to its basic strength the ten or more millions of votes that are cast for ideas and ideals, rather than because of the emblem at the top of the ticket.

Letter to the Young Democratic Clubs of America, Washington, D.C., April 19, 1939

5 / I do believe that the common denominator of our great men in public life has not been mere allegiance to one political party, but the disinterested devotion with which they have tried to serve the whole country, and the relative unimportance they have ascribed to politics, compared with the paramount importance of government.

By their motives may ye know them!

The relative importance of politics and government is something not always easy to see when you are in the frontline trenches of political organization. . . .

I have come to the conclusion that the closer people are to what may be called the front lines of government, of all kinds—local and state and federal—the easier it is to see the immediate underbrush, the individual tree trunks of the moment and to forget the nobility, the usefulness and the wide extent of the forest itself. . . .

They forget that back of the jockeying for party position—back of the party generals—hundreds of thousands of men and women—officers and privates, foremen and workmen—have to get a job done, have to put in day after day of honest, sincere work in carrying out the multitudinous functions that the policy-makers in modern democracy assign to administrators in modern democracy.

People tell me that I hold to party ties less tenaciously than most of my predecessors in the Presidency, that I have too many people in my administration who are not active party Democrats. I admit the soft impeachment.

My answer is that I do believe in party organization, but only in proportion to its proper place in government. I believe party organization —the existence of at least two effectively opposing parties—is a sound and necessary part of our American system; and that, effectively organized nationally and by states and by localities, parties are good instruments for the purpose of presenting and explaining issues, of drumming up interest in elections, and of improving the breed of candidates for public office.

But the future lies with those wise political leaders who realize that the great public is interested more in government than in politics; that the independent vote in this country has been steadily on the increase, at least for the past generation; that vast numbers of people consider themselves normally adherents of one party and still feel perfectly free to vote for one or more candidates of another party, come election day, and on the other hand, sometimes uphold party principles even when precinct captains decide to "take a walk." . . .

Most people, who are not on the actual firing line of the moment, have come to attach major importance only to the motives behind the leaders of the past. To them it matters, on the whole, very little what party label American statesmen bore, or what mistakes they made in smaller things, so long as they did the big job that their times demanded be done.

Address, Jackson Day dinner, Washington, D.C., Jan. 8, 1940

6 / The great social phenomenon of this depression, unlike others before it, is that it has produced but a few of the disorderly manifestations that too often attend upon such times.

Wild radicalism has made few converts, and the greatest tribute that I can pay to my countrymen is that in these days of crushing want there persists an orderly and hopeful spirit on the part of the millions of our people who have suffered so much. To fail to offer them a new chance is not only to betray their hopes but to misunderstand their patience.

To meet by reaction that danger of radicalism is to invite disaster. Reaction is no barrier to the radical. It is a challenge, a provocation. The way to meet that danger is to offer a workable program of reconstruction. . . .

This, and this only, is a proper protection against blind reaction on the one hand and an improvised, hit-or-miss, irresponsible opportunism on the other.

Acceptance speech, Democratic National Convention, Chicago, Ill., July 2, 1932

7 / We who seek to go forward must ever guard ourselves against a danger which history teaches. More than ever, we cherish the elective form of democratic government, but progress under it can easily be retarded by disagreements that relate to methods and to detail rather than to the broad objectives upon which we are agreed. It is as if all of us were united in the pursuit of a common goal, but that each and every one of us were marching along a separate road of our own. If we insist on choosing different roads, most of us will not reach our common destination. The reason that the forces of reaction so often defeat the forces of progress is that the Tories of the world are agreed and united in standing still on the same old spot and, therefore, never run the danger of getting lost on divergent trails. One might remark in passing that one form of standing still on the same spot consists in agreeing to condemn all progress and letting it go at that.

Radio message to the Young Democratic Clubs of America, Aug. 24, 1935

8 / The true conservative is the man who has a real concern for injustices and takes thought against the day of reckoning. The true conservative seeks to protect the system of private property and free enterprise by correcting such injustices and inequalities as arise from it. The most serious threat to our institutions comes from those who refuse to face the need for change. Liberalism becomes the protection for the far-sighted conservative.

Address before the Democratic state convention, Syracuse, N.Y., Sept. 29, 1936

9 / Wise and prudent men—intelligent conservatives—have long known that in a changing world worthy institutions can be conserved only by adjusting them to the changing time. In the words of the great essayist, "The voice of great events is proclaiming to us. Reform if you would preserve."

I am that kind of conservative because I am that kind of liberal.

Ibid.

10 / Conservatives admit that all of our recent policies are not wrong and that many of them should be retained—but their eyes are on the present;

they give no thought for the future and thus, without meaning to, are failing to solve even current social and economic problems by declining to consider the needs of tomorrow. Radicals of all kinds have some use to humanity because they have at least the imagination to think up many kinds of answers to problems even though their answers are wholly impracticable of fulfillment in the immediate future.

> Letter to the convention of the Young Democratic Clubs of America, Pittsburgh, Pa., Aug. 8, 1939

11 / Liberals . . . are those who, unlike the radicals who want to tear up everything by the roots and plant new and untried seeds, desire to use the existing plants of civilization, to select the best of them, to water them and make them grow—not only for the present use of mankind, but also for the use of generations to come. That is why I call myself a liberal, and that is why . . . an overwhelming majority of younger men and women throughout the United States are on the liberal side of things.

> *Ibid.*

12 / Years ago President Wilson told me a story. He said that the greatest problem that the head of a progressive democracy had to face was not the criticism of reactionaries or the attacks of those who would set up some other form of government, but rather to reconcile and unite progressive liberals themselves. The overwhelming majority of liberals all seek the same end, the same ultimate objectives. But because most liberals are able to see beyond the end of their own noses, they are very apt to want to reach their goal by different roads. People who do not want to move forward in the improvement of civilization are perfectly content to stand in one spot, and those people find it easy to remain united in demanding inaction. Liberals, therefore, in order to make their efforts successful, must find common ground and a common road, each making some concession as to form and method in order that all may obtain the substance of what all desire.

> Address on democratic processes, Los Angeles, Calif., Oct. 1, 1935

13 / A few days ago a brilliant newspaper writer came to the White House and asked me to illustrate the difference between a liberal and a conservative. I will condense for you what I told her.

For example, "Mr. A." is a composite conservative. He admitted that in 1933 interest rates charged by private banking to ordinary citizens who wanted to finance a farm or a home were altogether too high; he admitted that there were excesses, sharp practices and abuses in issuing securities and buying and selling stocks; he admitted that the hours of work in his factory and a great many other factories were too long; he admitted that old people, who became destitute through no fault of their own, were a problem; he admitted that national and international economic conditions and speculation made farming and fishing extremely hazardous occupations; and he even admitted that the buying power of farmers and fishermen had not kept pace with the buying power of many other kinds of workers.

But conservative "Mr. A." not only declined to take any lead in solving these problems in cooperation with his government, but found fault with and opposed, openly or secretly, almost every suggestion that was put forward by those who belonged to the liberal school of thought.

"Mr. B.," on the other hand, was the composite of a liberal. He not only agreed with "Mr. A." on the needs and the problems, but he put his shoulder under the load, he gave active study and active support to working out methods, in cooperation with government, for the solving of the problems and the filling of the needs.

"Mr. B." did not claim that the remedies were perfect but he knew that we had to start with something less than perfect in this imperfect world. And, my friends, if we have a government run by the "Mr. A.'s" of this life, it is obvious that the nation will slip behind once more in the march of civilization—bump along from one 1929 crisis to another. Yours is the choice of what kind of a government you want.

Address on liberalism and conservatism, Denton, Md., Sept. 5, 1938

14 / Too many of those who prate about saving democracy are really only interested in saving things as they were. Democracy should concern itself also with things as they ought to be.

I am not talking mere idealism; I am expressing realistic necessity.

Radio address on social justice and economic democracy, Hyde Park, N.Y., Nov. 4, 1938

15 / Extreme Rightists and extreme Leftists ought not to be taken out by us and shot against the wall, for they sharpen the argument, and make us realize the value of the democratic middle course—especially if that middle course, in order to keep up with the times, is, and I quote what I have said before, "just a little bit left of center."

I am reminded of four definitions:

A Radical is a man with both feet firmly planted—in the air.

A Conservative is a man with two perfectly good legs who, however, has never learned to walk forward.

A Reactionary is a somnambulist walking backwards.

A Liberal is a man who uses his legs and his hands at the behest—at the command—of his head.

Radio address to the New York *Herald Tribune* Forum, Oct. 26, 1939

16 / It has been said that some of you are Communists. That is an unpopular term these days. As Americans you have a right to call yourselves Communists. You have a right peacefully and openly to advocate certain ideals of theoretical communism; but as Americans you have not only a right but a sacred duty to confine your advocacy of changes in law to the methods prescribed by the Constitution of the United States—and you have no American right, by act or deed of any kind, to subvert the government and the Constitution of this nation.

Address to the American Youth Congress, Washington, D.C., Feb. 10, 1940

17 / I have not sought, I do not seek, I repudiate the support of any advocate of communism or of any other alien "ism" which would by fair means or foul change our American democracy.

That is my position. It always has been my position. It always will be my position.

Address before the Democratic state convention, Syracuse, N.Y., Sept. 29, 1936

18 / No dictator in history has ever dared to run the gauntlet of a really free election.

Address on the 200th anniversary of the founding of the University of Pennsylvania, Philadelphia, Sept. 20, 1940

19 / You sometimes find something good in the lunatic fringe. In fact, we have got as part of our social and economic government today a whole lot of things which in my boyhood were considered lunatic fringe, and yet they are now part of everyday life.

Press conference, May 30, 1944

20 / I call myself a little left of center.

Ibid., Dec. 9, 1944

21 / The life blood of this republic is the integrity and independence of the electorate. You American farmers and American workmen are entitled,

by all of the fundamental rights that you have acquired in generations of fighting, to a free and untrammeled choice on election day. The politician or employer who tries to deny to you these rights and to use a gospel of fear to blind you to the true facts presented in this campaign is an enemy, not only of fairness and sportsmanship in politics, but the very principles upon which this country has been established. To protect these rights men have suffered and died. The principles they have won in such a bitter fight are chiseled for all the centuries to come on the granite walls of our American system of government. The man who tries, for political or economic advantage, to chip away these rights is an untrustworthy leader in business and politics.

Campaign address, St. Louis, Mo., Oct. 21, 1932

22 / The ballot is the indispensable instrument of a free people. It should be the true expression of their will; and it is intolerable that the ballot should be coerced—whatever the form of coercion, political or economic.

The autocratic will of no man—be he President, or general, or captain of industry—shall ever destroy the sacred right of the people themselves to determine for themselves who shall govern them.

Campaign address, Boston, Mass., Oct. 31, 1932

23 / I must admit that I agree . . . [in] the superior ability of the whole of the voters to pass upon political and social issues in free and unhampered elections, as against the exclusive ability of a smaller group of individuals at the top of the social structure.

Address on the 200th anniversary of the founding of the University of Pennsylvania, Philadelphia, Sept. 20, 1940

24 / Inside the polling booth every American man and woman stands as the equal of every other American man and woman. There they have no superiors. There they have no masters save their own minds and consciences. There they are sovereign American citizens.

Campaign address, Worcester, Mass., Oct. 21, 1936

25 / When you and I stand in line tomorrow for our turn at the polls, we shall stand in a line which reaches back across the entire history of our nation.

Washington stood in that line and Jefferson and Jackson and Lincoln. And in later days Cleveland stood there and Theodore Roosevelt and

Woodrow Wilson. All these—in their day—waited their turn to vote. And rubbing elbows with them—their voting equals—is a long succession of American citizens whose names are not known to history but who, by their vote, helped to make history.

Every man and every woman who has voted in the past has had a hand in the making of the United States of the present. Every man and woman who votes tomorrow will have a hand in the making of the United States of the future. To refuse to vote is to say: "I am not interested in the United States of the future."

We who live in a free America know that our democracy is not perfect. But we are beginning to know also that, in self-government as in many other things, progress comes from experience. People do not become good citizens by mandate. They become good citizens by the exercise of their citizenship and by the discussions, the reading, the campaign give-and-take which help them make up their minds how to exercise that citizenship.

Final campaign radio address, Nov. 2, 1936

26 / All of the great freedoms which form the basis of our American democracy are part and parcel of that concept of free elections, with free expression of political choice between candidates of political parties. For such elections guarantee that there can be no possibility of stifling freedom of speech, freedom of the press and the air, freedom of worship.

These are the eternal principles which are now being threatened by the alliance of dictator nations.

Ours is the responsibility of defending these principles which have come to us as our national heritage. Ours is the responsibility of passing them on—not only intact, but stronger than ever, to all the generations yet to come.

We Americans realize how tenuous would be the existence of our party system, our freedom of elections, our freedom of living, if the doctrines of dictatorship were to prevail. For if they were to prevail, it would not be in Europe alone.

Radio address to Jackson Day dinners, from Fort Lauderdale, Fla., March 29, 1941

27 / When you and I step into the voting booth, we can proudly say: "I am an American, and this vote I am casting is the exercise of my highest privilege and my most solemn duty to my country."

We vote as free men, impelled only by the urgings of our own wisdom and our own conscience.

In our polling places are no storm troopers or secret police to look over our shoulders as we mark our ballots. . . .

It is that right, the right to determine for themselves who should be their own officers of government, that provides for the people the most powerful safeguard of our democracy. The right to place men in office, at definite, fixed dates of election for a specific term, is the right which will keep a free people always free.

Final campaign radio address, Hyde Park, N.Y., Nov. 4, 1940

28 / Nobody will ever deprive the American people of the right to vote except the American people themselves—and the only way they could do that is by not voting.

The continuing health and vigor of our democratic system depends on the public spirit and devotion of its citizens which find expression in the ballot box.

Every man and every woman in this nation—regardless of party—who have the right to register and to vote, and the opportunity to register and to vote, have also the sacred obligation to register and to vote. For the free and secret ballot is the real keystone of our American constitutional system. . . .

It is true that there are many undemocratic defects in voting laws in the various states; and some of these produce injustices which prevent a full and free expression of public opinion.

The right to vote must be open to our citizens irrespective of race, color, or creed—without tax or artificial restriction of any kind. The sooner we get to that basis of political equality, the better it will be for the country as a whole.

Candidates in every part of the United States are now engaged in running for office.

All of us are actuated by a normal desire to win. But, speaking personally, I should be very sorry to be elected President of the United States on a small turnout of voters. And by the same token, if I were to be defeated, I should be much happier to be defeated in a large out-pouring of voters. Then there could not be any question of doubt in anybody's mind as to which way the masses of the American people wanted this election to go.

The free and full exercise of our sacred right and duty to vote is more important than the personal hopes or ambitions of any candidate for any office in the land.

Campaign radio address, White House, Oct. 5, 1944

29 / It seems to me that we are most completely, most loudly, most proudly American around Election Day.

Because it is then that we can assert ourselves—voters and candidates alike. We can assert the most glorious, the most encouraging fact in all the world today—the fact that democracy is alive—and going strong.

We are telling the world that we are free—and we intend to remain free and at peace.

We are free to live and love and laugh.

We face the future with confidence and courage. We are American.

Campaign address, Boston, Mass., Oct. 30, 1940

30 / The Republican leaders have not been content with attacks on me, or my wife, or my sons. No . . . they now include my little dog, Fala. Well, of course, I don't resent attacks, and my family doesn't resent attacks, but Fala *does* resent them. . . . as soon as he learned that the Republican fiction writers in Congress and out had concocted a story that I had left him behind in the Aleutian Islands and had sent a destroyer to find him—at a cost to the taxpayers of two or three, or eight to twenty million dollars— his Scotch soul was furious. . . . I have a right to resent, to object to, libelous statements about my dog.

Address before the International Brotherhood of Teamsters, Washington, D.C., Sept. 23, 1944

4

Public Opinion and the Press

1 / The influence of a handful of political leaders is strong and so is the influence of private corporations when they see an opportunity to get something for nothing; but stronger than all of these put together is the influence of Mr. and Mrs. Average Voter. It may take a good many years to translate this influence of the people of the state into terms of law, but public opinion, when it understands a policy and supports it, is bound to win in the long run.

Radio address on passage of the St. Lawrence Power Development Bill, April 7, 1931

2 / There is no group in America that can withstand the force of an aroused public opinion.

Statement on signing the National Industrial Recovery Act, June 16, 1933

3 / A press association, collecting and disseminating news, enjoys a prominent place and exercises a tremendous influence in its field of operations. That it has functioned always without fear or favor, exercising the responsibilities for clean, factual and intelligent reporting, should be a matter of great pride to its builders, and its world-wide staff of workers. . . .

I personally find high satisfaction in the knowledge that it is possible in this land of ours for anyone to establish a newspaper or a news service and to enjoy the freedom of operation guaranteed by our fathers and which, I am glad to say, still prevails. I am glad, too, that our government never has seen fit to subsidize a newspaper or a news service and I dare to make the prediction that it never will.

> Letter to International News Service, Inc., New York City, April 13, 1934

4 / A government can be no better than the public opinion which sustains it.

> Address, Jackson Day dinner, Washington, D.C., Jan. 8, 1936

5 / The whole structure of democracy rests upon public opinion. Indeed under a government which functions through democratic institutions we are ruled by public opinion. Only through the full and free expression of public opinion can the springs of democracy be renewed and its institutions kept alive and capable of functioning. . . .

We have today three powerful agencies in the creation of public opinion: the press, motion pictures, radio. Ours then is the duty to see that these agencies through adherence to the highest ideals of truth, justice and fair play are maintained as public agencies for the creation of wholesome relationships among the various cultural, religious, racial and economic-interest groups which make up the American people. The sum of these complex and composite interests constitutes what we mean by American democracy.

> Letter to the Institute of Human Relations, National Conference of Jews and Christians, New York City, Aug. 20, 1937

6 / By a free press I mean a press which is untrammeled by prejudice and unfettered by selfish bias, which will serve no cause but that of truth and which will recognize no master but justice. . . .

Once the public realizes that its newspaper serves no interest save the that of truth it will give that paper an allegiance that neither depression nor ill-fortune nor any form of hard times can weaken. I have faith in the American press just as I have faith in the American people and in our democratic institutions. I venture the opinion that the straightforward pursuit of truth and justice points one way to prosperity and large influence of American newspapers both great and small.

> Letter to the *Brooklyn Daily Eagle* on the responsibilities of a free press, Sept. 2, 1938

7 / It is [a] corollary of our democracy that the public can be depended upon to assess problems and policies at their true value if facts are presented

as facts, and opinion as opinion—each in its true light. We are governed by public opinion. We cannot lay too much stress on the importance of truth in news.

Ibid.

8 / The constant free flow of communication among us—enabling the free interchange of ideas—forms the very blood stream of our nation. It keeps the mind and the body of our democracy eternally vital, eternally young.

Radio address to the New York *Herald Tribune* Forum, Oct. 24, 1940

9 / The people of a democracy are entitled to the essential facts and the government of a democracy must continuously have, in critical times as well as in peaceful times, the benefit of enlightened public criticism and enlightened public understanding.

Letter to the Director, Office of Facts and Figures, Washington, D.C., Dec. 2, 1941

5

Youth and Education

1 / The greatest single resource of this country is its youth, and no progressive government can afford to ignore the needs of its future citizens for adequate schooling and for that useful work which establishes them as a part of its economy. To ignore this need is to undermine the very basis of democracy which requires the constant renewal of its vitality through the absorption of its young people.

Message to Congress requesting appropriations for work relief, April 27, 1939

2 / The parents of our children are the guardians of our future citizens. They cannot evade the responsibility which is theirs through example and intelligent understanding to inspire and lay the ground work for that type of character which does what is right under any given circumstance, and is able to withstand temptation.

Parents as citizens might well set up standards for themselves as well as for their children. No group of parents can set itself up as immune from the problems of home and society which confront others. The soundness of our governmental institutions and of our economic system depends largely upon the standards which the majority of our citizens set up, and their desire to achieve them even at the cost of personal sacrifice.

Letter dated April 25, 1934, read at 13th annual dinner of the United Parents Associations, New York City, April 30, 1934

3 / We face the question of education and we find a mandate from the state as sovereign that the children of all shall be given opportunities to learn. In fact it is more than a state mandate, for the American system of

education is in fulfillment of a national purpose intimately associated with the great experiment in democracy we are still carrying on after the lapse of three centuries since our forefathers came here to undertake it and to pass its responsibilities on to us along with the inspired ideal which created them. The state's responsibility for education cannot be escaped by passing it on in one case to a city of teeming millions and in another to a dozen farmers scattered over miles of countryside. It is not solely on an altruistic basis that we consider the educational needs of a farm boy and girl as well as those of the tenement children in the city. The character and training of our fellow foot-loose Americans of the future are a matter of concern to us and to our descendants. They will have their part in making up the civilization in which we shall live a generation hence.

> Address on the finances and responsibilities of local government, University of Virginia, Charlottesville, July 6, 1931

4 / Knowledge—that is, education in its true sense—is our best protection against unreasoning prejudice and panic-making fear, whether engendered by special interests, illiberal minorities, or panic-stricken leaders.

> Campaign address, Boston, Mass., Oct. 31, 1932

5 / The ideals of young peoples are, on the whole, pretty fine and sound from the point of view of principle. Today they are making many changes in the methods, and many changes in the machinery of life, not just of government but of all human relationships, just as they will continue to make them; for a great many changes of government and human relationships are perfectly proper. But at the same time, the old-fashioned boyhood ideals, the old-fashioned boyhood principles, are going to keep the country going.

Every man and woman with an education has a twofold duty to perform. The first is to apply that education intelligently to problems of the moment; and the second is to obtain and maintain contact with and understanding of the average citizens of their own country.

> Extemporaneous remarks on receiving an honorary degree, Washington College, Chestertown, Md., Oct. 21, 1933

6 / There is in the spirit of a liberal education something of the self-confidence and the adaptability that is characteristic of our country. The pioneer does not call his life a failure if he comes to the end of one path. He knows that there are others, and with a sense of direction and a will to persevere, his life can go on with confidence into the uncertainties of the future.

All of us must honor and encourage those young men and young women whose ambitions lead them to seek specialization in science and in scholarship. Our great universities are properly providing adequate facilities for the development of specialists in science and in scholarship. The Nation is using their services in every form of human activity. Private business employs them. Private enterprise and government will continue to do so.

But at the same time there is a definite place in American life—an important place—for broad, liberal and non-specialized education. Every form of cooperative human endeavor cries out for men and women who, in their thinking processes, will know something of the broader aspects of any given problem. Government is using many men and women of this type—people who have the non-specialized point of view and who at the same time have a general and extraordinarily comprehensive knowledge not of the details, but of the progress and purposes which underlie the work of the specialists themselves.

Address on receiving an honorary degree, College of William and Mary, Williamsburg, Va., Oct. 20, 1934

7 / Human resources are above physical resources. The purposes which inspire the college youth of today will determine largely the value of the human resources of tomorrow.

Letter to the National Students Federation, Boston, Mass., Dec. 27, 1934

8 / The very objectives of young people have changed. In the older days a great financial fortune was too often the goal. To rule through wealth, or through the power of wealth, fired our imagination. This was the dream of the golden ladder—each individual for himself.

It is my firm belief that the newer generation of America has a different dream. You place emphasis on sufficiency of life, rather than on a plethora of riches. You think of the security for yourself and your family that will give you good health, good food, good education, good working conditions, and the opportunity for normal recreation and occasional travel. Your advancement, you hope, is along a broad highway on which thousands of your fellow men and women are advancing with you.

Radio message to the Young Democratic Clubs of America, Aug. 24, 1935

9 / One of the surest safeguards of American democracy is the fact that a million young people year by year study America's historic ideals in the colleges and universities.

Letter to the students of the University of Pennsylvania, Philadelphia, Sept. 26, 1935

10 / The youth of today are our sole investment in tomorrow. Let us guard and nurture that investment so that it may pay rich dividends in the good things of life.

Remarks to a committee from the National Students Federation, Washington, D.C., Nov. 11, 1935

11 / The qualities of a true education remain what they were when Washington insisted upon its importance.

First among these qualities is a sense of fair play among men.

As education grows, men come to recognize their essential dependence one upon the other. There is revealed to them the true nature of society and of government which, in a large measure, culminates in the art of human cooperation.

The second great attribute of education is peculiarly appropriate to a great democracy. It is a sense of equality among men when they are dealing with the things of the mind. Inequality may linger in the world of material things, but great music, great literature, great art and the wonders of science are, and should be, open to all.

Finally, a true education depends upon freedom in the pursuit of truth. No group and no government can properly prescribe precisely what should constitute the body of knowledge with which true education is concerned. The truth is found when men are free to pursue it. Genuine education is present only when the springs from which knowledge comes are pure. It is this belief in the freedom of the mind, written into our fundamental law, and observed in our everyday dealings with the problems of life, that distinguishes us as a nation, the United States of America, above every nation in the world.

In our ability to keep pure the sources of knowledge, in our mind's freedom to winnow the chaff from the good grain, in the even temper and in the calmness of our everyday relationships, in our willingness to face the details of fact and the needs of temporary emergencies—in all of these lie our future and our children's future.

Address on receiving an honorary degree, Temple University, Philadelphia, Pa., Feb. 22, 1936

12 / The temper of our youth has become more restless, more critical, more challenging. Flaming youth has become a flaming question. And youth comes to us wanting to know what we propose to do about a society that hurts so many of them.

There is much to justify the inquiring attitude of youth. You have a right to ask these questions—practical questions. No man who seeks to evade or to avoid deserves your confidence.

Many older people seem to take unmerited pride in the mere fact that they are adults. When youth comes crashing in on them with enthusiasms and ideals, they put on their most patronizing smiles, and pat the young man or the young woman on the shoulder, and in a worldly wise sort of way send them out with what they call their blessings. But—as every young person knows—that is not a blessing; it is a cold shower. What they have really said to you is this: "You're young. Enjoy your enthusiasms and your ideals while you can. For when you grow up and get out in the world you will know better." And the tragedy is that so many young people do just that: they do grow up and, growing up, they grow away from their enthusiasms and from their ideals. That is one reason why the world into which they go gets better so slowly.

Your objective, I take it, in the widest sense is this: an opportunity to make an honest living; a reasonable chance to improve your condition in life as you grow older; a practical assurance against want and suffering in your old age; and with it all the right to participate in the finer things of life—good health, clean amusement, and your share in the satisfactions of the arts, the sciences and religion.

Faced with that objective, it is clear that many of the old answers are not the right answers. No answer, new or old, is fit for your thought unless it is framed in terms of what you face and what you desire, unless it carries some definite prospect of a practical down-to-earth solution of your problems.

Address to the Young Democratic Club, Baltimore, Md., April 13, 1936

13 / No greater obligation faces the government than to justify the faith of its young people in the fundamental rightness of our democratic institutions and to preserve their strength, loyalty and idealism against the time when they must assume the responsibilities of citizenship.

Letter to the National Youth Administration, Washington, D.C., June 26, 1936

14 / [We] should train men to be citizens in that high Athenian sense which compels a man to live his life unceasingly aware that its civic significance is its most abiding, and that the rich individual diversity of the truly civilized state is born only of the wisdom to choose ways to achieve which do not hurt one's neighbors.

I am asking . . . [them] to dedicate themselves not only to the perpetuation, but also to the enlargement of that spirit. To pay ardent reverence to the past but to recognize no less the direction of the future, to understand philosophies we do not accept and hopes we find it difficult to share, to account the service of mankind the highest ambition a man can follow, and to know that there is no calling so humble that it cannot be instinct with that ambition; never to be indifferent to what may affect our neighbors; always, as Coleridge said, to put truth in the first place and not in the second; these I would affirm are the qualities by which the "real" is distinguished from the "nominal" scholar.

It is only when we have attained this philosophy that we can "above all find a friend in truth." When America is dedicated to that end by the common will of all her citizens, then America can accomplish her highest ideals.

Address at the Harvard University tercentenary celebration, Cambridge, Mass., Sept. 18, 1936

15 / It is the peculiar task of . . . every . . . university and college in this country to foster and maintain not only freedom within its own walls but also tolerance, self-restraint, fair dealing and devotion to the truth throughout America.

Ibid.

16 / The most priceless of our human assets are the young men and women of America—the raw material out of which the United States must shape its future.

Nature's deepest instinct is the concern in every parent's heart for the welfare of the children. It is a law of nature which equals even the instinct for the preservation of life itself. Indeed it is part of that law, for without the preservation of youth, the race itself would perish. And so, the highest duty of any government is to order public affairs so that opportunities for youth shall be made ever broader and firmer.

We Americans have never lost our sense of this obligation. To a greater degree than any other peoples we have sought to give each rising generation a little better chance in life than the one that preceded it. The little red schoolhouse for the education of the young, and the church for the training of their spiritual qualities, have always been the first structures to rise in every new settlement, as our ancestors pushed new frontiers through the wilderness. The school is the last expenditure upon which America should be willing to economize.

Campaign address, Kansas City, Mo., Oct. 13, 1936

17 / No body of citizens bears greater responsibility for the successful functioning of a democracy than the educational administrators and teachers. It is the responsibility of government to carry out the will of the people.

But it is the responsibility of organized education to make sure that the people understand their problems and are prepared to make intelligent choices when they express their will.

It is of great importance to the future of our democracy that ways and means be devised to engage the maximum number of young people and adults in a continuous, fearless and free discussion and study of public affairs. This should be the natural postgraduate program of all citizens whether they leave the fulltime school early or late. We have meeting places in every community, built by the people and used for day school work. Thousands of new buildings have been erected in the last few years. We now face the problem of promoting educational programs to make the most of our physical and human resources. The planning of such programs is a major responsibility of the educational profession. The result of such programs will be to strengthen the fabric of democracy.

Letter to Dr. J. W. Studebaker, U.S. Commissioner of Education, Feb. 18, 1937

18 / It is my conviction that, through work with our youth, we shall secure the greatest assurance of maintaining our democracy in the face of those forces which advocate forms of government not consistent with our cherished American traditions.

Radio greetings to the Boy Scouts of America, Feb. 7, 1938

19 / Freedom to learn is the first necessity of guaranteeing that man himself shall be self-reliant enough to be free.

Such things did not need as much emphasis a generation ago; but when the clock of civilization can be turned back by burning libraries, by exiling scientists, artists, musicians, writers and teachers, by dispersing universities, and by censoring news and literature and art, an added burden is placed upon those countries where the torch of free thought and free learning still burns bright.

If the fires of freedom and civil liberties burn low in other lands, they must be made brighter in our own.

If in other lands the press and books and literature of all kinds are censored, we must redouble our efforts here to keep them free.

If in other lands the eternal truths of the past are threatened by intolerance we must provide a safe place for their perpetuation.

There may be times when men and women in the turmoil of change lose touch with the civilized gains of centuries of education: but the gains of education are never really lost. Books may be burned and cities sacked, but truth, like the yearning for freedom, lives in the hearts of humble men and women. The ultimate victory of tomorrow is with democracy, and through democracy with education, for no people in all the world can be kept eternally ignorant or eternally enslaved.

Address before the National Education Association, New York City, June 30, 1938

20 / We have believed wholeheartedly in investing the money of all the people on the education of the people. That conviction, backed up by taxes and dollars, is no accident, for it is the logical application of our faith in democracy.

Man's present day control of the affairs of Nature is the direct result of investment in education. And the democratization of education has made it possible for outstanding ability, which would otherwise be completely lost, to make its outstanding contribution to the commonweal. We cannot afford to overlook any source of human raw material. Genius flowers in most unexpected places; "It is the impetus of the undistinguished host that hurls forth a Diomed or a Hector."

No government can create the human touch and self-sacrifice which the individual teacher gives to the process of education. But what government can do is to provide financial support and to protect from interference the freedom to learn.

No one wants the federal government to subsidize education any more than is absolutely neecssary. It has been and will be the traditional policy of the U.S. to leave the actual management of schools and their curricula to state and local control.

But we know that in many places local government unfortunately cannot adequately finance either the freedom or the facilities to learn. And there the federal government can properly supplement local resources. . . .

We know that the weakest educational link in the system lies in those communities which have the lowest taxable values, therefore, the smallest per capita tax receipts, and, therefore, the lowest teachers' salaries and most inadequate buildings and equipment. We do not blame these latter communities. They want better educational facilities, but simply have not enough money to pay the cost.

There is probably a wider divergence today in the standard of education between the richest communities and the poorest communities than there was one hundred years ago; and it is, therefore, our immediate task to seek to close that gap—not in any way by decreasing the facilities of the richer communities but by extending aid to those less fortunate. We all know that if we do not close this gap it will continue to widen, for the best brains in the poor communities will either have no chance to develop or will migrate to those places where their ability will stand a better chance.

To continue the parallel between natural and human resources, it is well to remember that our poorest communities exist where the land is most greatly eroded, where farming does not pay, where industries have moved out, where flood and drought have done their work, where transportation facilities are of the poorest and where cheap electricity is unavailable for the home. . . .

Our aid, for many reasons, financial and otherwise, must be confined to lifting the level at the bottom rather than to giving assistance at the top. Today we cannot do both, and we must therefore confine ourselves to the greater need.

Ibid.

21 / Democracy cannot succeed unless those who express their choice are prepared to choose wisely. The real safeguard of democracy, therefore, is education. It has been well said that no system of government gives so much to the individual or exacts so much as a democracy. Upon our educational system must largely depend the perpetuity of those institutions upon which our freedom and our security rest. To prepare each citizen to choose wisely and to enable him to choose freely are paramount functions of the schools in a democracy.

Statement on the observance of Education Week, Sept. 27, 1938

22 / Education in our democracy teaches the practice of reason in human affairs.

I refer not only to education that may come from books. I include education in fair play on the athletic field and on the debating platform; I include education for tolerance through participation in full, free discussion in the classroom. Practice in the scientific method by our young people may be more important than learning the facts of science. From kindergarten through college our schools train us to use the machinery of reason; parliamentary practice; the techniques of cooperation; how to accept with good grace the will of a majority; how to defend by logic and facts our deep convictions. This is education for the American way of life.

Our schools also bring us face to face with men and women with whom we shall share life's struggles. In their lives and ours, struggle will never be absent; the struggle of every individual against the stream of life; the struggle and competition among individuals, groups, institutions, states and nations. To the resolution of conflicts and struggles of life, democracy supplies no easy answer. The easy answer, the quick but incomplete answer, is force; tanks and torpedoes, guns and bombs. Democracy calls instead for the application of the rule of reason to solve conflicts. It calls for fair play in canvassing facts, for discussion, and for calm and orderly handling of difficult problems. These vital skills we Americans must acquire in our schools.

In our schools our coming generations must learn the most difficult art in the world—the successful management of democracy. Let us think of our schools . . . not only as buildings of stone and wood and steel; not only as places to learn how to use hand and brain; but as training centers in the use and application of the rule of reason in the affairs of men. And let us hope that out of our schools may come a generation which can persuade a bleeding world to supplant force with reason.

Ibid., Oct. 2, 1939

23 / No American child, merely because he happens to be born where property values are low and where local taxes do not, even though they should, support the schools, should be placed at a disadvantage in his preparation for citizenship.

Certainly our future is endangered when nearly a million children of elementary school age are not in school; when thousands of school districts and even some entire states do not pay for good schools. . . . I should like to put on the front page of every newspaper in the United States, a list of the most backward school districts and the most backward school states in the United States.

That is rough treatment, but if every person in the United States could know where the conditions are worst—education and health—those areas would get the sympathy, the understanding and the help for improving those conditions. . . .

I believe . . . that if anywhere in the country any child lacks opportunity for home life, for health protection, for education, for moral or spiritual development, the strength of the nation and its ability to cherish and advance the principles of democracy are thereby weakened.

Address before the White House Conference on Children in a Democracy, Washington, D.C., Jan. 19, 1940

24 / Our Boy Scouts represent a cross-section of all American boys, from large cities and from villages and farms, from seaport towns and ranches, boys of all blood origins—all enrolled under the banner of Scouting. Moreover, our movement embraces all sects and creeds and is above all class or sectional consciousness. It is, in a word, democratic and therefore truly American. God grant that it may ever remain so.

I like to think of Scouting as a kind of family group. This is as it should be, for the United States is a family nation. The family is the very base of our national life and the scouting movement does not take the individual away from it. Rather, it extends the spirit of the family into the activities of the boy outside home. Our twelfth scout law effectively expresses the spiritual ideals of scouting. It constitutes an excellent basis for citizenship. It affirms the importance of religion in the life of the individual and the life of the nation and emphasizes the neecssity of respect for the convictions of other people.

Radio address to the Boy Scouts of America on their 30th anniversary, Feb. 8, 1940

25 / The great achievements of science and even of art can be used in one way or another to destroy as well as create; they are only instruments by which men try to do the things they most want to do. If death is desired, science can do that. If a full, rich, and useful life is sought, science can do that also.

Address before the Eighth Pan American Scientific Conference, Washington, D.C., May 10, 1940

26 / Eternal truths will be neither true nor eternal unless they have fresh meaning for every new social situation.

It is the function of education, the function of all of the great institutions of learning in the United States, to provide continuity for our national life—to transmit to youth the best of our culture that has been tested in the fire of history. It is equally the obligation of education to train the minds and the talents of our youth; to improve, through creative citizenship, our American institutions in accord with the requirements of the future.

We cannot always build the future for our youth, but we can build our youth for the future.

It is in great universities . . . that the ideas which can assure our national safety and make tomorrow's history, are being forged and shaped. Civilization owes most to the men and women, known and unknown, whose free, inquiring minds and restless intellects could not be subdued by the power of tyranny.

This is no time for any man to withdraw into some ivory tower and proclaim the right to hold himself aloof from the problems and the agonies of his society. The times call for bold belief that the world can be changed by man's endeavor, and that this endeavor can lead to something new and better. No man can sever the bonds that unite him to his society simply by averting his eyes. He must ever be receptive and sensitive to the new; and have sufficient courage and skill to face novel facts and to deal with them.

If democracy is to survive, it is the task of men of thought, as well as men of action, to put aside pride and prejudice; and with courage and single-minded devotion—and above all with humility—to find the truth and teach the truth that shall keep men free.

We may find in that sense of purpose, the personal peace, not of repose, but of effort, the keen satisfaction of doing, the deep feeling of achievement for something far beyond ourselves, the knowledge that we build more gloriously than we know.

Address on the 200th anniversary of the founding of the University of Pennsylvania, Philadelphia, Sept. 20, 1940

27 / New schools symbolize two modern government functions in America, each of which is proving itself more and more vital to the continuance of our democracy.

One of them is an old function, based on the ideal and the understanding of the Founding Fathers that true democratic government cannot long endure in the midst of widespread ignorance. They recognized that democratic government would call for the intelligent participation of all of its people, as enlightened citizens—citizens equipped with what we used to call "a schooling." From their time to our own, it has always been recognized as a responsibility of government that every child have the right to a free and liberal education. These buildings can well be dedicated to that old function—the American institution of universal education.

In the last decade, this right of free education, which has become a part of the national life in our land, has taken on additional significance from events in certain other lands. For a large portion of the world the right no longer exists. Almost the first freedom to be destroyed, as dictators take control, is the freedom of learning. Tyranny hates and fears nothing more than the free exchange of ideas, the free play of the mind that comes from education.

In these schools and in other American schools, the children of today and of future generations will be taught, without censorship or restriction, the facts of current history and the whole context of current knowledge. Their textbooks will not be burned by a dictator who disagrees with them; their teachers will not be banished by a ruler whom they have offended; their schools will not be closed if they teach unpalatable truths; and their daily instruction will not be governed by the decrees of any central bureau of propaganda. They will get not all of the story part of the time, or only part of the story all of the time—they will get all of the story all of the time.

Here will be trained the young people of a nation—not for enforced labor camps or for regimentation as an enslaved citizenry, but for the intelligent exercise of the right of suffrage, and for participation as free human beings in the life of the nation.

These buildings are also a symbol of a second and a newer responsibility which our democracy has assumed as one of its major functions. As you know, they have been paid for, in part by the taxpayers of the consolidated district, and in part, by the federal government.

Address at the dedication of new schools in Hyde Park, N.Y., Oct. 5, 1940

28 / If our boys or girls on reaching employment age have been unable to get a job in private industry, the government owes them the duty of furnishing them with the necessary training to equip them for employment.

Campaign address, Philadelphia, Pa., Oct. 23, 1940

29 / We, at home, owe a special and continuing obligation to these men and women in the armed services.

During the war we have seen to it that they have received the best training and equipment, the best food, shelter, and medical attention, the best protection and care which planning, ingenuity, physical resources, and money could furnish in time of war. But after the war shall have been won, the best way that we can repay a portion of that debt is to see to it, by planning and by action now, that those men and women are demobilized into an economy which is sound and prosperous, with a minimum of unemployment and dislocation; and that, with the assistance of government, they are given the opportunity to find a job for which they are fitted and trained, in a field which offers some reasonable assurance of well-being and continuous employment.

For many, what they desire most in the way of employment will require special training and further education. As a part of a general program for the benefit of the members of our armed services, I believe that the nation is morally obligated to provide this training and education and the necessary financial assistance by which they can be secured. It is an obligation which should be recognized now; and legislation to that end should be enacted as soon as possible.

Message to Congress on educational opportunities for war veterans, Oct. 27, 1943

30 / There are many things which we have learned in this war. Among the most important are those which we have learned through our Selective Service System about the health and education of the youth of our nation. We have found that among those examined for selective service 4½ percent can be classed as illiterate; and that 40 percent of all registrants for selective service have not gone beyond an elementary school education. . . .

I believe that the federal government should render financial aid where it is needed, and only where it is needed—in communities where farming does not pay, where land values have depreciated through erosion or through flood or drought, where industries have moved away, where transport facilities are inadequate or where electricity is unavailable for power and light.

Such government financial aid should never involve government interference with state and local administration and control. It must purely and simply provide the guarantee that this country is great enough to give to all of its children the right to a free education.

Address before the Conference on Rural Education, Washington, D.C., Oct. 4, 1944

31 / The training and educational programs of the Army, the Navy, and civilian agencies during this war have broadened our conception of the role that education should play in our national life. The records of Selective Service reveal that we have fallen far short of a suitable standard of elementary and secondary education. If a suitable standard is to be maintained in all parts of the country, the federal government must render aid where it is needed—but only where it is needed. Such financial aid should involve no interference with state and local control and administration of educational programs. It should simply make good our national obligation to all our children. This country is great enough to guarantee the right to education adequate for full citizenship.

Annual budget message to Congress, Jan. 3, 1945

6

Religion and the Arts

1 / With every passing year I become more confident that humanity is moving forward to the practical application of the teachings of Christianity as they affect the individual lives of men and women. . . .

The people of the United States still recognize, and, I believe, recognize with firmer faith than ever before, that spiritual values count in the long run more than material values. Those who have sought by edict to eliminate the right of mankind to believe in God and to practice that belief, have, in every case, discovered sooner or later that they are tilting in vain against an inherent, essential, undying quality, and indeed necessity, of the human race—a quality and a necessity which in every century have proved an essential to permanent progress.

Address before the National Conference of Catholic Charities, New York City, Oct. 4, 1933

2 / Christianity was born in and of an era notable for the great gulf that separated the privileged from the underprivileged of the world of two thousand years ago—an era of lines of demarcation between conquerors and conquered; between caste and caste; between warring philosophies based on the theories of logicians rather than on practical humanities. The early churches were united in a social ideal.

Although through all the centuries we know of many periods when civilization has slipped a step backward, yet I am confident that over the sum of the centuries we have gained many steps for every one we have lost.

Now, once more, we are embarking on another voyage into the realm of human contacts. That human agency which we call government is seeking through social and economic means the same goal which the churches are seeking through social and spiritual means.

If I were asked to state the great objective which church and state are both demanding for the sake of every man and woman and child in this country, I would say that that great objective is "a more abundant life."

The early Christians challenged the pagan ethics of Greece and of Rome; we are wholly ready to challenge the pagan ethics that are represented in many phases of our boasted modern civilization. We have called on enlightened business judgment, on understanding labor and on intelligent agriculture to provide a more equitable balance of the abundant life between all elements of the community.

> Address before the Federal Council of Churches of Christ in America, Washington, D.C., Dec. 6, 1933

3 / The supreme values are spiritual. The hope of the world is that character which, built upon the solid rock, withstands triumphantly all the storms of life.

To build this exemplary character is our great task. Without it the abundant life cannot be realized, and the best citizens and best soldiers of a country are those who have put on the armor of righteousness.

[Those] who by word and life are advancing the cause of idealism and true religion are doing a commendable work, one that is absolutely essential to the life of the nation.

> Letter to the chaplains of military and naval services, War Department, Washington, D.C., Feb. 13, 1934

4 / In the United States we regard it as axiomatic that every person shall enjoy the free exercise of his religion according to the dictates of his conscience. Our flag for a century and a half has been the symbol of the principles of liberty of conscience, of religious freedom and of equality before the law; and these concepts are deeply ingrained in our national character.

> Address, San Diego Exposition, San Diego, Calif., Oct. 2, 1935

5 / In the formative days of the republic the directing influence [that] the Bible exercised upon the fathers of the nation is conspicuously evident. To Washington it contained the sure and certain moral precepts that constituted the basis of his action. That which proceeded from it transcended all other books, however elevating their thought. To his astute mind moral and religious principles were the "indispensable supports" of political prosperity,

the "essential pillars of civil society." Learned as Jefferson was in the best of the ancient philosophers, he turned to the Bible as the source of his higher thinking and reasoning. Speaking of the lofty teachings of the Master, he said: "He pushed His scrutinies into the heart of man; erected His tribunal in the region of his thoughts, and purified the waters at the fountain head." Beyond this he held that the Bible contained the noblest ethical system the world has known. His own compilation of the selected portions of this book, in what is known as "Jefferson's Bible," bears evidence of the profound reverence in which he held it.

Statement on the 400th anniversary of the printing of the first English Bible, Oct. 6, 1935

6 / We who have faith cannot afford to fall out among ourselves. The very state of the world is a summons to us to stand together. For as I see it, the chief religious issue is not between our various beliefs. It is between belief and unbelief. It is not your specific faith or mine that is being called into question—but all faith. . . .

No greater thing could come to our land today than a revival of the spirit of religion—a revival that would sweep through the homes of the nation and stir the hearts of men and women of all faiths to a reassertion of their belief in God and their dedication to His will for themselves and for their world. I doubt if there is any problem—social, political or economic—that would not melt away before the fire of such a spiritual awakening.

Radio address on Brotherhood Day, Feb. 23, 1936

7 / In the whole history of mankind, far back into the dim past before man knew how to record thoughts or events, the human race has been distinguished from other forms of life by the existence, the fact, of religion. Periodic attempts to deny God have always come and will always come to naught.

Address before the Inter-American Conference for the Maintenance of Peace, Buenos Aires, Argentina, Dec. 1, 1936

8 / In a world perplexed by doubt and fear and uncertainty, there is need for a return to religion, religion as exemplified in the Sermon on the Mount. We need more and more a consciousness of the fact that in the highest and the noblest sense we are our brother's keeper and I want to reiterate the belief I have already affirmed many times that there is not a problem, social, political or economic, that would not find full solution in the fire of a religious awakening. . . .

Today when we see religion challenged in wide areas of the earth we who hold to [the] old ideals of the fatherhood of God and the brotherhood of man must be steadfast and united in bearing unceasing witness to our faith in things of the spirit.

Greetings to the United Methodist Council, Chicago, Ill., Jan. 17, 1938

9 / After all, the majority of Americans, whether they adhere to the ancient teaching of Israel or accept the tenets of the Christian religion, have a common source of inspiration in the Old Testament. In the spirit of brotherhood we should, therefore, seek to emphasize all those many essential things in which we find unity in our common biblical heritage.

Acknowledgement of the award of the American Hebrew Medal, March 6, 1939

10 / Our modern democratic way of life has its deepest roots in our great common religious tradition, which for ages past has taught to civilized mankind the dignity of the human being, his equality before God, and his responsibility in the making of a better and fairer world.

Everywhere in the world there are men of stout heart and firm faith now engaged in a great spiritual struggle to test whether that ancient wisdom is to endure, or whether it must give way to the older, discarded doctrine that some few men shall dominate multitudes of others and dictate to them their thinking, their religion, their living. This conflict has found its most terrible expression in a war which has now engulfed a large portion of humanity. In its more peaceful aspects, the same struggle also pervades all efforts of men of good will who are seeking through democracy the way to the world to come.

In teaching this democratic faith to American children, we need the sustaining, buttressing aid of those great ethical religious teachings which are the heritage of our modern civilization. For "not upon strength nor upon power, but upon the spirit of God" shall our democracy be founded.

Letter to the Jewish Education Committee, New York City, Dec. 16, 1940

11 / All of recorded history bears witness that the human race has made true advancement only as it has appreciated spiritual values. Those unhappy peoples who have placed their sole reliance on the sword have inevitably perished by the sword in the end.

Physical strength can never permanently withstand the impact of spiritual force.

Address at the dedication of Woodrow Wilson's birthplace, Staunton, Va., May 4, 1941

12 / Religion, by teaching man his relationship to God, gives the individual a sense of his own dignity and teaches him to respect himself by respecting his neighbors.

State of the Union Message, Jan. 4, 1939

13 / When men dedicate a new edifice for a common enterprise, they are at once celebrating an achievement and announcing a purpose. They cannot refrain nor could they properly be excused from making clear what that purpose is. . . . The mission of this Museum is plain. We are dedicating this building to the cause of peace and to the pursuits of peace. The arts that ennoble and refine life flourish only in the atmosphere of peace. And in this hour of dedication we are glad again to bear witness before all the world to our faith in the sanctity of free institutions. For we know that only where men are free can the arts flourish and the civilization of national culture reach full flower.

The arts cannot thrive except where men are free to be themselves and to be in charge of the discipline of their own energies and ardors. The conditions for democracy and for art are one and the same. What we call liberty in politics results in freedom in the arts. There can be no vitality in the works gathered in a museum unless there exists the right of spontaneous life in the society in which the arts are nourished.

A world turned into a stereotype, a society converted into a regiment, a life translated into a routine, make it difficult for either art or artists to survive. Crush individuality in society and you crush art as well. Nourish the conditions of a free life and you nourish the arts, too.

In encouraging the creation and enjoyment of beautiful things we are furthering democracy itself. That is why this Museum is a citadel of civilization.

As the Museum of Modern Art is a living museum, not a collection of curious and interesting objects, it can, therefore, become an integral part of our democratic institutions—it can be woven into the very warp and woof of our democracy. Because it has been conceived as a national institution the Museum can enrich and invigorate our cultural life by bringing the best of modern art to all of the American people.

Address at the dedication of the Museum of Modern Art, New York City, May 10, 1939

14 / Great works of art have a way of breaking out of private ownership into public use. They belong so obviously to all who love them—they are so clearly the property not of their single owners but of all men everywhere—that the private rooms and houses where they are hung become in time too

narrow for their presence. The true collectors are the collectors who understand this—the collectors of great paintings who feel that they can never
truly own, but only gather and preserve for all who love them, the treasures
they have found. . . .

There was a time when the people of this country would not have
thought that the inheritance of art belonged to them or that they had
responsibilities to guard it. A few generations ago, the people of this country
were taught by their writers and by their critics and by their teachers to
believe that art was something foreign to America and to themselves—
something imported from another continent and from an age which was
not theirs—something they had no part in, save to go to see it in a guarded
room on holidays or Sundays.

But recently, within the last few years, they have discovered that they
have a part. They have seen in their own towns, in their own villages, in
schoolhouses, in post offices, in the back rooms of shops and stores, pictures
painted by their sons, their neighbors—people they have known and lived
beside and talked to. They have seen, across these last few years, rooms full
of painting and sculpture by Americans, walls covered with painting by
Americans—some of it good, some of it not good, but all of it native,
human, eager, and alive—all of it painted by their own kind in their own
country, and painted about things they know and look at often and have
touched and loved.

The people of this country know now, whatever they were taught or
thought they knew before, that art is not something just to be owned but
something to be made: that it is the act of making and not the act of owning
which is art. And knowing this they know also that art is not a treasure in
the past or an importation from another country, but part of the present
life of all the living and creating peoples—all who make and build; and,
most of all, the young and vigorous peoples who have made and built our
present wide country.

It is for this reason that the people of America accept the inheritance
of these ancient arts. Whatever these paintings may have been to men who
looked at them a generation back—today they are not *only* works of art.
Today they are the symbols of the human spirit, and of the world the
freedom of the human spirit made—a world against which armies now are
raised and countries overrun and men imprisoned and their work destroyed.

To accept, today, the work of German painters such as Holbein and
Dürer and of Italians like Botticelli and Raphael, and of painters of the Low
Countries like Van Dyck and Rembrandt, and of famous Frenchmen,
famous Spaniards—to accept this work today on behalf of the people of
this democratic nation is to assert the belief of the people of this nation in a
human spirit which now is everywhere endangered and which, in many

countries where it first found form and meaning, has been rooted out and broken and destroyed.

To accept this work today is to assert the purpose of the people of America that the freedom of the human spirit and human mind which has produced the world's great art and all its science—shall not be utterly destroyed.

Address at the dedication of the National Art Gallery, Washington, D.C., March 17, 1941

7

Immigrants—Racial Minorities—Tolerance

1 / [Immigrants] believed that men, out of their intelligence and their self-discipline, could create and use forms of government that would not enslave the human spirit, but free it and nourish it throughout the generations. They did not fear government, because they knew that government in the New World was their own.

> Address commemorating the coming of the first white pioneer to the area, Green Bay, Wisc., Aug. 9, 1934

2 / We can and should, without further delay, extend to the Indian the fundamental rights of political liberty and local self-government and the opportunities of education and economic assistance that they require in order to attain a wholesome American life. This is but the obligation of honor of a powerful nation toward a people living among us and dependent upon our protection.

Certainly the continuance of autocratic rule, by a federal department, over the lives of more than two hundred thousand citizens of this nation is incompatible with American ideals of liberty. It also is destructive of the character and self-respect of a great race.

> Statement to Senate and House committees on Indian affairs, April 28, 1934

3 / It is truly remarkable, the things which the Negro people have accomplished within living memory—their progress in agriculture and in-

dustry, their achievement in the field of education, their contributions to the arts and sciences and, in general, to good citizenship.

It is my hope and belief that the Negro, inspired by the achievements of the race to date, will go forward to even greater things in the years to come. All of us should keep in mind the words of the immortal Lincoln— "In giving freedom to the slave we assure freedom to the free—honorable alike in what we give and what we preserve."

Letter to Cleveland G. Allen on progress of the Negro race since Emancipation, Dec. 26, 1935

4 / Religion in wide areas of the earth is being confronted with irreligion; our faiths are being challenged. It is because of that threat that you and I must reach across the lines between our creeds, clasp hands and make common cause.

Radio address on Brotherhood Day, Feb. 23, 1936

5 / The overwhelming majority of those who came from the nations of the Old World to our American shores were not the laggards, not the timorous, not the failures. They were men and women who had the supreme courage to strike out for themselves, to abandon language and relatives, to start at the bottom without influence, without money and without knowledge of life in a very young civilization. . . .

They came to us speaking many tongues—but a single language, the universal language of human aspiration.

Address on the 50th anniversary of the dedication of the Statue of Liberty, New York City, Oct. 28, 1936

6 / The lesson of religious toleration—a toleration which recognizes complete liberty of human thought, liberty of human conscience—is one which, by precept and example, must be inculcated in the hearts and minds of all Americans if the institutions of our democracy are to be maintained and perpetuated.

We must recognize the fundamental rights of man. There can be no true national life in our democracy unless we give unqualified recognition to freedom of religious worship and freedom of education. . . .

Rarely before in our history have prospects for achieving permanent harmony among the various elements composing our nation been so propitious as at the present time. . . . I pledge myself . . . with all the resources at my command, to work for so happy a consummation. My prayer shall ever be that this nation, under God, may vindicate through all coming time the sanctity of the right of all within our borders to the free exercise of religion according to the dictates of conscience.

Letter to Michael Williams, publisher of *The Commonweal*, March 30, 1937

7 / No democracy can long survive which does not accept as fundamental to its very existence the recognition of the rights of minorities.

Letter to the National Association for the Advancement of Colored People, Columbus, Ohio, June 25, 1938

8 / Remember, remember always that all of us, and you and I especially, are descended from immigrants and revolutionists.

Address to the Daughters of the American Revolution, Washington, D.C., April 21, 1938

9 / We in the United States, and, indeed, in all the Americas . . . remember that our population stems from many races and kindreds and tongues. Often, I think, we Americans offer up the silent prayer that on the continent of Europe, from which the American hemisphere was principally colonized, the years to come will break down many barriers of intercourse between nations—barriers which may be historic, but which so greatly, through the centuries, have led to strife and hindered friendship and normal intercourse.

Address at the opening of the New York World's Fair, April 30, 1939

10 / Perhaps the highest service we Americans can render at this time is to demonstrate that our personal liberty, our democratic ways of life, our free representative government, make it possible for us to disagree among ourselves over many things without bitterness and find quickly the means of settlement and adjustment of controversy when it has gone far enough. A world emergency such as the present gives us new realization of the blessings of democracy and liberty. In the presence of these blessings and in the face of this world necessity we must adjourn our small grudges, our differences, and find the way to peace and good will within our borders in every department of life. So we become a free and fearless nation with people of all shades of opinion and walks of life, united in common purpose to maintain and to practice and to protect this American way of life.

Letter to the annual convention of the American Federation of Labor, Cincinnati, Ohio, Sept. 30, 1939

11 / One of the great achievements of the American commonwealth has been the fact that race groups which were divided abroad are united here. Enmities and antagonisms were forgotten; former opponents met here as friends. Groups which had fought each other overseas here work together; their children intermarry; they have all made contributions to democracy and peace.

Because of the very greatness of this achievement we must be constantly vigilant againt the attacks of intolerance and injustice. We must scrupulously guard the civil rights and civil liberties of all citizens, whatever their background. We must remember that any oppression, any injustice, any hatred, is a wedge designed to attack our civilization. If reason is to prevail against intolerance, we must always be on guard.

Letter to the American Committee for Protection of the Foreign-Born, New York City, Jan. 9, 1940

12 / It is now more than ever important that the place of a minority group in a democracy not be obscured by ignorance and prejudice. It is important that members of a minority group consider together their special problems in order that these problems may find expression for the benefit of all. It is of even greater importance that the whole people consider with open and sympathetic mind these problems of the minority in order that the processes of democracy may work to bring about their solution. For it is obvious that the political, social and economic well-being of the whole people depends upon the achievement of the well-being for all sections of the population regardless of color, creed or geography.

Letter of greeting, dated March 29, 1940, to the Third National Negro Congress, Washington, D.C., April 26–28, 1940

13 / In every representative American meeting there will be men and women and children with names like Jackson and Lincoln and Isaac and Schultz and O'Brien and Stuyvesant and Olson and Kovacs and Satori and Jones and Smith. These varied Americans with varied backgrounds are all immigrants or the descendants of immigrants. All of them are inheritors of the same stalwart tradition—a tradition of unusual enterprise, of adventurousness, of courage "to pull up stakes and git moving." That has been the great, compelling force in our history.

Radio address to the New York *Herald Tribune* Forum, Oct. 24, 1940

14 / In our own American community we have sought to submerge all the old hatreds, all the old fears, of the old world.

We are Anglo-Saxon and Latin, we are Irish and Teuton and Jewish and Scandinavian—we are American. We belong to many races and colors and creeds—we are American.

And it seems to me that we are most completely, most loudly, American around Election Day.

Campaign address, Boston, Mass., Oct. 30, 1940

15 / We are a nation of many nationalities, many races, many religions— bound together by a single unity, the unity of freedom and equality.

Whoever seeks to set one nationality against another, seeks to degrade all nationalities.

Whoever seeks to set one race against another seeks to enslave all races.

Whoever seeks to set one religion against another, seeks to destroy all religion.

Campaign address, Brooklyn, N.Y., Nov. 1, 1940

16 / Religious intolerance, social intolerance and political intolerance have no place in our American life. . . .

Today, in this war, our fine boys are fighting magnificently all over the world and among those boys are the Murphys and the Kellys, the Smiths and the Joneses, the Cohens, the Carusos, the Kowalskis, the Schultzes, the Olsens, the Swobodas, and—right in with all the rest of them—the Cabots and the Lowells.

All of these and others like them are the life-blood of America. They are the hope of the world.

It is our duty to them to make sure that, big as this country is, there is no room in it for racial or religious intolerance—and that there is no room for snobbery.

Our young men and young women are fighting not only for their existence, and their homes and their families. They also are fighting for a country and a world where men and women of all races, colors, and creeds can live, work, speak, and worship—in peace, freedom, and security.

Campaign address, Boston, Mass., Nov. 4, 1944

8

Individualism—
Private Enterprise

1 / I, too, believe in individualism; but I mean it in everything that the word implies.

I believe that our industrial and economic system is made for individual men and women, and not individual men and women for the benefit of the system.

I believe that the individual should have full liberty of action to make the most of himself; but I do not believe that in the name of that sacred word a few powerful interests should be permitted to make industrial cannon fodder of the lives of half of the population of the United States.

I believe in the sacredness of private property, which means that I do not believe that it should be subjected to the ruthless manipulation of professional gamblers in the stock markets and the corporate system.

Campaign address, Columbus, Ohio, Aug. 20, 1932

2 / Private enterprise in times such as these cannot be left without assistance and without reasonable safeguards lest it destroy not only itself but also our processes of civilization.

Radio address (Fireside Chat) on the record of his administration, Sept. 30, 1934

3 / I need not tell you that true wealth is not a static thing. It is a living thing made out of the disposition of men to create and to distribute the good things of life with rising standards of living. Wealth grows when

men cooperate; but it stagnates in an atmosphere of misunderstanding and misrepresentation. Here, in America, the material means are at hand for the growth of true wealth. It is in the spirit of American institutions that wealth should come as the reward of hard labor—hard labor, I repeat—of mind and hand. That is a pretty good definition of what we call the profit system.

Address before the District of Columbia Bankers' convention, Washington, D.C., Oct. 24, 1934

4 / No wise man has any intention of destroying what is known as the profit motive; because by the profit motive we mean the right by work to earn a decent livelihood for ourselves and for our families.

We have, however, a clear mandate from the people, that Americans must forswear that conception of the acquisition of wealth which, through excessive profits, creates undue private power over private affairs and, to our misfortune, over public affairs as well. In building toward this end we do not destroy ambition, nor do we seek to divide our wealth into equal shares on stated occasions. We continue to recognize the greater ability of some to earn more than others. But we do assert that the ambition of the individual to obtain for him and his a proper security, a reasonable leisure, and a decent living throughout life, is an ambition to be preferred to the appetite for great wealth and great power.

State of the Union Message, Jan. 4, 1935

5 / Let me emphasize that serious as have been the errors of unrestrained individualism, I do not believe in abandoning the system of individual enterprise. The freedom and opportunity that have characterized American development in the past can be maintained if we recognize the fact that the individual system of our day calls for the collaboration of all of us to provide, at the least, security for all of us. Those words "freedom" and "opportunity" do not mean a license to climb upwards by pushing other people down.

Any paternalistic system which tries to provide for security for everyone from above only calls for an impossible task and a regimentation utterly uncongenial to the spirit of our people. But government cooperation to help make the system of free enterprise work, to provide that minimum security without which the competitive system cannot function, to restrain the kind of individual action which in the past has been harmful to the community—that kind of governmental cooperation is entirely consistent with the best traditions of America.

Radio message to the Young Democratic Clubs of America, Aug. 24, 1935

6 / I believe, I have always believed, and I will always believe in private enterprise as the backbone of economic well-being in the United States.

But I know, and you know, and every independent businessman who has had to struggle against the competition of monopolies knows, that this concentration of economic power in all-embracing corporations does not represent private enterprise as we Americans cherish it and propose to foster it. On the contrary, it represents private enterprise which has become a kind of private government, a power unto itself—a regimentation of other people's money and other people's lives.

Campaign address, Chicago, Ill., Oct. 14, 1936

7 / The struggle against private monopoly is a struggle for, and not against, American business. It is a struggle to preserve individual enterprise and economic freedom.

I believe in individualism. I believe in it in the arts, the sciences and professions. I believe in it in business. I believe in individualism in all of these things—up to the point where the individualist starts to operate at the expense of society. The overwhelming majority of American business-men do not believe in it beyond that point. We have all suffered in the past from individualism run wild. Society has suffered and business has suffered.

Ibid.

8 / We can make our machinery of private enterprise work only so long as it does not benefit one group at the expense of another.

No one in the United States believes more firmly than I in the system of private business, private property and private profit. No Administration in the history of our country has done more for it. It was this Administration which dragged it back out of the pit into which it had fallen in 1933.

If the Administration has had the slightest inclination to change that system, all that it would have had to do was to fold its hands and wait— let the system continue to default to itself and to the public.

Instead . . . we acted quickly and drastically to save it. It was because of our belief in private enterprise that we acted, because of our faith in the essential and fundamental virtue of democracy and our conviction that individual initiative and private profit served it best. . . .

But as your profits return and the values of your securities and invest-ments come back, do not forget the lessons of the past. We must hold constantly to the resolve never again to become committed to the philos-ophy of the boom era, to individualism run wild, to the false promise that American business was great because it had built up financial control of industrial production and distribution in the hands of a few individuals and corporations by the use of other people's money; that government should be ever ready to purr against the legs of high finance; that the benefits of the free competitive system should trickle down by gravity from the top to the bottom; and above all, that government had no right, in any way, to interfere with those who were using the system of private profit to the damage of the rest of the American citizens.

Collapse of business was the price we paid for not facing intelligently the problems of private enterprise in a modern world.

There were those who advised extreme courses in the days of the crisis in 1933. Many said that deflation should take its course, wiping out in bankruptcy all but a handful of the strongest.

Some, including many businessmen, urged that the only solution was for government to take everything over and run things itself.

We took the middle road. We used the facilities and resources available only to government, to permit individual enterprise to resume its normal functions in a socially sound competitive order. We provided credit at one end of the business mechanism and purchasing power at the other. The broken pipes of the circulatory system of business have been welded together again.

An overwhelming majority of independent individual businessmen approve in their hearts what we did to save American business. I am equally sure that a handful of monopolistic businessmen hate what we did for American business. Business had become regimented. Free enterprise was being gobbled up piece by piece. Economic control of business in these few persons had developed into political control of government itself. They did not want us to take American business out of their grip.

But we not only have freed government from their domination; we are now freeing business also from their domination.

We have loosened the grip of monopoly by taking from monopolists their chief tools—the devices of high finance. . . .

All we ask of business and for business is the greater good of the greater number—fair treatment by it and fair treatment for it. We are reaching for the security which comes from an intelligent and honorable system of interdependent economics which every businessman as well as everyone else can trust and into which he can venture with confidence.

We seek to guarantee the survival of private enterprise by guaranteeing conditions under which it can work.

Campaign radio address to the businessmen of the nation, Oct. 23, 1936

9 / Big manufacturers talk about control of production by the farmer as an indefensible "economy of scarcity." And yet these same manufacturers

never hesitate to shut down their own huge plants, throw men out of work, and cut down the purchasing power of whole communities whenever they think they must adjust their production to the oversupply of the goods they make. When it is their baby who has the measles, they call it not "an economy of scarcity" but "sound business judgment."

Radio address (Fireside Chat) announcing a call for a special session of Congress, Oct. 12, 1937

10 / From our earliest days we have had a tradition of substantial government help to our system of private enterprise. But today the government no longer has vast tracts of rich land to give away and we have discovered that we must spend large sums to conserve our land from further erosion and our forests from further depletion. The situation is also very different from the old days, because now we have plenty of capital, banks and insurance companies loaded with idle money; plenty of industrial productive capacity and several millions of workers looking for jobs. It is following tradition as well as necessity, if government strives to put idle money and idle men to work, to increase our public wealth and to build up the health and strength of the people—and to help our system of private enterprise to function.

Radio address (Fireside Chat) on the economic situation, April 14, 1938

11 / Private enterprise is ceasing to be free enterprise and is becoming a cluster of private collectivisms: masking itself as a system of free enterprise after the American model, it is in fact becoming a concealed cartel system after the European model.

Message to Congress on the concentration of economic power, April 29, 1938

12 / Among us today a concentration of private power without equal in history is growing.

This concentration is seriously impairing the economic effectiveness of private enterprise as a way of providing employment for labor and capital and as a way of assuring a more equitable distribution of income and earnings among the people of the nation as a whole. . . .

No man of good faith will misinterpret these proposals [to correct the situation]. They derive from the oldest American traditions. Concentration of economic power in the few and the resulting unemployment of labor and capital are inescapable problems for a modern "private enterprise" democracy. I do not believe that we are so lacking in stability that we will lose faith in our own way of living just because we seek to find out how to make that way of living work more effectively.

This program should appeal to the honest common sense of every independent business man interested primarily in running his own business at a profit rather than in controlling the business of other men. . . .

It is a program to preserve private enterprise for profit by keeping it free enough to be able to utilize all our resources of capital and labor at a profit.

It is a program whose basic purpose is to stop the progress of collectivism in business and turn business back to the democratic competitive order.

It is a program whose basic thesis is not that the system of free private enterprise for profit has failed in this generation, but that it has not yet been tried.

Once it is realized that business monopoly in America paralyzes the system of free enterprise on which it is grafted, and is as fatal to those who manipulate it as to the people who suffer beneath its impositions, action by the government to eliminate these artificial restraints will be welcomed by industry throughout the nation.

For idle factories and idle workers profit no man.

Ibid.

13 / It is an unfortunate human failing that a full pocketbook often groans more loudly than an empty stomach.

I am, as you know, a firm believer in private enterprise and in private property. I am a firm believer in the American opportunity of men and women to rise in private enterprise.

But, of course, if private opportunity is to remain safe, average men and women must be able to have it as a part of their own individual satisfaction in life and their own stake in democracy.

Campaign address, Brooklyn, N.Y., Nov. 1, 1940

14 / I am certain that private enterprise will be able to provide the vast majority of those jobs [for the veterans returning from the war]—and, in those cases where this cannot be accomplished, that the Congress will pass the legislation which will make good the assurance of jobs.

Address at the White House Correspondents' Association dinner, Washington, D.C., Feb. 12, 1943

15 / I believe in free enterprise—and always have.

I believe in the profit system—and always have.

I believe that private enterprise can give full employment to our people. . . .

Beware of that profound enemy of the free enterprise system who pays lip-service to free competition—but also labels every anti-trust prosecution as a "persecution."

Campaign address, Chicago, Ill., Oct. 28, 1944

9

Agriculture

1 / To devote to agriculture the same interest and intelligence that is now being given to industry will mean new recruits for farming, better living conditions, and the breaking down of artificial and unnecessary barriers between the rural and the urban communities.

Second annual message to the N.Y. State Legislature, Jan. 1, 1930

2 / The practical way to help the farmer is by an arrangement that will, in addition to lightening some of the impoverishing burdens from his back, do something toward the reduction of the surpluses of staple commodities that hang on the market. It should be our aim to add to the world prices of staple products the amount of a reasonable tariff protection, to give agriculture the same protection that industry has today.

And in exchange for this immediately increased return I am sure that the farmers of this nation would agree ultimately to such planning of their production as would reduce the surpluses and make it unnecessary in later years to depend on dumping those surpluses abroad in order to support domestic prices. That result has been accomplished in other nations; why not in America, too?

Acceptance speech, Democratic National Convention, Chicago, Ill., July 2, 1932

3 / It is a moral as well as an economic question [the condition of agriculture] that we face—moral because we want to reestablish the standards that in times past were our goal. We want the opportunity to live in comfort, reasonable comfort, out of which we may build spiritual values. The consequences of poverty bring a loss of spiritual and moral values. And even more important is the loss of the opportunity that we had hoped to

give to the younger generation. We want our children to have a chance for an education, for the sound development of American standards to be applied in their daily lives at play and work. Those opportunities can come only if the condition of agriculture is made more prosperous.

Campaign address, Sioux City, Iowa, Sept. 29, 1932

4 / Congress is about to pass legislation that will greatly ease the mortgage distress among the farmers and the home owners of the nation, by providing for the easing of the burden of debt now bearing so heavily upon millions of our people. . . .

The Farm Relief Bill [A.A.A.] seeks by the use of several methods, alone or together, to bring about an increased return to farmers for their major farm products, seeking at the same time to prevent in the days to come disastrous overproduction which so often in the past has kept farm commodity prices far below a reasonable return. This measure provides wide powers for emergencies. The extent of its use will depend entirely upon what the future has in store. . . .

I am certain that the people of this country understand and approve the broad purposes behind these new governmental policies relating to agriculture and industry and transportation. We found ourselves faced with more agricultural products than we could possibly consume ourselves and surpluses which other nations did not have the cash to buy from us except at prices ruinously low. . . . All of this has been caused in large part by a complete lack of planning and a complete failure to understand the danger signals that have been flying ever since the close of the World War. The people of this country have been erroneously encouraged to believe that they could keep on increasing the output of farm and factory indefinitely and that some magician would find ways and means for that increased output to be consumed with reasonable profit to the producer. . . .

It is wholly wrong to call the measures that we have taken Government control of farming, industry and transportation. It is rather a partnership between government and farming and industry and transportation, not partnership in profits, for the profits would still go to the citizens, but rather a partnership in planning and partnership to see that the plans are carried out.

Radio address (Fireside Chat) on achievements and plans of the new administration, May 7, 1933

5 / I have just signed the Farm Relief Bill [A.A.A.], which includes the refinancing of farm debts.

The Act extends relief not only to farmer borrowers, but to mortgage creditors as well.

Holders of farm mortgages will have the privilege of exchanging them for Federal Land Bank bonds, the interest payments upon which are to be guaranteed by the Treasury of the United States.

Farmers whose mortgages are to be exchanged for these bonds will reap the benefit of lower interest rates and more liberal terms of payment.

It is to the interest of all the people of the United States that the benefits of this Act should be extended to all who are in need of them and that none should be deprived of them through ignorance or precipitate action.

Statement on signing the Farm Relief Bill, May 12, 1933

6 / Remember, the government's part in this [farm] program is merely to supply the unifying element that the farmers themselves, in their past efforts, found so essential to success. That, it seems to me, is the true function of government under our Constitution—to promote the general welfare, not by interfering unduly with individual liberties, but by bringing to the aid of the individual those powers of government which are essential to assure the continuance of the inalienable rights which the Constitution is intended to guarantee. It is democracy in the good old American sense of the word.

The government's policy toward agriculture has been evolving ever since the days of the first President of the United States, George Washington. I know it will continue to evolve, and I hope no one thinks that the present machinery is perfect and cannot be improved. What counts is not so much the methods of the moment as the pathways that are marked out down the years. I like to think of the Agricultural Adjustment Act, not merely as a temporary means of rescue for a great industry, but as the expression of an enduring principle carved in stone by a nation which has come to maturity—a nation which has forever left behind the old irresponsible ways of its youth, a nation facing the realities of today and prudently taking thought for the morrow. I like to think that never again will this nation let its agriculture fall back into decay, and that, instead, the farmers of America will always be able to guard the principles of liberty and democracy for which their farmer ancestors fought. I like to think that agricultural adjustment is an expression, in concrete form, of the human rights those farmer patriots sought to win when they stood at the bridge at Concord, when they proclaimed the Declaration of Independence, and when they perpetuated these ideals by the adoption of the Constitution of the United States. Methods and machinery may change, but principles go on, and I have faith that, no matter what attempts may be made to tear it down, the principle of farm equality expressed by agricultural adjustment will not die.

Address on agriculture, Fremont, Neb., Sept. 28, 1935

7 / When three and a half years ago the Administration undertook to meet the desperate and long neglected needs of agriculture, we turned to the cooperative idea, and called to Washington representatives of the great cooperatives and other farm organizations to work out a program with us.

The Triple A itself had as its foundation and its essence the cooperative idea. Administered locally by community committees selected by the farmers themselves, it was a picture of economic democracy in action. I pay my tribute—with the rest of the nation—to the patriotic zeal of the committees of farmers who did so much through their earnest cooperation for our adjustment and conservation program. The farmers of America will not forget what they have done, and what they are doing.

Campaign address, St. Paul, Minn., Oct. 9, 1936

8 / In the past three and one-half years, the government has helped farmers to meet emergencies of two kinds. The first was a collapse of prices resulting from huge surpluses for which the foreign markets disappeared. The second was a failure of crops in wide areas resulting from drought. Each of these emergencies, except for government action to assist farmers, would have had devastating consequences to consumers and business as well as to farmers.

The time has come to work out permanent measures guarding farmers and consumers against disasters of both kinds. Crop insurance and a system of storage reserves should operate so that the surpluses of fat years could be carried over for use in the lean years.

Measures of this kind should make three important contributions to the general welfare of the country as a whole; first, protection of the individual farmer's income against the hazards of crop failure or price collapse; second, protection of consumers against shortages of food supplies and against extremes of prices; and third, assistance to both business and employment through providing an even flow of farm supplies and the establishing of stability in farm buying power. Since 1933, the A.A.A. payments have proved their usefulness to agriculture as well as business in assuring farmers some income both in time of price collapse and in time of crop failure.

Letter to Secretary of Agriculture Henry A. Wallace on the establishment of a crop insurance committee, Sept. 19, 1936

9 / An enduring agricultural civilization must be built on the firm foundation of home and farm ownership. Any long-time improvement of the welfare of the nation and of farm people involves improvement of the tenancy situation.

Letter to Senator John H. Bankhead and Representative Marvin Jones on farm tenancy, Sept. 21, 1936

10 / The American dream of the family-size farm, owned by the family which operates it, has become more and more remote. The agricultural ladder, on which an energetic young man might ascend from hired man to tenant to independent owner, is no longer serving its purpose. . . .

Owners of family-size farms have been slipping down. Thousands of farmers commonly considered owners are as insecure as tenants. The farm owner-operator's equity in his property is, on the average, 42 percent, and in some of our best farming sections is as little as one fifth.

When fully half the total farm population of the United States no longer can feel secure, when millions of our people have lost their roots in the soil, action to provide security is imperative, and will be generally approved. . . .

The attack on the problem of farm tenancy and farm security is a logical continuation of the agricultural program this administration has been developing since March 4, 1933. Necessarily, whatever program the Congress devises will have to be closely integrated with existing activities for maintaining farm income and for conserving and improving our agricultural resources.

Obviously action by the states alone and independently cannot cure the widespread ill. A nationwide program under federal leadership and with the assistance of states, counties, communities, and individuals is the only solution. Most Americans believe that our form of government does not prohibit action on behalf of those who need help.

Message to Congress on farm tenancy, Feb. 16, 1937

11 / Crop insurance and a system of storage reserves should operate so that surpluses in years of good weather might be carried over for use in years of unfavorable growing conditions. Crop insurance and a system of storage reserves would help to protect the income of individual farmers against the hazards of crop failure; it would help to protect consumers against shortages of food supplies and against extremes of prices; and finally, it would assist in providing a more nearly even flow of farm supplies, thus stabilizing farm buying power and contributing to the security of business and employment. . . .

A program of crop insurance and storage of reserves should be part of the foundation of agricultural policy which we are building and which must include the conservation of soil and water, better land use, increased farm income, and alleviation of distress in rural areas arising out of factors beyond the control of individual producers.

Message to Congress on crop insurance, Feb. 18, 1937

12 / We must continue in our efforts toward abundance without waste. We need legislation which will not only prevent new farm surpluses from causing new collapse in farm prices, but which will also safeguard farmers and consumers against the hazards of crop failure. We need an "all-weather farm plan"—a plan that uses the reasonable surpluses of a year of good weather to carry over food supplies to make up for the shortages of a year of bad weather.

Out of the experience of the last five years we have learned that with the aid of the government, farmers can successfully guard themselves against economic disaster.

Message to the Special Session of Congress proposing farmer and consumer legislation, Nov. 15, 1937

13 / The new law has three major objectives which are inseparably and of necessity linked with the national welfare. The first of these aims is conservation of the soil itself through wise and proper land use. The second purpose is the reestablishment and maintenance of farm income at fair levels so that the great gains made by agriculture in the past three years can be preserved and national recovery can continue. The third major objective is the protection of consumers by assuring adequate supplies of food and fiber now and in the future. . . .

The history of every nation is eventually written in the way in which it cares for its soil. The United States, as evidenced by the progressive public opinion and vigorous demand which resulted in the enactment of this law, is now emerging from its youthful stage of heedless exploitation and is beginning to realize the supreme importance of treating the soil well.

Statement on signing the Soil Conservation and Domestic Allotment Act, March 1, 1936

14 / If we would avoid the poverty of the past, we must strive today—not tomorrow—toward two objectives.

The first is called "better land use"—using the land in such a way that we do not destroy it or harm it for future generations, and in such a way that it will bring to us the best year-in and year-out return as a reward for our labors. . . .

The other objective is the control, with the approval of what I believe is the overwhelming sentiment of the farmers themselves, of what is known as crop surplus.

Address on farm legislation, Grand Forks, N.D., Oct. 4, 1937

15 / In formulating a farm program there are certain things we must keep in mind.

We must keep in mind the fertility of our soil. We have begun to assist farmers to stop the waste of soil and save the good soil that remains. Any sound, long-time program must have soil conservation as a principal goal.

We must keep in mind the economic welfare of farm families. As a long-time national policy, farmers must have a fair share in the national income to supply farmers' buying to keep city factories running.

We must keep in mind the consumers of the nation. . . . Consumers should have the same protection against the under-production of years of scarcity as the farmers should have against the over-production of years of glut.

We must keep in mind the American democratic way. Farm programs cannot long succeed unless they have the active support of the farmers who take part in them. Our program should continue to be one planned and administered, so far as possible, by the farmers themselves.

Message to the Special Session of Congress proposing farmer and consumer legislation, Nov. 15, 1937

16 / Gradually, through these years, the basic principles of national farm policy have become clear. By experience we have learned what must be done to assure to agriculture a fair share of an increasing national income, to provide consumers with abundant supplies of food and fiber, to stop waste of soil, and to reduce the gap between huge surpluses and disastrous shortages. The nation is now agreed that we must have greater reserves of food and feed to use in years of damaging weather and to help iron out extreme ups and downs of price. We are agreed that the real and lasting progress of the people of farm and city alike will come, not from the old familiar cycle of glut and scarcity, not from the succession of boom and collapse, but from the steady and sustained increases in production and fair exchange of things that human beings need.

Statement on signing the Agricultural Adjustment Act, Feb. 16, 1938

17 / The farm program is a splendid example of what 6,000,000 American families can do, when they have the will and the leadership to do it.

The farmers have had a long hard struggle to get laws and programs which give them an opportunity to obtain economic and social justice, to make it possible for them to conserve the good earth which, next to our people and our tradition of freedom, is our greatest heritage. . . .

Many years ago I was told by men of experience in state and national affairs that American farmers could never agree on a program. I did not share that pessimistic belief. My friends and I went out to disprove it and the farmers of America showed clearly that we were right. To them go the honor and the glory.

Radio address to farm dinners throughout the nation, March 8, 1940

18 / [Representative Joseph Martin] is one of that great historic trio which has voted consistently against every measure for the relief of agriculture—Martin, [Bruce] Barton, and [Hamilton] Fish.

Campaign address, Boston, Mass., Oct. 30, 1940

19 / The American farmer is a great producer; and he must have the means to be also a great consumer. For more farm income means more jobs everywhere in the nation. . . .

In 1932 the American farmers' net income was only two and one-quarter billion dollars.

In 1940—a year before we were attacked—farm income was more than doubled to five and a half billion dollars.

This year—1944—it will be approximately thirteen and one-half billion dollars.

Campaign address, Chicago, Ill., Oct. 28, 1944

10

Interrelation of Labor, Industry, and Government

1 / In our generation, a new idea has come to dominate thought about government—the idea that the resources of the nation can be made to produce a far higher standard of living for the masses if only government is intelligent and energetic in giving the right direction to economic life.

That idea—or more properly that ideal—is wholly justified by the facts. It cannot be thrust aside by those who want to go back to the conditions of ten years ago or even preserve the conditions of today. It puts all forms of government to proof.

That ideal makes understandable the demands of labor for shorter hours and higher wages, the demands of farmers for a more stable income, the demands of the great majority of businessmen for relief from disruptive trade practices, the demands of all for the end of that kind of license, often mistermed "liberty," which permits a handful of the population to take far more than their tolerable share from the rest of the people.

Radio address on the 150th anniversary of the Constitution, Washington, D.C., Sept. 17, 1937

2 / Organizations of workers, wisely led, temperate in their demands and conciliatory in their attitude, make not for industrial strife, but for industrial peace. The whole tendency of our modern civilization has been toward cooperation. Employers and employees alike have learned that in union there is strength, that a coordination of individual effort means an elimination of waste, a bettering of living conditions, and is, in fact, the father of

prosperity. . . . Capital is realizing that without the friendly and intelligent cooperation of labor it cannot exist, and labor has learned that without the aid of capital it cannot earn its daily bread. Indeed, so successful has this new principle of arbitration, calm discussion, and willingness to look fairly at the arguments on the other side proved in our industrial affairs that it has led to a general demand for its adoption between nations as the surest guarantee for the peace of the world.

Address before the N.Y. Women's Trade Union League, June 8, 1929

3 / The times and the present needs call for a leadership which insists on the permanence of our fundamental institutions and at the same time demands that by governmental and community effort our business and industry be nourished and encouraged back to a basis made more sound and more firm by the lessons of the experience through which we are passing. Let us not seek merely to restore. Let us restore and at the same time remodel. . . . This is the duty of all of us—leaders in business, finance, agriculture, labor and government.

Fourth annual message to the N.Y. State Legislature, Jan. 6, 1932

4 / It is well within the inventive capacity of man, who has built up this great social and economic machine capable of satisfying the wants of all, to insure that all who are willing and able to work receive from it at least the necessities of life. In such a system, the reward for a day's work will have to be greater, on the average, than it has been, and the reward to capital, especially capital which is speculative, will have to be less.

Address, Oglethorpe University, Atlanta, Ga., May 22, 1932

5 / Never in history have the interests of all the people been so united in a single economic problem [depression]. Picture to yourself, for instance, the great groups of property owned by millions of our citizens, represented by credits issued in the form of bonds and mortgages—government bonds of all kinds, federal, state, county, municipal; bonds of industrial companies, of utility companies; mortgages on real estate in farms and cities, and finally the vast investments of the nation in the railroads. What is the measure of the security of each of those groups? We know well that in our complicated, interrelated credit structure if any one of these credit groups collapses they may all collapse. Danger to one is danger to all. . . .

Statesmanship and vision, my friends, require relief to all at the same time.

Acceptance speech, Democratic National Convention, Chicago, Ill., July 2, 1932

6 / We must set up some new objectives; we must have new kinds of management. Business must think less of its own profit and more of the national function it performs. Each unit of it must think of itself as a part of a greater whole; one piece in a large design.

> Radio address to luncheon meetings of the Business and Professional Men's League, Oct. 6, 1932

7 / There can be only one great principle to guide our course in the coming years. We have learned the lesson that extravagant advantage for the few ultimately depresses the many. To our cost we have seen how, as the foundations of the false structure are undermined, all come down together. We must put behind us the idea that an uncontrolled, unbalanced economy, creating paper profits for a relatively small group, means or ever can mean prosperity.

> Campaign address, New York City, Nov. 5, 1932

8 / The relations between government and business will necessarily be in process of definition during the coming years. . . . Business leaders are now expected to assume the responsibilities which accompany their power. It must be the policy of the government to see that they do it. A good deal can be done in this way, especially if we mobilize public opinion. It is a way we must honestly try. The time has come when industrial leadership must serve the public interest. . . .

We are engaged in a national enterprise. There are no sacred highly privileged special interests which we are pledging ourselves to protect.

> Radio address to luncheon meetings of the Business and Professional Men's League, Oct. 6, 1932

9 / Faith is a delicate though powerful factor in our economic life, and a party that sounds a note of alarm from high places is performing no decent service to the American nation.

> Campaign address, St. Louis, Mo., Oct. 21, 1932

10 / There has been long overdue a reduction of the hours of work and a reduction of the number of working days per week. After all, the greatest justification of modern industry is the lessening of the toil of men and women. These fruits will be dead fruits unless men earn enough so that they can buy the things that are produced, so that they can have the leisure

for the cultivation of body, mind and spirit, which the great inventions are supposed to make possible. That means that government itself must set an example in the case of its own employees. It means also that government must exert its persuasive leadership to induce industry to do likewise.

Campaign address, Boston, Mass., Oct. 31, 1932

11 / We can make possible by democratic self-discipline in industry general increases in wages and shortening of hours sufficient to enable industry to pay its own workers enough to let those workers buy and use the things that their labor produces. This can be done only if we permit and encourage cooperative action in industry, because it is obvious that without united action a few selfish men in each competitive group will pay starvation wages and insist on long hours of work. Others in that group must either follow suit or close up shop. We have seen the result of action of that kind in the continuing descent into the economic hell of the past four years.

There is a clear way to reverse that process: If all employers in each competitive group agree to pay their workers the same wages—reasonable wages—and require the same hours—reasonable hours—then higher wages and shorter hours will hurt no employer. Moreover, such action is better for the employer than unemployment and low wages, because it makes more buyers for his product. That is the simple idea which is the very heart of the Industrial Recovery Act.

On the basis of this simple principle of everybody doing things together, we are starting out on this nationwide attack on unemployment. . . . There is nothing complicated about it and there is nothing particularly new in the principle. It goes back to the basic idea of society and of the nation itself that people acting in a group can accomplish things which no individual acting alone could even hope to bring about.

Radio address (Fireside Chat) on the purposes and foundations of the recovery program, July 24, 1933

12 / There are the perfectly natural problems of selfish individuals who seek personal gain by running counter to the calm judgment of sound leadership. There are hot-heads who think that results can be obtained by noise or violence; there are insidious voices seeking to instill methods or principles which are wholly foreign to the American form of democratic government.

On the part of employers there are some who shudder at anything new. There are some who think in terms of dollars and cents instead of in terms of human lives; there are some who themselves would prefer government by a privileged class instead of by majority rule.

Address at dedication of the Samuel Gompers Memorial, Washington, D.C., Oct. 7, 1933

13 / The employer who turns away from impartial agencies of peace, who denies freedom of organization to his employees, or fails to make every reasonable effort at a peaceful solution of their differences, is not fully supporting the recovery effort of his government. The workers who turn away from these same impartial agencies and decline to use their good offices to gain their ends are likewise not fully cooperating with their government.

Radio address (Fireside Chat) on the record of his administration, Sept. 30, 1934

14 / True wealth is not a static thing. It is a living thing made out of the disposition of men to create and to distribute the good things of life with rising standards of living. Wealth grows when men cooperate; but it stagnates in an atmosphere of misunderstanding and misrepresentation. Here, in America, the material means are at hand for the growth of true wealth. It is in the spirit of American institutions that wealth should come as the reward of hard labor of mind and hand. That is what we call a profit system. Its real fulfillment comes in the general recognition of the rights of each factor of the community. It is not in the spirit of partisans, but partners, that America has progressed. The time is ripe for an alliance of all forces intent upon the business of recovery. In such an alliance will be found business and banking, agriculture and industry, and labor and capital. What an all-American team that is! The possibilities of such a team kindle the imagination—they encourage our determination—they make easier the tasks of those in your government who are leading it.

Address before the District of Columbia Bankers' Convention, Washington, D.C., Oct. 24, 1934

15 / If an industry fails voluntarily to agree within itself, unquestioned power must rest in the government to establish in any event certain minimum standards of fair competition in commercial practices, and, especially, adequate standards in labor relations. For example, child labor must not be allowed to return; the fixing of minimum wages and maximum hours is practical and necessary.

The rights of employees freely to organize for the purpose of collective bargaining should be fully protected.

Message to Congress on progress under the National Recovery Act and recommendation for its extension, Feb. 20, 1935

16 / The individual does not create the product of his industry with his own hands; he utilizes the many processes and forces of mass production to meet the demands of a national and international market.

Therefore, in spite of the great importance in our national life of the efforts and ingenuity of unusual individuals, the people in the mass have inevitably helped to make large fortunes possible. Without mass cooperation great accumulations of wealth would be impossible save by unhealthy speculation. . . . People know that most personal incomes come not only through the effort or ability or luck of those who receive them, but also because of the opportunities for advantage which government itself contributes.

Message to Congress on tax methods and policies, June 19, 1935

17 / It is now beyond partisan controversy that it is a fundamental individual right of a worker to associate himself with other workers and to bargain collectively with his employer. New laws, in themselves, do not bring a millennium; new laws do not pretend to prevent labor disputes, nor do they cover all industry and all labor. But they do constitute an important step toward the achievement of just and peaceable labor relations in industry. This right of the federal government is well established. Every President of the United States in this generation has been faced by the fact that when labor relations are strained to the breaking point there remains but one high court of conciliation—the government of the United States.

Address, San Diego Exposition, San Diego, Calif., Oct. 2, 1935

18 / In our national life, public and private, the very nature of free government demands that there must be a line of defense held by the yeomanry of business and industry and agriculture. I do not mean the generalissimos, but the small men, the average men in business and industry and agriculture —those who have an ownership in their business and a responsibility which gives them stability. Any elemental policy, economic or political, which tends to eliminate these dependable defenders of democratic institutions, and to concentrate control in the hands of a few small, powerful groups, is directly opposed to the stability of government and to democratic government itself.

Address at the Texas Centennial Exposition, Dallas, June 12, 1936

19 / What is of vast importance at this critical time is the fact that we have a common heritage of principle and that we are bound, with millions of our fellow Americans, in a common determination to preserve human

freedom and enlarge its sphere and to prevent forever a return to that despotism which comes from unlicensed power to control and manipulate the resources of our nation, and the destiny of human lives.

Letter to Labor's Non-Partisan League, Washington, D.C., Aug. 3, 1936

20 / Labor Day in this country has never been a class holiday. It has always been a national holiday. It has never had more significance as a national holiday than it has now. . . .

Labor Day belongs to all of us. . . . Labor Day symbolizes the hope of all Americans. Anyone who calls it a class holiday challenges the whole concept of American democracy.

The Fourth of July commemorates our political freedom—a freedom which without economic freedom is meaningless indeed. Labor Day symbolizes our determination to achieve an economic freedom for the average man which will give his political freedom reality.

Radio address (Fireside Chat) on the evening before Labor Day, Sept. 6, 1936

21 / The interest of every businessman is bound to the interest of every wage earner. Whether he is running a store on the corner or is a stockholder in a corporation, big or little, he is financially better off when wages and working conditions are good than when wages and working conditions are poor. . . .

Remember that when men and women are idle, they are not in the market for the products of industry. When wages are low and the working week is long, their purchasing power is limited.

It is to the real advantage of every producer, every manufacturer and every merchant to cooperate in the improvement of working conditions, because the best customer of American industry is the well-paid worker. And the best guarantee of corporate dividends is a rising standard of living.

Campaign address, Cleveland, Ohio, Oct. 16, 1936

22 / It is the problem of government to harmonize the interests of . . . groups which are often divergent and opposing, to harmonize them in order to guarantee security and good for as many of their individual members as may be possible. The science of politics, indeed, may properly be said to be in large part the science of the adjustment of conflicting group interests.

Address on receiving an honorary degree, Rollins College, Winter Park, Fla., March 23, 1936

23 / Those of us who are in government and those whom government serves must all do their part by placing at the service of capital and labor the necessary machinery to facilitate the adjustment of disputes, and thereby eliminate the need for strikes and interference with the flow of wages and of commerce. Such machinery must be perfected if we are to deal with this problem in a manner that is in keeping with our heritage of human reason and intelligence. On the exercise of this intelligence we must base our hopes for peace.

Labor Day statement, Hyde Park, N.Y., Sept. 5, 1937

24 / Government can be expected to cooperate in every way with the business of the nation provided the component parts of business abandon practices which do not belong to this day and age, and adopt price and production policies appropriate to the times.

State of the Union Message, Jan. 3, 1938

25 / Government can deal and should deal with blindly selfish men. But that is a comparatively small part—the easier part of our problem. The larger, more important and more difficult part of our problem is to deal with men who are not selfish and who are good citizens, but who cannot see the social and economic consequences of their actions in a modern economically interdependent community. They fail to grasp the significance of some of our most vital social and economic problems because they see them only in the light of their own personal experience and not in perspective with the experience of other men and other industries. They, therefore, fail to see these problems for the nation as a whole.

Message to Congress on the concentration of economic power, April 29, 1938

26 / The modern interdependent industrial and agricultural society is like a large factory. Each member of the organization has his own job to perform on the assembly line, but if the conveyor belt breaks or gets tangled up, no one in the factory, no matter how hard he tries, can do his own particular job. Each of us—farmer, businessman or worker—suffers when anything goes wrong with the conveyor belt.

If our democracy is to survive it must give the average man reasonable assurance that the belt will be kept moving.

Radio address on social justice and economic democracy, Hyde Park, N.Y., Nov. 4, 1938

27 / The first duty of our statesmanship today is to bring capital and manpower together.

Dictatorships do this by main force. By using main force they apparently succeed at it—for the moment. However we abhor their methods, we are compelled to admit that they have obtained substantial utilization of all their material and human resources. Like it or not they have solved, for a time at least, the problem of idle men and idle capital. Can we compete with them by boldly seeking methods of putting idle men and idle capital together and, at the same time, remain within our American way of life, within the Bill of Rights, and within the bounds of what is, from our point of view, civilization itself?

Ibid., Jan. 4, 1939

28 / Not one of you who are good Americans and practical Americans believe that we could repeat the catastrophe of those years immediately preceding and following 1929 and emerge from it with our economic and social system unchanged. No businessman, big or little, can fairly or patriotically ask his government to take a course of action that runs that risk.

That is why our school of thought—the conservative school—holds the view that an intelligent nation should rest its faith in arithmetic rather than in a hunch.

Today, in order to provide customers for business, your government uses government capital to provide jobs, to prevent farm prices from collapsing and to build up purchasing power when private capital fails to do it. . . .

We also use what we call social legislation—such as legislation to encourage better pay for low-paid labor and thereby provide more and better customers for you; such as legislation to protect investors so that they may continue to be your customers without losing their savings in worthless stocks and bonds.

Address before the American Retail Federation, Washington, D.C., May 22, 1939

29 / It is one of the characteristics of a free and democratic modern nation that it have free and independent labor unions. In country after country in other lands, labor unions have disappeared as the iron hand of the dictator has taken command. Only in free lands have free labor unions survived. When union workers assemble with freedom and independence in a convention like this, it is proof that American democracy has remained unimpaired; it is a symbol of our determination to keep it free.

Address before the Teamsters' Union convention, Washington, D.C., Sept. 11, 1940

30 / The present position of labor in the United States as an interdependent unit in the life of the nation has not come about by chance. It has been an evolutionary process of a healthy democracy at work.

Labor Day radio address, Sept. 1, 1941

31 / There isn't much difference between labor and management actually. I suppose that a very large proportion of management has come, in this country, from the ranks of labor. It's like the old Kipling saying about "Judy O'Grady an' the Colonel's Lady." They are both the same under the skin. That is true in this country, especially in this country, and we want to keep it so.

Informal remarks to the members of the management-labor conference, Washington, D.C., Dec. 17, 1941

II

Housing

1 / You have just cause for pride in what you have achieved—the tall, slim buildings standing white and clear against the sky—but too often around their feet cluster the squalid tenements that house the very poor—buildings that should have been destroyed years ago, full of dark rooms where the sunlight never enters, stifling in the hot summer days, no fit habitation for any man, far less for the thousands of children that swarm up and down their creaking stairways.

Address on housing, New York City, Feb. 28, 1930

2 / The Federal Housing Administration, in the last two years, has been responsible for the building or improvement of over five hundred million dollars' worth of homes. Let it be made perfectly clear that this money was not government money. It was all private money from private lending agencies and all the government did was to insure a portion of the loan. And, incidentally, it was a pretty good business proposition, because the loans are now being paid back, for the simple reason that people now have work.

Extemporaneous campaign remarks at Grand Rapids, Mich., Oct. 15, 1936

3 / Many millions of Americans still live in habitations which not only fail to provide the physical benefits of modern civilization but breed disease and impair the health of future generations. The menace exists not only in the slum areas of the very large cities, but in many smaller cities as well. It exists on tens of thousands of farms, in varying degrees, in every part of the country.

State of the Union Message, Jan. 6, 1937

4 / We have come to realize that a nation cannot function as a healthy democracy with part of its citizens living under good conditions and part forced to live under circumstances inimical to the general welfare.

Greetings to the National Public Housing Conference, New York City, Jan. 14, 1937

5 / Revival of housing construction must be based on reduction of the costs of building and the payment for buildings rather than on a resumption of the rising costs. . . . Housing must be produced at prices, rates and rents that the mass of our people can afford to pay.

The government has made provision, through assistance to municipal housing, for many of the most needy. But private enterprise and private capital must bear the burden of providing the great bulk of new housing.

Message to Congress recommending housing legislation, Nov. 27, 1937

6 / Under the National Housing Act [1934] the Congress established the Federal Housing Administration, which insures mortgages on certain types of housing, but itself makes no loans. The agency is designed to become self-sustaining through the operation of a mortgage insurance fund, into which premiums are paid by borrowers who obtain loans under the provisions of the Act from private lending institutions.

Ibid.

7 / Millions today are living in urban and rural habitations which fail to comply with minimum standards of health, safety and decency. The continued existence of these conditions breeds disease and crime and impairs the health and vitality of our present and future generations.

Letter to the governors of several states urging housing legislation, March 1, 1938

8 / The demand for homes and our capacity to build them call for a program of well over a million homes a year for at least ten years. Private industry can build and finance the vast majority of these homes. Government can and will assist and encourage private industry to do this, as it has for many years. For those very low income groups that cannot possibly afford decent homes, the federal government should continue to assist local housing authorities in meeting that need.

Campaign address, Chicago, Ill., Oct. 28, 1944

12

Planning—Experimentation

1 / Land utilization involves more than a mere determination of what each and every acre of land can best be used for, or what crops it can best grow. That is the first step; but having made that determination, we arrive at once at the larger problem of getting men, women and children—in other words, population—to go along with a program and carry it out.

It is not enough to pass resolutions that land must, or should, be used for some specific purpose; government itself must take steps, with the approval of the governed, to see that plans become realities.

Address before the Conference of Governors, French Lick, Ind., June 2, 1931

2 / Too many of us have been lazy-minded in this matter of government. We like to talk in large terms about the comparative advantages and defects of democracy and autocracy; we like to admire patriotically the work of our forefathers in devising our forms of government or to criticize them as too slavish imitators, but we are terrifically dilatory in following our forefathers' example by seeking to plan and devise for our own immediate needs and for the future; particularly, we hate the details of government.

Address on the finances and responsibilities of local government, University of Virginia, Charlottesville, July 6, 1931

3 / The question . . . is whether we cannot plan a better distribution of our population as between the larger city and the smaller country communities without any attempt to increase or any thought of increasing the number of those who are engaged in farming as an industry. Is it not possible that we might devise methods by which the farmer's market may be

brought closer to him and the industrial worker be brought closer to his food supply? A farm and a rural home are not necessarily the same thing.

Address before the American Country Life Conference, Ithaca, N.Y., Aug. 19, 1931

4 / One of the greatest values of this total regional planning is the fact that it dares us to make experiments. This country will remain progressive America just so long as we are willing to make experiments; just so long as we are able to say, "Here is a suggestion that sounds good. We cannot guarantee it. Let's try it out somewhere and see if it works."

Address on regional planning, New York City, Dec. 11, 1931

5 / I am not speaking of an economic life completely planned and regimented. I am speaking of the necessity, however, in those imperative interferences with the economic life of the nation that there be a real community of interest, not only among the sections of this great country, but among its economic units and the various groups in these units. . . . I plead not for a class control but for a true concert of interests.

The plans we may make for this emergency, if we plan wisely and rest our structure upon a base sufficiently broad, may show the way to a more permanent safeguarding of our social and economic life to the end that we may in a large number avoid the terrible cycle of prosperity crumbling into depression. In this sense I favor economic planning, not for this period alone but for our needs for a long time to come.

Address, Jefferson Day dinner, St. Paul, Minn., April 18, 1932

6 / That which seems most important to me in the long run is the problem of controlling by adequate planning the creation and distribution of those products which our vast economic machine is capable of yielding. It is true that capital, whether public or private, is needed in the creation of new enterprise and that such capital gives employment.

But think carefully of the vast sums of capital or credit which in the past decade have been devoted to unjustified enterprises—to the development of unessentials and to the multiplying of many products far beyond the capacity of the nation to absorb. . . . I do not mean to intimate that we have come to the end of this period of expansion. We shall continue to need capital for the production of newly-invented devices, for the replacement of equipment worn out or rendered obsolete by our technical progress; we need better housing in many of our cities and we still need in many parts of the country more good roads, canals, parks and other improvements. . . .

The country needs and, unless I mistake its temper, the country demands bold, persistent experimentation. It is common sense to take a method and try it: If it fails, admit it frankly and try another. But above all, try something. The millions who are in want will not stand by silently forever while the things to satisfy their needs are within easy reach.

We need enthusiasm, imagination and the ability to face facts, even unpleasant ones, bravely. We need to correct, by drastic means if necessary, the faults in our economic system from which we now suffer. We need the courage of the young.

Address, Oglethorpe University, Atlanta, Ga., May 22, 1932

7 / We must have, I assert with all possible emphasis, national planning in agriculture. We must not have, as now, the scattering of our efforts through the heterogeneous and disassociated activities of our governmental agencies dealing with the problem. On the other hand, we must avoid the present tendency to jump from one temporary expedient to another. We need unity of planning, coherence in our Administration and emphasis upon cures rather than upon drugs. . . .

Planning of that kind, designed primarily to gain a better and less wasteful distribution of agricultural productive effort, inevitably will point the way to readjustments in the distribution of the population in general. . . .

The . . . tariff policy consists, in large measure, of negotiating agreements with individual countries permitting them to sell goods to us in return for which they will let us sell to them goods and crops which we produce. An effective application of this principle will restore the flow of international trade; and the first result of that flow will be to assist substantially the American farmer in disposing of his surplus. . . .

One fact I want to make clear, with all possible emphasis. There is no reason to despair merely because defects have been found in all of these plans; or because some of them have been discarded by responsible leaders in favor of new plans. The fact that so much earnest study and investigation of this problem has been made, from so many angles, and by so many men is, in my opinion, ground for assurance rather than despair. Such a wealth of information has been accumulated, so many possibilities explored, so many able minds enlisted, and, more important still, so much education on the subject provided for and by the farmers themselves, that the time has come when able and thoughtful leaders who have followed this development from the beginning are now focusing on the basic elements of the problem and the practical nature of its solution.

Campaign address, Topeka, Kan., Sept. 14, 1932

8 / It is wholly wrong to call the measures that we have taken government control of farming, industry, and transportation. It is rather a partnership between government and farming and industry and transportation, not partnership in profits, for the profits still go to the citizens, but rather a partnership in planning, and a partnership to see that the plans are carried out. . . .

I have no expectation of making a hit every time I come to bat. What I seek is the highest possible batting average, not only for myself but for the team. Theodore Roosevelt once said to me: "If I can be right 75 percent of the time I shall come up to the fullest measure of my hopes."

Radio address (Fireside Chat) on achievements and plans of the new administration, May 7, 1933

9 / It has been remarked of late . . . that those who are today in charge of your national government are guilty of great experimentation. And they are right. If I read my history correctly, the same suggestion was used when Englishmen, two centuries ago, protesting in vain against intolerable conditions at home, founded new colonies in the American wilderness as an experiment. And the same suggestion was used during the period in 1776 when the Washingtons, the Adamses, the Bullocks and other people of that time conducted another experiment.

Address on the bicentennial celebration of the founding of Georgia, Savannah, Nov. 18, 1933

10 / I do not see why there is not greater enthusiasm for planning, except perhaps for this reason: that the word planning does not signify anything very spectacular about it and it takes a good many years to see results from it. We are all very apt in this life to go after the things that we can throw up our hats and cheer about. We are very apt to favor the panaceas, suggested legislation which would cure all of our troubles in thirty days. We do not like to think ahead. And yet, this is the only solution!

Informal speech at the Subsistence Homes Exhibition, Washington, D.C., April 24, 1934

11 / It is going to take planning; and I am not the least bit afraid of that. If we had started planning a generation ago, we would not have had so much trouble today. Prosperity is coming back, and when it comes back we want to be quite sure that it does not disappear again overnight.

Extemporaneous remarks on the drought situation, Jacksonville, Ill., Sept. 4, 1936

12 / While it is certain that much of the unemployment caused by the march of technical advance is absorbed by new occupations born of new

industries, it is equally true that in the meantime labor may pay a very heavy price through the readjustment and adaptations necessary on the part of workers whose jobs are affected by change. Employers likewise are deeply affected by swift technological changes producing obsolescence and displacement of capital investment.

More than jobs and investment are affected by technical change: Family, church, community, state and all industry are subject to its influence. Study and investigation of technological advances and their social implications constitute one of our most important American planning problems.

Statement on the report by the National Resources Committee, July 12, 1937

13 / The more we study the water resources of the nation, the more we accept the fact that their use is a matter of national concern, and that in our plans for their use our line of thinking must include great regions as well as narrower localities.

Had we known as much and acted as effectively twenty and thirty and forty years ago as we do today in the development of the use of land in that great semi-arid strip in the center of the country which runs from the Canadian border to Texas, we could have prevented in great part the abandonment of thousands and thousands of farms in portions of ten states and thus prevented the migration of thousands of destitute families from those areas into the states of Washington and Oregon and California.

We would have done this by avoiding the plowing up of vast areas which should have been kept in grazing range and by stricter regulations to prevent overgrazing. At the same time we would have checked soil erosion, stopped the denudation of our forests, and controlled disastrous fires.

Some of my friends who talk glibly of the right of any individual to do anything he wants with any of his property take the point of view that it is not the concern of the federal or state or local government to interfere with what they miscall "the liberty of the individual." With them I do not agree and never have agreed, because, unlike them, I am thinking of the future of the United States. My conception of liberty does not permit an individual citizen or group of citizens to commit acts of depredation against nature in such a way as to harm their neighbors, and especially to harm the future generations of Americans.

Address on conservation of water resources, Bonneville Dam, Ore., Sept. 28, 1937

14 / Nationwide thinking, nationwide planning and nationwide action are the three great essentials to prevent nationwide crises for future generations to struggle through.

Address, Thomas Jefferson dinner, New York City, April 25, 1936

13

Conservation

1 / We have been . . . a wasteful nation, a nation that has wasted its natural resources and very often wasted its human resources.

> Extemporaneous remarks on the conservation of natural resources, Boise, Idaho, Sept. 27, 1937

2 / We have been fighting Nature. Now it is time for us to cooperate with Nature.

> Extemporaneous remarks on the drought situation, Aberdeen, S.D., Aug. 28, 1936

3 / We believe that the material resources of America should serve the human resources of America.

> Campaign address, Providence, R.I., Oct. 21, 1936

4 / For centuries European countries have been renewing and caring for their forests so as to get the maximum of benefit from them. They treat timber as a crop. We treat our timber resources as if they were a mine, from which the ore can be taken once and once only. The United States is using timber today four times as fast as it is being grown.

> Radio address on N.Y. State constitutional amendments providing for reforestation, Oct. 26, 1931

5 / Every European nation has a definite land policy, and has had one for generations. We have none. Having none, we face a future of soil erosion

and timber famine. It is clear that economic foresight and immediate employment march hand in hand in the call for the reforestation of these vast areas.

Acceptance speech, Democratic National Convention, Chicago, Ill., July 2, 1932

6 / I propose to create a civilian conservation corps [CCC] to be used in simple work, not interfering with normal employment, and confining itself to forestry, the prevention of soil erosion, flood control and similar projects. I call your attention to the fact that this type of work is of definite, practical value, not only through the prevention of great present financial loss, but also as a means of creating future national wealth. . . .

This enterprise is an established part of our national policy. It will conserve our precious natural resources. It will pay dividends to the present and future generations. It will make improvements in national and state domains which have been largely forgotten in the past few years of industrial development.

Message to Congress proposing the creation of the Civilian Conservation Corps, March 21, 1933

7 / In creating this civilian conservation corps we are killing two birds with one stone. We are clearly enhancing the value of our natural resources, and we are relieving an appreciable amount of actual distress. This great group of men has entered upon its work on a purely voluntary basis; no military training is involved and we are conserving not only our natural resources, but our human resources.

Radio address (Fireside Chat) on achievements and plans of the new administration, May 7, 1933

8 / The passage of this Act [Federal Regulation of Grazing on Public Lands] marks the culmination of years of effort to obtain from Congress express authority for federal regulation of grazing on the public domain in the interests of national conservation and of the livestock industry.

It authorizes the Secretary of the Interior to provide for the protection, orderly use, and regulation of the public ranges, and to create grazing districts with an aggregate area of not more than 80 million acres. It confers broad powers on the Secretary of the Interior to do all things necessary for the preservation of these ranges, including, amongst other powers, the right to specify from time to time the number of livestock which may graze within such districts and the seasons when they shall be permitted to do so. The authority to exercise these powers is carefully safeguarded against impairment by state or local action. Creation of a grazing district by the Secretary of the Interior and promulgation of rules and regulations respecting it will supersede state regulation of grazing on that part of the public domain included with such district.

Water development, soil erosion work, and the general improvement of such lands are provided for in the Act.

> Statement on signing the Act for Federal Regulation of Grazing on Public Lands, June 28, 1934

9 / There is the imperative need of saving those lands of the country now being rapidly turned into virtual deserts through wind and water erosion, and the relocation of those who are trying to wrest a living from this rapidly deteriorating land. Such lands include the flat prairie lands of the West where drought and wind combine to carry away the remaining fertile top-soil and hill land where, after land has been cleared, rain has washed the formerly fertile hillsides clean of productive soil, with consequent gullying and virtual ruin of the land for productive purposes. Such lands can be saved by returning them to forest, or utilizing them for grazing rather than attempting to raise clean-tilled crops, which induce rapid erosion.

> Statement on the establishment of the National Resources Board, July 3, 1934

10 / We should remember that the development of our national park system over a period of many years has not been a simple bed of roses. As is the case in the long fight for the preservation of national forests and water power and mineral deposits and other national possessions, it has been a long and fierce fight against many private interests which were entrenched in political and economic power. So, too, it has been a constant struggle to continue to protect the public interest, once it was saved from private exploitation at the hands of the selfish few.

It took a bitter struggle to teach the country at large that our national resources are not inexhaustible and that, when public domain is stolen, a twofold injury is done, for it is a theft of the treasure of the present and at the same time bars the road of opportunity to the future.

> Address, Glacier National Park, Mont., Aug. 5, 1934

11 / During the three or four centuries of white men on the American continent, we find a continuous striving of civilization against Nature. It is only in recent years that we have learned how greatly by these processes we have harmed Nature and Nature in turn has harmed us. . . .

Furthermore, it is only within our own generation that the development of science, leaping forward, has taught us where and how we have violated Nature's immutable laws, and where and how we can commence to repair such havoc as man has wrought. . . . Men and Nature must work hand in hand. . . .

For the first time in our national history we have made an inventory of our national assets and the problems relating to them. For the first time we have drawn together the foresight of the various planning agencies of the federal government and suggested a method and a policy for the future.

Message to Congress on natural resources, Jan. 24, 1935

12 / A forest is not solely so many thousand board feet of lumber to be logged when market conditions make it profitable. It is an integral part of our natural land covering, and the most potent factor in maintaining Nature's delicate balance in the organic and inorganic worlds. In his struggle for selfish gain, man has often needlessly tipped the scales so that Nature's balance has been destroyed, and the public welfare has usually been on the short-weighted side. Such public necessities, therefore, must not be destroyed because there is profit for someone in their destruction. The preservation of the forests must be lifted above mere dollars and cents considerations. . . . The forests are also needed for mitigating extreme climatic fluctuations, holding the soil on the slopes, retaining the moisture in the ground, and controlling the equable flow of water in our streams. The forests are the "lungs" of our land, purifying the air and giving fresh strength to our people. Truly, they make the country more livable.

Statement on receiving the Schlich Forestry Medal, Jan. 29, 1935

13 / We must start at the bottom and persuade the farmer that he must only take off his woodlot each year the amount of trees—lumber, logs, cordwood, whatever it may be—equivalent to the growth made in that woodlot that year. And so with the larger lumbering operations. There are more and more lumber companies with very large acreage who are coming to this annual crop theory. With that, we shall eliminate some of the terrific evils of the past. . . . If timber is treated as an annual crop, it becomes an asset on which you can raise money.

Remarks at celebration of 50th anniversary of N.Y. State Conservation, Lake Placid, Sept. 14, 1935

14 / You and I are enlisted today in a great crusade in every part of the land to cooperate with Nature and not to fight her, to cooperate to stop destructive floods, to prevent dust storms, to prevent the washing away of

our precious soils, to grow trees, to give thousands of farm families a chance
to live, and to seek to provide more and better food for the city dwellers
of the nation.

> Address, Atlanta, Ga., Nov. 29, 1935

15 / Our objective must be so to manage the physical use of the land that
we will not only maintain soil fertility but will hand on to the next generation a country with better productive power and a greater permanency of
land use than the one we inherited from the previous generation. The opportunity is as vast as is the danger.

> Message to Congress on the control and use of land and water resources, Jan. 30,
> 1936

16 / The remarkable thing was that the people of the United States were so
complacent for so long in the face of exploitation, waste and mismanage-
ment, yes, and even larceny of the natural wealth that belongs to all the
people.

But not everybody remained insensible to what was happening. On
occasion there came as cries from the wilderness warnings against the
ravaging of our forests, the waste of our topsoil and our water supplies, and
the dissipation of our oil reserves and mineral deposits. Theodore Roosevelt,
for one . . . rose up and battled against this squandering of our patrimony.
He, for the first time, made the people as a whole conscious that the vast
national domain and the natural resources of the country were the property
of the nation itself and not the property of any class, regardless of its
privileged status.

> Address at the dedication of the new Department of the Interior Building, Wash-
> ington, D.C., April 16, 1936

17 / Government itself cannot close its eyes to the pollution of waters, to
the erosion of soil, to the slashing of forests, any more than it can close its
eyes to the need for slum clearance and schools and bridges.

> Address at the dedication of the Triborough Bridge, New York City, July 11, 1936

18 / If a nation were to establish in its social balance sheet a capital account
for its energy assets, and were to charge against that account the water that
it permits to go unused, as well as the coal and the oil that are used; or if
the petroleum industry were charged with the gas that it permits to go to
waste—a quantity, by the way, that is enormous in these United States; then

perhaps all citizens would perceive that public policy and private conduct in respect of our natural resources should be quite different from what they now are.

Address before the Third World Power Conference, Washington, D.C., Sept. 11, 1936

19 / No part of our conservation work is more important than the protection of our wildlife. It is a work into which we can all enter, heart and soul, because there is no political partisanship in an activity whose object is to preserve and restore the life of our great out-of-doors. . . . One of the earliest concerns of my administration on assuming office was to provide a national wildlife restoration program and a policy that would make certain that the conservation of our wild animals, birds and fishes would thereafter take rank with the conservation of the other great renewable resources of the nation. . . .

We have evolved a national wildlife conservation program which proposed, largely in conjunction with giving work to the unemployed, to provide abundantly for the needs of wildlife by purchase and retirement of agricultural lands that were submarginal in character, by the purchase of other suitable lands, and by making generous allocations of public lands, all to be set aside as sanctuaries. . . .

We have outlined and enacted a legislative program to give effect to our policy:

1. The Duck Stamp Bill, which has raised about $700,000 a year for the protection of migratory birds.

2. The Coordination Bill, requiring active cooperation of each department of the administration and Cabinet officers in the enforcement of game laws.

3. The Robinson Bill, creating game sanctuaries on all public properties—a big step forward. . . .

The nation has acquired and set aside in these past three years some 4,800,000 acres of land and dedicated them to the restoration and perpetuation of valuable wildlife. Many of the refuges have been located on the principal resting and breeding grounds of wild fowl of all kinds; others are placed along the main migratory flight lanes, while still others afford rest and food and safety to the birds in their winter quarters.

Out in the Western country great ranges have been established to perpetuate the big-game species—the elk, antelope, mountain sheep and the deer. All these sanctuaries afford shelter and security to hosts of song and insectivorous birds and to a great variety of other wild creatures.

Campaign address, Elkins, W.Va., Oct. 1, 1936

20 / The dust storms and floods of the last few years have underscored the importance of programs to control soil erosion. I need not emphasize . . . the seriousness of the problem and the desirability of our taking effective action, as a nation and in several states, to conserve the soil as our basic asset. The nation that destroys its soil destroys itself.

Letter to the governors urging uniform soil conservation laws, Feb. 26, 1937

21 / Nature has given recurrent and poignant warnings through dust storms, floods and droughts that we must act while there is yet time if we would preserve for ourselves and our posterity the natural sources of a virile national life.

Experience has taught us that the prudent husbandry of our national estate requires farsighted management. Floods, droughts and dust storms are in a very real sense manifestations of Nature's refusal to tolerate continued abuse of her bounties. Prudent management demands not merely works which will guard against these calamities, but carefully formulated plans to prevent their occurrence. Such plans require coordination of many related activities.

For instance, our recent experiences of floods have made clear that the problem must be approached as one involving more than great works on main streams at the places where major disasters threaten to occur. There must also be measures of prevention and control among tributaries and throughout the entire headwaters areas.

A comprehensive plan of flood control must embrace not only downstream levees and floodways, and retarding dams and reservoirs on major tributaries, but also smaller dams and reservoirs on the lesser tributaries, and measures of applied conservation throughout an entire drainage area, such as restoration of forests and grasses on inferior lands, and encouragement of farm practices which diminish runoff and prevent erosion on arable lands.

Message to Congress recommending the creation of regional authorities for the development of natural resources, June 3, 1937

22 / A good many of us probably think of our forests as having the primary function of saving our timber resources, but they do far more than that; much of the timber in them is cut and sold under scientific methods, and replaced on the system of rotation by new stands of many types of useful trees. The National Forests, in addition, provide forage for livestock and game; they husband our water at the source; they mitigate our floods and prevent the erosion of our soil. Last but not least, our National Forests will provide constantly increasing opportunity for recreational use.

Address on conservation of forest resources, Timberline Lodge, Mount Hood National Forest, Ore., Sept. 28, 1937

23 / Forests are intimately tied into our whole social and economic life. They grow on more than one-third of the land area of the continental United States. Wages from forest industries support five to six million people each year. Forests give us building materials and thousands of other things in everyday use. Forest lands furnish food and shelter for much of our remaining game, and healthful recreation for millions of our people. Forests help prevent erosion and floods. They conserve water and regulate its use for navigation, for power, for domestic use and for irrigation. Woodlands occupy more acreage than any other crop on American farms, and help support two and one-half million farm families. . . .

When in 1933 I asked the Congress to provide for the Civilian Conservation Corps I was convinced that forest lands offered one source for worth-while work, non-competitive with industry, for large numbers of our unemployed. Events of the past five years have indicated that my earlier conviction was well founded. In rebuilding and managing those lands, and in the many uses of them and their resources, these exists a major opportunity for new employment and for increasing the national wealth.

Creation of the National Forest system, which now extends to thirty-eight states, has been a definite step toward constructive solution of our forest problem. From national forest lands comes domestic water for more than six million people. Forage, occurring largely in combination with timber, contributes stability to one-fourth the western range livestock industry. Through correlated and coordinated public management of timber and all other resources, these public properties already help support almost a million people and furnish healthful recreation to more than thirty million each year. By means of exchanges and purchases, the Congress has for many years encouraged additions to this system. These measures should very definitely be continued as funds and facilities are available.

The Congress has also provided that the national government shall cooperate with the various states in matters of fire protection on privately owned forest lands and farm woodlands. The states are in turn cooperating with private owners. Among other measures the Congress has also authorized an extensive program of forest research, which has been initiated and projected; federal cooperation in building up a system of state forests; cooperative activities with farmers to integrate forest management with the general farm economy; the planting of trees in the Prairie-Plains states—an activity which has heretofore been carried on as an emergency unemployment relief measure with outstanding success and material benefit; and—under the Omnibus Flood Control Bill—measures to retard run-off and erosion on forested and other watersheds.

Progress has been made—and such measures as these should be continued. They are not adequate, however, to meet the present situation. We are still exploiting our forest lands. Forest communities are still being crippled: still being left desolate and forlorn. Watersheds are still being denuded. Fertile valleys and industrial cities below such watersheds still suffer from erosion and floods. We are still liquidating our forest capital, still cutting our accessible forests faster than they are being replaced.

Our forest budget still needs balancing. . . .

As a nation we now have the accumulated experience of three centuries of use and abuse as guides in determining broad principles. The public has certain responsibilities and obligations with respect to private forest lands, but so also have private owners with respect to the broad public interests in those same lands. Particular consideration might therefore be given in these studies, which I hope will form the basis for essential legislation during the next session of Congress, to the situation with respect to private forest lands, and to consideration of such matters as:

1. The adequacy and effectiveness of present activities in protecting public and private forest lands from fire, insects, and diseases, and of cooperative efforts between the federal government and the states.

2. Other measures, federal and state, which may be necessary and advisable to insure that timber cropping on privately owned forest lands may be conducted as continuous operations, with the productivity of the lands built up against future requirements.

3. The need for extension of federal, state, and community ownership of forest lands, and of planned public management of them.

4. The need for such public regulatory controls as will adequately protect private as well as the broad public interests in all forest lands.

5. Methods and possibilities of employment in forestry work on private and public forest lands, and possibilities of liquidating such public expenditures as are or may be involved.

Message to Congress recommending a study of the forest land problem, March 14, 1938

24 / The soil of the United States faces a continuing loss of its productive capacity.

That is a challenging statement. It would seem, therefore, to be the part of wisdom for the government and the people of the United States to adopt every possible method to stop this loss and begin to rebuild soil fertility.

We give the name of "soil conservation" to the problem as a whole; and we are already active in our efforts to retard and prevent soil erosion, and by the more intelligent use of land to build up its crop, its pasturage and its tree producing capacity.

As a result of the studies and tests of modern science it has come to be recognized that phosphorus is a necessary element in human, in animal and

in plant nutrition. The phosphorus content of our land, following generations of cultivation, has greatly diminished. It needs replenishing. The
necessity for wider use of phosphates and the conservation of our supplies
of phosphates for future generations is, therefore, a matter of great public
concern. We cannot place our agriculture upon a permanent basis unless we
give it heed. . . .

To the end that continuous and adequate supplies be insured, and that
efficient forms of this key element, phosphorus, be available at the lowest
cost throughout the country, I recommend that a joint committee of the
Senate and of the House of Representatives be named to give study to the
entire subject of phosphate resources, their use and service to American
agriculture, and to make report to the next Congress.

Message to Congress on soil conservation, May 20, 1938

25 / Money spent for the building of ponds and small lakes, for the
damming of rivers, for planting shelterbelts, for other forms of afforestation, for putting plough land back into grass, that is money well spent. It
pays to do it, not only for this generation but for the children who will
succeed to the land a few years hence.

People who are ignorant and people who think only in terms of the
moment scoff at our efforts and say: "Oh, let the next generation take care
of itself—if people out in the dry parts of the country cannot live there let
them move out and hand the land back to the Indians." That is not your idea
nor mine. We seek permanently to establish this part of the nation as a fine
and safe place which a large number of Americans can call home.

Address on the conservation of natural resources, Amarillo, Tex., July 11, 1938

26 / Our resources of coal, oil, gas and water power provide the energy
to turn the wheels of industry, to service our homes and to aid in national
defense. . . .

Our energy resources are not inexhaustible, yet we are permitting
waste of their use and production. In some instances, to achieve apparent
economies today future generations will be forced to carry the burden of
unnecessarily high costs and to substitute inferior fuels for particular purposes. National policies concerning these vital resources must recognize the
availability of all of them; the location of each with respect to its markets;
the costs of transporting them; the technological developments which will
increase the efficiency of their production and use; the use of the lower
grade coals; and the relationships between the increased use of energy and
the general economic development of the country.

In the past the federal government and the states have undertaken various measures to conserve our heritage in these resources. In general, however, each of these efforts has been directed toward the problems in a single field: toward the protection of the public interest in the power of flowing water in the nation's rivers; toward the relief of economic and human distress in the mining of coal; or toward the correction of demoralizing and wasteful practices and conditions in the industries producing oil and natural gas. It is time now to take a larger view: to recognize—more fully than has been possible or perhaps needful in the past—that each of our great natural resources of energy affects the others.

It is difficult in the long run to envisage a national coal policy, or a national petroleum policy, or a national water-power policy without also in time a national policy directed toward all of these energy producers—that is, a national energy resources policy. . . .

The widening interest and responsibility on the part of the federal government for the conservation and wise use of the nation's energy resources raises many perplexing questions of policy determination. Clearly, there must be adequate and continuous planning and provision for studies which will reflect the best technical experience available, as well as full consideration for both regional and group interests.

Message to Congress on national energy resources, Feb. 16, 1939

14

Public Utilities—
Holding Companies

1 / The water power of the state should belong to all the people. There was, perhaps, some excuse for careless legislative gift of power sites in the days when it was of no seemingly great importance. There can be no such excuse now. The title to this power must vest forever in the people of this state. No commission, no, not the legislature itself has any right to give, for any consideration whatever, a single potential kilowatt in virtual perpetuity to any person or corporation whatsoever. The legislature in this matter is but the trustee of the people, and it is its solemn duty to administer such heritage so as most greatly to benefit the whole people. On this point there can be no dispute.

It is also the duty of our legislative bodies to see that this power, which belongs to all the people, is transformed into usable electrical energy and distributed to them at the lowest possible cost. It is our power; and no inordinate profits must be allowed to those who act as the people's agents in bringing this power to their homes and workshops. If we keep these two fundamental facts before us, half of the problem disappears.

First Inaugural Address as governor of New York, Jan. 1, 1929

2 / It is becoming more and more clear that the families of this state, whether they live in the cities, in the villages or on the farms, have been paying too much for their electricity, and are therefore not in a position to use to a proper degree the many labor-saving devices of modern invention.

Furthermore, rates between different localities show much too great variance, and rural installations are in many cases prohibitive.

Whether mere regulation of electric utilities in the future can be made more successful than it has proved in the past remains a serious question. In the meantime the development of the great state-owned natural resources offers a definite method of relief.

Second annual message to the N.Y. State Legislature, Jan. 1, 1930

3 / As a result of a long course of judicial decisions and of newly invented methods of financing, the householders and businessmen of the nation, in a great many cases, must now pay exorbitant rates, measured not in terms of reasonableness for legitimate investors but rather in terms of speculative profit. We can, of course, have no objection to a reasonable return for the real investor in stocks of utility companies; indeed we should actually do everything possible to safeguard such reasonable return for him. The difficulty is rather with those who seek unreasonably to inflate profits and promote speculative trading by so pyramiding capital structures in holding companies and otherwise that profits are made on stock which is not always represented by actual investment.

Third annual message to the N.Y. State Legislature, Jan. 7, 1931

4 / In this great task of reordering the dislocated American economics, we must constantly strive for three ends: efficiency of service, safety of financial structure, and permanence of employment. The railroad mesh is the warp on which our economic web is largely fashioned. It has made a continent into a nation. It has saved us from splitting, like Europe, into small, clashing, warring units. It has made possible the rise of the West. It is our service of supply. These are not matters of private concern; they have no place in the excesses of speculation, nor can they be allowed to become springboards of financial ambition. Such readjustments as must be made, should be so made that they will not have to be done again; and the system must become, as it should be, secure, serviceable, national in the best sense of that word.

Campaign address, Salt Lake City, Utah, Sept. 17, 1932

5 / [In the state of New York] I laid down the principle that this task of transmission and of distribution [of electricity] should be offered in the first instance to private capital and private management, but under very definite terms. These terms were intended to carry out the purpose of getting the electricity into the homes of the people at the lowest reasonable price. This price would be made up of the following items: First, a payment

to the state at the power house of an amount necessary to pay the interest and amortization on the cost of the plant; second, an item representing the actual cost of transmission and a reasonable return on the actual money wisely and necessarily invested in transmission lines; and third, the cost of distribution plus a reasonable return on the amount wisely and necessarily invested in the properties engaged in distribution.

The sum of these three items would represent the actual cost of electricity to the home owner, and we have believed that this cost would be far below the average price now charged to the home owners in the state. The very definite plan has been to invite private capital to contract with the state to do this transmitting and distribution on these entirely proper and reasonable terms. But at that point it became necessary to provide an alternative in the event that private capital was unwilling to undertake transmission and distribution on terms involving only a reasonable profit to that private capital. . . . The net result of our blindness, of our failure to regulate, and of our failure to say that if private capital will not operate for a reasonable profit, government will have to operate itself, is that in most places in the United States the householders and the farmer and the small businessman are paying vastly more for that very necessary part of our modern life—electricity—than they should be paying. It is neither radical, nor a violation of any principle of sound business, for me to state in definite terms that public servants with a proper regard for the interests of the people themselves must exert every effort to restore the fundamentals of public control. And this applies not only in every state capitol, but also in the control by the national government over those great sources of power which fall under its jurisdiction.

Address, Jefferson Day dinner, St. Paul, Minn., April 18, 1932

6 / I do not hold with those who advocate government ownership or government operation of all utilities. I state to you categorically that as a broad general rule the development of utilities should remain, with certain exceptions, a function for private initiative and private capital.

But the exceptions are of vital importance, local, state and national, and I believe that the overwhelming majority of the people in this country agree with me.

Again we must go back to first principles: A utility is in most cases a monopoly, and it is by no means possible, in every case, for government to insure at all times by mere inspection, supervision and regulation that the public get a fair deal—in other words, to insure adequate service and reasonable rates.

I therefore lay down the following principle: That where a community—a city or county or a district—is not satisfied with the service rendered or the rates charged by the private utility, it has the undeniable basic right, as one of its functions of government, one of its functions of home rule, to set up, after a fair referendum to its voters has been had, its own governmentally owned and operated service. . . .

State owned or federal owned power sites can and should and must properly be developed by government itself. . . . When so developed by government, private capital should, I believe, be given the first opportunity to transmit and distribute the power on the basis of the best service and the lowest rates to give a reasonable profit only. The right of the federal government and state governments to go further and to transmit and distribute where reasonable and good service is refused by private capital, gives to government—in other words, the people—that very same essential "birch rod" in the cupboard.

Campaign address, Portland, Ore., Sept. 21, 1932

7 / I have been watching with great interest the fight being waged against public utility holding-company legislation. I have watched the use of investors' money to make the investor believe that the efforts of government to protect him are designed to defraud him. I have seen much of the propaganda prepared against such legislation—even down to mimeographed sheets of instruction for propaganda to exploit the most far-fetched and fallacious fears. . . .

We seek to establish the sound principle that the utility holding company so long as it is permitted to continue should not profit from dealings with subsidiaries and affiliates where there is no semblance of actual bargaining to get the best value and the best price. If a management company is equipped to offer a genuinely economic management service to the smaller operating utility companies, it ought not to own stock in the companies it manages, and its fees ought to be reasonable. The holding company should not be permitted to establish a sphere of influence from which independent engineering, construction and other private enterprise are excluded by a none too benevolent private paternalism. . . .

We do not seek to prevent the legitimate diversification of investment in operating utility companies by legitimate investment companies. But the holding company in the past has confused the function of control and management with that of investment and in consequence has more frequently than not failed in both functions. Possibly some holding companies may be able to divest themselves of the control of their present subsidiaries and become investment trusts. But an investment company ceases to be an investment company when it embarks into business and management. Investment judgment requires the judicial appraisal of other people's management. . . .

Where the utility holding company does not perform a demonstrably useful and necessary function in the operating industry and is used simply as a means of financial control, it is idle to talk of the continuation of holding companies on the assumption that regulation can protect the public against them. Regulation has small chance of ultimate success against the kind of concentrated wealth and economic power which holding companies have shown the ability to acquire in the utility field. No government effort can be expected to carry out effective, continuous, and intricate regulation of the kind of private empires within the nation which the holding company device has proved capable of creating.

Except where it is absolutely necessary to the continued functioning of a geographically integrated operating utility system, the utility holding company with its present powers must go . . . it offers too well-demonstrated temptation to and facility for abuse to be tolerated as a recognized business institution. That temptation and that facility are inherent in its very nature. It is a corporate invention which can give a few corporate insiders unwarranted and intolerable powers over other people's money. In its destruction of local control and its substitution of absentee management, it has built up in the public utility field what has justly been called a system of private socialism which is inimical to the welfare of a free people. . . .

I am against private socialism of concentrated private power as thoroughly as I am against governmental socialism. The one is equally as dangerous as the other; and the destruction of private socialism is utterly essential to avoid governmental socialism.

Message to Congress on the Public Utility Holding Company Bill, March 12, 1935

8 / Under holding company domination the utility industry has long been hopelessly at war within itself and with public sentiment. . . . The absentee management of unnecessary holding company control has lost touch with, and has lost the sympathy of, the communities it pretends to serve. Even more significantly it has given the country as a whole an uneasy apprehension of overconcentrated economic power.

A business that loses the confidence of its customers and the good-will of the public cannot long continue to be a good risk for the investor. This legislation [Holding Company Bill] will serve the investor by ending the conditions which have caused that lack of confidence and good-will. It will put the public utility operating industry on a sound basis for the future, both in its public relations and in its internal relations.

This legislation will not only in the long run result in providing lower electric and gas rates to the consumer but it will protect the actual value and earning power of properties now owned by thousands of investors who have little protection under the old laws against what used to be called frenzied finance. It will not destroy values.

Radio address (Fireside Chat) on democratic government, April 28, 1935

9 / The great majority of local or regional operating utility companies can come to an understanding with the government and with the people of the territories which they serve. That would enable them to obtain, within their own localities or regions, all of the new capital necessary for the extension or improvement of their services.

But most of these operating companies are owned by holding companies—pyramided holding companies—which are finance companies, not operating utility companies. Very few investors in the operating companies have lost money. But thousands of investors have lost their money in buying holding company securities which had Blue Sky above them instead of tangible assets behind them.

That evil of the utility holding company control will not grow in the days to come because this government has now passed laws to prevent similar occurrences in the future. But we have not yet corrected the existing evils that flow from mistakes of the past. We cannot condone their continuance.

It has been estimated, I think fairly accurately, that there are outstanding some $13,000,000,000 worth of electric utility securities and that the substantial control of this total is vested in the hands of owners of less than $600,000,000 of the total. That means that the ownership of about four per cent of the securities controls the other ninety-six per cent.

There, my friends, is a 96-inch dog being wagged by a four-inch tail.

Address, Jackson Day dinner, Washington, D.C., Jan. 8, 1938

10 / We have seen the multiplied evils which have arisen from the holding company system in the case of public utilities, where a small minority ownership has been able to dominate a far-flung system.

We do not want those evils repeated in the banking field, and we should take steps now to see that they are not. . . .

I recommend that the Congress enact at this session legislation that will effectively control the operation of bank holding companies; prevent holding companies from acquiring control of any more banks, directly or indirectly; prevent banks controlled by holding companies from establishing any more branches; and make it illegal for a holding company, or any corporation or enterprise in which it is financially interested, to borrow from or sell securities to a bank in which it holds stock.

I recommend that this bank legislation make provision for the gradual separation of banks from holding company control or ownership, allowing a reasonable time for this accomplishment—time enough for it to be done in an orderly manner and without causing inconvenience to communities served by holding company banks.

Message to Congress on the concentration of economic power, April 29, 1938

15

TVA—Other Regional Authorities

1 / I am determined on two things as a result of what I have seen today. The first is to put Muscle Shoals to work. The second is to make of Muscle Shoals a part of an even greater development that will take in all of that magnificent Tennessee River from the mountains of Virginia down to the Ohio and the Gulf.

Muscle Shoals is more today than a mere opportunity for the federal government to do a kind turn for the people in one small section of a couple of states. Muscle Shoals gives us the opportunity to accomplish a great purpose for the people of many states and, indeed, for the whole Union. Because there we have an opportunity of setting an example of planning, not just for ourselves but for the generations to come, tying in industry and agriculture and forestry and flood prevention, tying them all into a unified whole over a distance of a thousand miles so that we can afford better opportunities and better places for living for millions of yet unborn in the days to come.

Remarks during Muscle Shoals inspection trip, Montgomery, Ala., Jan. 21, 1933

2 / It is clear that the Muscle Shoals development is but a small part of the potential public usefulness of the entire Tennessee River. Such use, if envisioned in its entirety, transcends mere power development; it enters the wide fields of flood control, soil erosion, afforestation, elimination from agricultural use of marginal lands, and distribution and diversification of industry. In short, this power development of war days leads logically to

national planning for a complete river watershed involving many states and the future lives and welfare of millions. It touches and gives life to all forms of human concerns.

I, therefore, suggest to the Congress legislation to create a Tennessee Valley Authority, a corporation clothed with the power of government but possessed of the flexibility and initiative of a private enterprise. It should be charged with the broadest duty of planning for the proper use, conservation and development of the natural resources of the Tennessee River drainage basin and its adjoining territory for the general social and economic welfare of the nation. This Authority should also be clothed with the necessary power to carry these into effect. Its duty should be the rehabilitation of the Muscle Shoals development and the coordination of it with the wider plan.

Many hard lessons have taught us the human waste that results from lack of planning. Here and there a few wise cities and counties have looked ahead and planned. But our nation has "just grown." It is time to extend planning to a wider field, in this instance comprehending in one great project many states directly concerned with the basin of one of our greatest rivers.

This in a true sense is a return to the spirit and vision of the pioneer. If we are successful here we can march on, step by step, in a like development of other great natural territorial units within our borders.

Message to Congress suggesting legislation for establishment of a Tennessee Valley Authority, April 10, 1933

3 / The TVA is primarily intended to change and to improve the standards of living of the people of that valley. Power is . . . a secondary consideration. Of course it is an important one because, if you can get cheap power to those people, you hasten the process of raising the standard of living.

Press conference, Warm Springs, Ga., Nov. 23, 1934

4 / Government power projects will affect not only the development of agriculture and industry and mining in the sections that they serve, but they will also prove useful yardsticks to measure the cost of power throughout the United States.

Address at the dedication of Boulder Dam, Sept. 30, 1935

5 / The public interest demands that the power that is being or soon will be generated by the Tennessee Valley Authority and at the Bonneville Dam

and other Public Works projects should be made to serve the greatest number of our people at the lowest cost and, as far as possible, without injury to existing actual investment. . . .

This objective can best be attained by cooperative pooling of power facilities within each region, including those of the federal projects, the privately owned utilities and the municipal plants, through the joint use of the existing transmission line networks under the control of the members of the pool. Such a pool, it appears, will smooth out the peaks and valleys of separate system operations, reduce the amount of necessary reserve capacity and postpone the need for investment in new generating facilities.

> Statement regarding a conference to provide for the pooling of power in the Tennessee Valley area, Sept. 19, 1936

6 / The original objective of the [TVA] law included . . . the planting of water-retaining forests near the headwaters of the many rivers and streams, the terracing of farm hillsides, the building of small check-dams, the development of fertilizer, the diversification of crops and other soil building methods, the improvement of highways and other forms of transportation, the bringing in of small industries, the extension of rural electric lines, and many other similar activities.

In other words, it is time that people should understand that power development was only a part—and ultimately only a relatively small part —of a great social and economic experiment in one of our major watersheds.

> Message to Congress on the program of the Tennessee Valley Authority, Jan. 15, 1940

7 / This Chickamauga Dam, the sixth in the series of mammoth structures built by the Tennessee Valley Authority for the people of the United States, is helping to give to all of us human control of the watershed of the Tennessee River in order that it may serve in full the purposes of mankind.

The chain of man-made inland seas may well be named "The Great Lakes of the South." Through them we are celebrating the opening of a new artery of commerce, new opportunities for recreation, relief from the desolation of floods, and new low-cost energy which has begun to flow to the homes and farms and industries in seven American states. . . .

Today we see the progress that we have made, that we are making and that we propose to continue to make. We have come far along the road. In this valley, as in the nation, we do not propose to abandon the goal that is directly before our eyes, either by sitting down or by going back.

These splendid changes have not come by compulsion—for thousands of farmers and thousands of townspeople have met together in the common effort. They have debated and discussed. Participating in the processes of their government, they have altered the looks of their towns. They have added fertilizer to their soil. They have improved their industries. No farmer was forced to join this conservation movement. No workman was compelled to labor here under onerous conditions, or for less than a rightful wage. No citizen has lost a single one of these human liberties we prize so highly in this democracy. This is a demonstration of what a democracy at work can do, of what a people uniting in a war against waste and insecurity can and propose to do.

There were and are those who maintain that the development of the enterprise that lies largely in this state is not a proper activitiy of government. As for me, I glory in it as one of the great social and economic achievements of the United States.

Address at the dedication ceremonies of the Chickamauga Dam, near Chattanooga, Tenn., Sept. 2, 1940

8 / We might give consideration to the creation of seven regional authorities or agencies; one on the Atlantic seaboard; a second for the Great Lakes and Ohio Valley; a third for the drainage basin of the Tennessee and Cumberland Rivers; a fourth embracing the drainage basins of the Missouri River and the Red River of the north; a fifth embracing the drainage basins of the Arkansas, Red, and Rio Grande Rivers; a sixth for the basins of the Colorado River and rivers flowing into the Pacific south of the California-Oregon line; and a seventh for the Columbia River Basin. And in addition I should leave undisturbed the Mississippi River Commission which is well equipped to handle the problems immediately attending the channel of that great river.

Apart from the Tennessee Valley Authority, the Columbia Valley Authority, and the Mississippi River Commission, the work of these regional bodies, at least in their early years, would consist chiefly in developing integrated plans to conserve and safeguard the prudent use of waters, water-power, soils, forests and other resources of the areas entrusted to their charge.

Message to Congress recommending the creation of regional authorities for the development of natural resources, June 3, 1937

16

Consumer—Depositor— Investor

1 / Somebody, of course, must strike the equitable balance between conflicting interests and especially must protect the . . . consumer. And that word "consumer" means the whole American people.

Remarks to the Code Authorities of 600 industries, Washington, D.C., March 5, 1934

2 / I believe that we are at the threshold of a fundamental change in our popular economic thought, that in the future we are going to think less about the producer and more about the consumer. Do what we may have to do to inject life into our ailing economic order, we cannot make it endure for long unless we can bring about a wiser, more equitable distribution of the national income.

Address, Oglethorpe University, Atlanta, Ga., May 22, 1932

3 / The honor of the producers in a country ought to be the invariable ingredient of the products produced in it. The various qualities of goods require a kind of discrimination which is not at the command of consumers. They are likely to confuse outward appearance with inward integrity. In such a situation as has grown up through our rising level of living and our multiplication of goods, consumers are prevented from choosing intelligently and producers are handicapped in any attempt to maintain higher standards. Only the scientific and disinterested activity of government can

protect this honor of our producers and provide the possibility of discriminating choice to our consumers.

Message to Congress on proposed pure foods and drugs legislation, March 22, 1935

4 / We are keeping before us the objectives of protecting, on the one hand, industry against chiselers from within its own ranks, and, on the other hand, the consumer through the maintenance of reasonable competition for the prevention of the unfair sky-rocketing of retail prices.

Radio address (Fireside Chat) on the problems of government, June 28, 1934

5 / The broader the base of consumers of a product that is now classed as a necessity, the lower would be its cost and the greater its stability. A great many years ago Dr. Steinmetz observed that electricity is expensive because it is not widely used, and at the same time it is not widely used because it is expensive. Notwithstanding reductions in rates and increase of consumption since his day—which, by the way, have demonstrated the truth of his words—his observation still holds true. There is a vicious circle which must be broken, and a wise public policy will help to break it.

Address before the Third World Power Conference, Washington, D.C., Sept. 11, 1936

6 / Industrialists kill the goose which lays the golden egg when they keep prices up at the expense of employment and purchasing power . . . [and] when they cut wages and thereby reduce purchasing power. Either policy is self-defeating and suicidal.

Press conference, Jan. 25, 1938

7 / Some of our bankers had shown themselves either incompetent or dishonest in their handling of the people's funds. They had used the money entrusted to them in speculations and unwise loans. This was, of course, not true in the vast majority of our banks, but it was true in enough of them to shock the people for a time into a sense of insecurity and to put them into a frame of mind where they did not differentiate, but seemed to assume that the acts of a comparative few had tainted them all. It was the government's job to straighten out this situation and to do it as quickly as possible.

Radio address (Fireside Chat) on the national economic crisis, March 12, 1933

8 / In the ten years before the crash of 1929, the years of the so-called prosperity boom, bank failures averaged over six hundred a year. The number of bank failures last year [1939] was only forty-two, and of those forty-two, thirty-two were not under federal deposit insurance [Act of June 16, 1933]. Ten were. . . . In those ten banks, ninety-nine per cent of the depositors did not lose one dollar.

Campaign address, Philadelphia, Pa., Oct. 23, 1940

9 / Government cannot prevent some individuals from making errors of judgment. But government can prevent to a very great degree the fooling of sensible people through misstatements and through the withholding of information on the part of private organizations, great and small, which seek to sell investments to the people of the nation.

First—Toward that end and to inspire truth telling, I propose that every effort be made to prevent the issue of manufactured and unnecessary securities of all kinds which are brought out merely for the purpose of enriching those who handle their sale to the public; and I further propose that with respect to legitimate securities the sellers shall tell the uses to which the money is to be put. This truth telling requires that definite and accurate statements be made to the buyers in respect to the bonuses and commissions the sellers are to receive; and, furthermore, true information as to the investment of principal, as to the true earnings, true liabilities and true assets of the corporation itself.

Second—We are well aware of the difficulty and often the impossibility under which state governments have labored in the regulation of holding companies that sell securities in interstate commerce. It is logical, it is necessary and it is right that federal power be applied to such regulation.

Third—For the very simple reason that the many exchanges in the business of buying and selling securities and commodities can by the practical expedient of moving elsewhere avoid regulation by any given state, I propose the use of federal authority in the regulation of these exchanges.

Fourth—The events of the past three years prove that the supervision of national banks for the protection of the public has been ineffective. I propose vastly more rigid supervision.

Fifth—We have witnessed not only the unrestrained use of bank deposits in speculation to the detriment of local credit, but we are also aware that this speculation was encouraged by the government itself. I propose that such speculation be discouraged and prevented.

Sixth—Investment banking is a legitimate business. Commercial banking is another wholly separate and distinct business. Their consolidation and mingling are contrary to public policy. I propose their separation.

Seventh—Prior to the panic of 1929 the funds of the Federal Reserve System were used practically without check for many speculative enterprises. I propose the restriction of Federal Reserve Banks in accordance with the original plans and earlier practices of the Federal Reserve System under Woodrow Wilson.

Finally, my friends, I propose two new policies for which legislation is not required. They are policies of fair and open dealing on the part of the officials of the American government with the American investing public.

In the first place, I promise you that it will no longer be possible for international bankers or others to sell foreign securities to the investing public of America on the implied understanding that these securities have been passed on or approved by the State Department or any other agency of the federal government.

In the second place, I assure you that high public officials in the next Administration will neither by word nor by deed seek to influence the prices of stocks and bonds.

Campaign address, Columbus, Ohio, Aug. 20, 1932

10 / True regulation is for the equal benefit of the consumer and the investor. The only man who will suffer from true regulation is the speculator, or the unscrupulous promoter who levies tribute equally from the man who buys the service and from the man who invests his savings.

Campaign address, Portland, Ore., Sept. 21, 1932

11 / The money changers have fled from their high seats in the temple of our civilization. We may now restore that temple to the ancient truths. The measure of the restoration lies in the extent to which we apply social values more noble than mere monetary profit. . . .

Finally, in our progress toward a resumption of work we require two safeguards against a return of the evils of the old order: there must be a strict supervision of all banking and credits and investments, so that there will be an end to speculation with other people's money; and there must be provision for an adequate but sound currency.

First Inaugural Address, March 4, 1933

12 / The big objective is to restore the old idea that a person who uses other people's money does so in a fiduciary capacity. That applies whether he is a dealer in new securities or whether he is a dealer in old securities. The same thing applies to commodities. In other words, a person who

works in either a stock or a commodity exchange is acting as the agent for other people in a fiduciary capacity.

Press conference, March 29, 1933

13 / I recommend to the Congress legislation for federal supervision of traffic in investment securities in interstate commerce.

In spite of many state statutes the public in the past has sustained severe losses through practices neither ethical nor honest on the part of many persons and corporations selling securities.

Of course, the federal government cannot and should not take any action which might be construed as approving or guaranteeing that newly issued securities are sound in the sense that their value will be maintained or that the properties which they represent will earn profit.

There is, however, an obligation upon us to insist that every issue of new securities to be sold in interstate commerce shall be accompanied by full publicity and information, and that no essentially important element attending the issue shall be concealed from the buying public.

This proposal adds to the ancient rule of *caveat emptor*, the further doctrine "let the seller also beware." It puts the burden of telling the whole truth on the seller. It should give impetus to honest dealing in securities and thereby bring back public confidence.

The purpose of the legislation I suggest is to protect the public with the least possible interference with honest business.

This is but one step in our broad purpose of protecting investors and depositors. It should be followed by legislation relating to the better supervision of the purchase and sale of all property dealt in on exchanges, and by legislation to correct unethical and unsafe practices on the part of offices and directors of banks and other corporations.

What we seek is a return to a clearer understanding of the ancient truth that those who manage banks, corporations and other agencies handling or using other people's money are trustees acting for others.

Message to Congress recommending legislation for federal supervision of traffic in investment securities in interstate commerce, March 29, 1933

14 / This bill requires the publicity necessary for sound investment. It is, of course, no insurance against errors of judgment. That is the function of no government. It does give assurance, however, that, within the limit of its powers, the federal government will insist upon knowledge of the facts on which alone judgment can be based.

The new law will also safeguard against the abuses of high-pressure salesmanship in security flotations. It will require full disclosure of all the private interests on the part of those who seek to sell securities to the public.

The Act is thus intended to correct some of the evils which have been so glaringly revealed in the private exploitation of the public's money. This law and its effective administration are steps in a program to restore some old-fashioned standards of rectitude. Without such an ethical foundation, economic well-being cannot be achieved.

Statement on signing the securities bill, May 27, 1933

15 / This Congress has performed a useful service in regulating the investment business on the part of financial houses and in protecting the investing public in its acquisition of securities.

There remains the fact, however, that outside the field of legitimate investment, naked speculation has been made far too alluring and far too easy for those who could and for those who could not afford to gamble.

Such speculation has run the scale from the individual who has risked his pay envelope or his meager savings on a margin transaction involving stocks with whose true value he was wholly unfamiliar, to the pool of individuals or corporations with large resources, often not their own, who sought by manipulation to raise or depress market quotations far out of line with reason. All of this has resulted in loss to the average investor who is of necessity personally uninformed.

The exchanges in many parts of the country which deal in securities and commodities conduct, of course, a national business because their customers live in every part of the country. The managers of these exchanges have, it is true, often taken steps to correct certain obvious abuses. We must be certain that abuses are eliminated and to this end a broad policy of national regulation is required.

It is my belief that exchanges for dealing in securities and commodities are necessary and of definite value to our commercial and agricultural life. Nevertheless, it should be our national policy to restrict, as far as possible, the use of these exchanges for purely speculative operations.

I therefore recommend to the Congress the enactment of legislation providing for the regulation by the federal government of the operations of exchanges dealing in securities and commodities for the protection of investors, for the safeguarding of values, and so far as it may be possible, for the elimination of unnecessary, unwise and destructive speculation.

Message to Congress recommending the creation of the Securities and Exchange Commission, Feb. 9, 1934

16 / Because kidnappers and bank robbers could in high-powered cars speed across state lines, it became necessary, in order to protect our people,

to invoke the power of the federal government. In the same way speculators and manipulators from across state lines, and regardless of state laws, have lured the unsuspecting and the unwary to financial destruction. In the same way across state lines, there have been built up intricate corporate structures, piling bond upon stock and stock upon bond—huge monopolies which were stifling independent business and private enterprise.

There was no power under Heaven that could protect the people against that sort of thing except a people's government at Washington. All that this administration has done, all that it proposes to do—and this it does propose to do—is to use every power and authority of the federal government to protect the commerce of America from the selfish forces which ruined it.

Campaign address, Chicago, Ill., Oct. 14, 1936

17 / Investment trusts should be brought under strict control to insure their operations in the interests of their investors rather than their managers. The Securities and Exchange Commission is to make a report to Congress on the results of a comprehensive study of investment trusts and their operations which it has carried on for nearly two years. The investment trust, like the holding company, puts huge aggregations of the capital of the public at the direction of a few managers. Unless properly restricted, it has potentialities of abuse second only to the holding company as a device for the further centralization of control over American industry and American finance.

The tremendous investment funds controlled by our great insurance companies have a certain kinship to investment trusts, in that these companies invest as trustees the savings of millions of our people. The Securities and Exchange Commission should be authorized to make an investigation of the facts relating to these investments with particular relation to their use as an instrument of economic power.

Message to Congress on the concentration of economic power, April 29, 1938

18 / . . . thousands of investors have lost their money in buying holding company securities which had Blue Sky above them instead of tangible assets behind them.

Address, Jackson Day dinner, Washington, D.C., Jan. 8, 1938

17

Public Welfare—Social and Economic Security

1 / Poverty in old age should not be regarded either as a disgrace or necessarily as a result of lack of thrift or energy. Usually it is a mere by-product of modern industrial life. An alarmingly increasing number of aged persons are becoming dependent on outside help for bare maintenance. While improved medical science has increased man's span of life, the rapid pace of modern industry has proportionately increased the number of years during which he is an unsought employee. While the worker of today on the average may look forward to a longer life than did his grandfather, he must necessarily count on a shorter period of industrial availability. No greater tragedy exists in modern civilization than the aged, worn-out worker who after a life of ceaseless effort and useful productivity must look forward for his declining years to a poorhouse. A modern social conscious-ness demands a more humane and efficient arrangement.

Message to the N.Y. State Legislature, proposing a commission to study the question of security against old age, poverty, and want, Feb. 28, 1929

2 / We should forever banish the black shadow of old-age want. For those who may no longer earn their daily bread, because of swift-falling accident or slow incurable disease, we have provided, and we are providing, hospitals, sanitaria, and institutions where, so far as is humanly possible, they may be restored to useful life, or, if that is not possible, receive care and comforts. But how about those whose bodies are not stricken by sudden disaster, who work hard and faithfully through long years, until time lays its heavy hand upon them? Is there no obligation on the part of the state to

look after these? It is through no fault of theirs that they cannot continue to add to our prosperity or to labor for the good of the whole state. And yet, what answer have we made, except the creation of that gloomy institution which haunts the thought of every aged worker, like some horrible nightmare, the poorhouse?

I do not believe it necessary, nor do those who have studied the matter long and thoughtfully, believe that it is an economic necessity that we herd our aged workers, dependent on their toil for their daily bread, in institutions of this character. It is not even an economic solution of the problem. It is the most wasteful and extravagant system that we could possibly devise. It belongs to that past barbaric age when we chained our insane to the walls of our madhouses. . . .

In the final analysis, good economics as well as a decent sense of humanity dictates that if the state is to aid them in their declining years that aid should be given to them under conditions where they may maintain their independent lives and hold up their heads as citizens of America.

Address before the N.Y. Women's Trade Union League, June 8, 1929

3 / The old idea of the right of an individual to be sick or of a community to have epidemics no longer exists. That right has been turned around and transferred to the state. I mean by "state" the general governing agencies, and they undoubtedly have the right to insist on good health. . . . We must bring home more and more to the average citizen the fact that health has become a part of government, that it is no longer a question of charity.

Address on public health and the development of Saratoga Springs, N.Y., June 25, 1929

4 / [Rehabilitation] is a problem that demands a crusade. The progress of the past fifty years has been great, but we have marched only a short way. The extension of the work must go on until every child in the United States can be assured of the best that science, government assistance and private aid can give.

It is a task that appeals to our humanity, but it is a task that appeals also to our future economic success. Every citizen, man, woman or child, who is unable to take his or her part in the normal life of modern civilization is a drag on our economic life. Good humanity and good economics demand that the work must go on.

Address on treatment of the handicapped, Chautauqua, N.Y., July 13, 1929

5 / The most striking and important difference between the civilization of today and the civilization of yesterday is the universal recognition that

the first duty of a state, and by that I mean a government, is to promote the welfare of the citizens of that state. It is no longer sufficient to protect them from invasion, from lawless and criminal acts, from injustice and persecution, but the state must protect them, so far as lies in its power, from disease, from ignorance, from physical injury, and from old-age want.

Address before the N.Y. State Charities Aid Association, New York City, Jan. 17, 1930

6 / Unemployment is a problem for the entire community. It is a major social tragedy for the individual who is denied the opportunity to work and earn, but it does not stop there, and if not soon corrected will have a long-time depressive effect on business and trade in the State.

Statement on unemployment and industry, March 29, 1930

7 / It is far better for all of us to have steady employment year in and year out, rather than to have periods where there is a demand for more labor than exists, followed by periods when a large percentage of workers are either entirely out of a job or are receiving pay for only one or two days' work a week. The feasts and plenty of yesterday will never dispel the famine and need of today . . . but it is wholly possible to set some portion of yesterday's feast aside in cold storage, as it were, to satisfy tomorrow's hunger.

Address before the N.Y. State Federation of Labor, Buffalo, N.Y., Aug. 27, 1930

8 / I look forward to the time when every young man and young woman entering industrial or agricultural or business activity will begin to insure himself or herself against the privations of old age. The premiums which that young man or young girl will pay should be supplemented by premiums to be paid by the employers of the state, as well as by the state itself. In that way, when the young man or young girl has grown to old and dependent age, he or she will have built up an insurance fund which will maintain them in comfort in their years of reduced activity. In this way, their assistance will be a result of their own efforts and foresightedness. They will be receiving not charity, but the natural profits of their years of labor and insurance.

Gubernatorial campaign address, Rochester, N.Y., Oct. 21, 1930

9 / Our American aged do not want charity, but rather old age comforts to which they are rightfully entitled by their own thrift and foresight in

the form of insurance. It is, therefore, my judgment that the next step to be taken should be based on the theory of insurance by a system of contributions commencing at an early age. In this way all men and women will, on arriving at a period when work is no longer practicable, be assured not merely of a roof overhead and enough food to keep body and soul together, but also enough income to maintain life during the balance of their days in accordance with the American standard of living.

Third annual message to the N.Y. State Legislature, Jan. 7, 1931

10 / The overwhelming majority of children who become crippled can with proper treatment be restored to a useful, active life in the community. . . .

We owe to every crippled child in the United States a chance to come back, not merely from the big, broad point of view of humanity. I want to emphasize again that by restoring all of these tens of thousands of children to useful, normal lives, we shall be doing a fine thing, carrying out a great objective for the nation.

Radio address on aid to the crippled, Feb. 18, 1931

11 / The success or failure of any government in the final analysis must be measured by the well-being of its citizens. Nothing can be more important to a state than its public health; the state's paramount concern should be the health of its people.

Report to the N.Y. State Legislature on public health, Feb. 19, 1931

12 / Today we are giving serious thought to still another form of insurable risk—that of providing some form of reserve for individual men and women to be used by them for their maintenance and support in times of involuntary unemployment. Here again, as was the case a quarter of a century ago when workmen's compensation was being considered, there is much unthinking opposition on the principal ground that the proposal is something new. It is not a sound argument to make that a new thing may prove unsound just because it is new.

Address on unemployment insurance, New York City, March 6, 1931

13 / Relief should not, of course, take the shape of a dole in any respect. The dole method of relief for unemployment is not only repugnant to all sound principles of social economics, but is contrary to every principle of American citizenship and of sound government. American labor seeks

no charity, but only a chance to work for its living. The relief which the workers of the state should be able to anticipate, when engulfed in a period of industrial depression, should be one of insurance, to which they themselves have in a large part contributed. Each industry itself should likewise bear a part of the premium for this insurance, and the state, in the interest of its own citizens, and to prevent a recurrence of the widespread hardship of these days, should at the least supervise its operations.

> Recommendations to the N.Y. State Legislature on unemployment insurance, March 25, 1931

14 / Public health is more than a local responsibility. Disease knows nothing about town lines, nor do bacilli undertake to inquire about local jurisdictions. Their carriers are on the public highways and riding in the railroad trains. If we care nothing about the fact that a farmer's children are dying of infection or malnutrition—and that can happen in the country, too— we can still give some thought to the weaklings and the sufferers whom we may have to support in some day not far off.

> Address on the finances and responsibilities of local government, University of Virginia, Charlottesville, July 6, 1931

15 / Other than the indifference of local governments, there is no reason for tuberculosis to be twice as prevalent in some communities as in others; for deaths and illnesses from diphtheria to continue to occur when some municipalities have been able to stamp it out entirely; for twice as many babies to die each year in some counties and cities as in the communities where a modern health program is in force; for certain death rates to be higher in rural communities, with no organized health services, than in urban communities where health service is available; and for those citizens of lower economic rank to suffer a higher death rate from practically *all* causes.

> Statement on the report of the N.Y. State Special Health Commission, April 6, 1932

16 / These unhappy times call for the building of plans that rest upon the forgotten, the unorganized but indispensable units of economic power, . . . that build from the bottom up and not from the top down, that put their faith once more in the forgotten man at the bottom of the economic pyramid.

> Radio address on national affairs, Albany, N.Y., April 7, 1932

17 / There are two theories of prosperity and of well-being: The first theory is that if we make the rich richer, somehow they will let a part of their prosperity trickle down to the rest of us. The second theory—and I suppose this goes back to the days of Noah—I won't say Adam and Eve, because they had a less complicated situation—but, at least, back to the days of the flood, there was the theory that if we make the average of mankind comfortable and secure, their prosperity will rise upward, just as yeast rises up, through the ranks. . . .

The philosophy of social justice that I am going to talk about . . . the philosophy of social justice through social action, calls definitely, plainly, for the reduction of poverty. And what do we mean when we talk about the reduction of poverty? We mean the reduction of the causes of poverty . . . [which] in the main are beyond the control of any one individual or any czar, either a czar of politics or a czar of industry. The followers of the philosophy of "social action for the prevention of poverty" maintain that if we set up a system of justice we shall have small need for the exercise of mere philanthropy. Justice, after all, is the first goal we seek. We believe that when justice has been done individualism will have a greater security to devote the best that individualism itself can give. . . .

And so, in these days of difficulty, we Americans everywhere must and shall choose the path of social justice—the only path that will lead us to a permanent bettering of our civilization, the path that our children must tread and their children must tread, the path of faith, the path of hope and the path of love toward our fellow men.

Campaign address, Detroit, Mich., Oct. 2, 1932

18 / We have two problems: first, to meet the immediate distress; second, to build up on a basis of permanent employment.

As to "immediate relief," the first principle is that this nation, this national government, if you like, owes a positive duty that no citizen shall be permitted to starve. That means that while the immediate responsibility for relief rests, of course, with local, public and private charity, in so far as these are inadequate the states must carry on the burden, and whenever the states themselves are unable adequately to do so the federal government owes the positive duty of stepping into the breach. . . .

In addition to providing emergency relief, the federal government should and must provide temporary work wherever that is possible. You and I know that in the national forests, on flood prevention, and on the development of waterway projects that have already been authorized and planned but not yet executed, tens of thousands, and even hundreds of thousands of our unemployed citizens can be given at least temporary employment. . . .

Finally, in that larger field that looks further ahead, we call for a coordinated system of employment exchanges, the advance planning of public works, and unemployment reserves.

Campaign address, Boston, Mass., Oct. 31, 1932

19 / Among our objectives I place the security of the men, women and children of the nation first.

This security for the individual and for the family concerns itself primarily with three factors. People want decent homes to live in; they want to locate them where they can engage in productive work; and they want some safeguard against misfortunes which cannot be wholly eliminated in this man-made world of ours. . . .

Security was attained in the earlier days through the interdependence of members of families upon each other and of the families within a small community upon each other. The complexities of great communities and of organized industry make less real these simple means of security. Therefore, we are compelled to employ the active interest of the nation as a whole through government in order to encourage a greater security for each individual who composes it. . . . If, as our Constitution tells us, our federal government was established among other things "to promote the general welfare," it is our plain duty to provide for that security upon which welfare depends. . . . We may well undertake the great task of furthering the security of the citizen and his family through social insurance. . . .

These three great objectives—the security of the home, the security of livelihood, and the security of social insurance—are, it seems to me, a minimum of the promise that we can offer to the American people. They constitute a right which belongs to every individual and every family willing to work. They are the essential fulfillment of measures already taken toward relief, recovery and reconstruction.

This seeking for a greater measure of welfare and happiness does not indicate a change in values. It is rather a return to values lost in the course of our economic development and expansion. . . .

We must dedicate ourselves anew to a recovery of the old and sacred possessive rights for which mankind has constantly struggled—homes, livelihood, and individual security. The road to these values is the way to progress.

Message to Congress reviewing the record of his administration, June 8, 1934

20 / The primary responsibility for community needs rests upon the community itself. . . . If every effort has been used by any given community and has proven insufficient, then it is the duty of the state to

supplement, with the resources of the state, the additional needs up to the limit of its power. . . . Finally, it is only when both of these efforts, taken together, prove insufficient that the federal government has any duty to add its resources to the common cause. . . .

> Address before the Conference on Mobilization for Human Needs, Washington, D.C., Sept. 28, 1934

21 / There is also the problem of economic loss due to sickness—a very serious matter for many families with and without incomes, and, therefore, an unfair burden upon the medical profession. Whether we come to this form of insurance soon or later on, I am confident that we can devise a system which will enhance and not hinder the remarkable progress which has been made and is being made in the practice of the professions of medicine and surgery in the United States.

> Address to the Advisory Council of the Committee on Economic Security, White House, Nov. 14, 1934

22 / I am not willing that the vitality of our people be further sapped by the giving of cash, of market baskets, of a few hours of weekly work cutting grass, raking leaves or picking up papers in the public parks. We must preserve not only the bodies of the unemployed from destitution but also their self-respect, their self-reliance and courage and determination.

> State of the Union Message, Jan. 4, 1935

23 / The establishment of sound means toward a greater future economic security of the American people is dictated by a prudent consideration of the hazards involved in our national life. No one can guarantee this country against the dangers of future depressions, but we can reduce these dangers. We can eliminate many of the factors that cause economic depressions, and we can provide the means of mitigating their results. This plan for economic security is at once a measure of prevention and a method of alleviation.

> Message to Congress on proposed social security legislation, Jan. 17, 1935

24 / The social objective, I should say, remains just what it was, which is to do what any honest Government of any country would do: to try to increase the security and the happiness of a larger number of people in all occupations of life and in all parts of the country; to give them more of the good things of life; to give them a greater distribution not only of

wealth in the narrow terms, but of wealth in the wider terms; to give them places to go in the summertime—recreation; to give them assurance that they are not going to starve in their old age; to give honest business a chance to go ahead and make a reasonable profit; and to give everyone a chance to earn a living.

Press conference, June 7, 1935

25 / Today a hope of many years' standing is in large part fulfilled. The civilization of the past hundred years, with its startling industrial changes, has tended more and more to make life insecure. Young people have come to wonder what would be their lot when they came to old age. The man with a job has wondered how long the job would last.

This social security measure gives at least some protection to thirty millions of our citizens who will reap direct benefits through unemployment compensations, through old-age pensions and through increased services for the protection of children and the prevention of ill health.

We can never insure one hundred per cent of the population against one hundred per cent of the hazards and vicissitudes of life, but we have tried to frame a law which will give some measure of protection to the average citizen and to his family against the loss of a job and against poverty-ridden old age.

This law, too, represents a cornerstone in a structure which is being built but is by no means complete. It is a structure intended to lessen the force of possible future depressions. It will act as a protection to future administrations against the necessity of going deeply into debt to furnish relief to the needy. The law will flatten out the peaks and valleys of deflation and of inflation. It is, in short, a law that will take care of human needs and at the same time provide for the United States an economic structure of vastly greater soundness.

What we are doing is good. But it is not good enough. To be truly national a social security program must include all those who need its protection. Today many of our citizens are still excluded from old-age insurance and unemployment compensation because of the nature of their employment. This must be set aright, and it will be.

Some time ago I directed the Social Security Board to give attention to the development of a plan for liberalizing and extending the old-age insurance system to provide benefits for wives, widows and orphans. More recently, a great national health conference has been held, held at my suggestion to consider ways and means of extending to the people of this country more adequate health and medical services and also to afford the people of this country some protection against the economic losses arising out of ill health.

I am hopeful that on the basis of studies and investigation now under way, the Congress will improve and extend the law. I am also confident that each year will bring further development in federal and state social security legislation—and that is as it should be.

Statement on signing the Social Security Act, Aug. 14, 1935

26 / We were opposed by many of the same organizations and the same individuals who are now crying aloud about the socialism involved in social security legislation, in bank deposit insurance, in farm credit, in the saving of homes, in the protection of investors and the regulation of public utilities. The reforms, however, for which we were condemned twenty-four years ago are taken today as a matter of course. And so, I believe, will be regarded the reforms that now cause such concern to the reactionaries of 1935. We come to an understanding of these new ways of protecting people because our knowledge enlarges and our capacity for organized action increases.

Radio message to the Young Democratic Clubs of America, Aug. 24, 1935

27 / Private enterprise, indeed, became too private. It became privileged enterprise, not free enterprise.

Acceptance speech, Democratic National Convention, Philadelphia, Pa., June 27, 1936

28 / This matter of economic security, I take it, is not to be achieved by aiming at restriction of national income—real national income—but by aiming for more abundant and more widely distributed national income. A satisfying standard of living and security for a national household of nearly 130 million people are to be realized only by high productivity, broadly and equitably distributed, and wisely proportioned with respect to its drain on national resources and to the variety of human wants that it is designed to satisfy.

Address before the Third World Power Conference, Washington, D.C., Sept. 11, 1936

29 / By security I do not mean just a living, just having enough to eat and a place to sleep. I mean living according to the American standard, a standard which provides a decent diet, a decent education and a reasonable amount of leisure and recreation. . . .

That kind of security, as we see it, applies not only to people with respect to their own individual family lives, but ought to apply to their occupation and ought to apply to the businesses which employ them.

Extemporaneous campaign remarks, Cincinnati, Ohio, Oct. 16, 1936

30 / Child labor, especially in low-paid unstandardized types of work, is increasing. I am convinced that nationwide minimum standards are necessary and that a way should be found promptly to crystallize in legal safeguards public opinion in behalf of the elimination of child labor.

Letter to several state governors urging the ratification of the Child Labor Amendment to the Constitution, Jan. 7, 1937

31 / A self-supporting and self-respecting democracy can plead no justification for the existence of child labor, no economic reason for chiseling workers' wages or stretching workers' hours.

Enlightened business is learning that competition ought not to cause bad social consequences which inevitably react upon the profits of business itself.

Message to Congress recommending wages and hours legislation, May 24, 1937

32 / The inherent right to work is one of the elemental privileges of a free people. Continued failure to achieve that right and privilege by anyone who wants to work and needs work is a challenge to our civilization and to our security. Endowed, as our nation is, with abundant physical resources, and inspired as it should be with the high purpose to make those resources and opportunities available for the enjoyment of all, we approach this problem of re-employment with the real hope of finding a better answer than we have now.

Radio address regarding an unemployment census, Nov. 14, 1937

33 / On a thousand fronts government—state and municipal as well as federal—is playing the same role of the insurer of security for the average man, woman and child that the Army detachments played in the early days of the old Northwest Territory. When you think it through, at the bottom most of the great protective statutes of today are in essence mutual insurance companies, and our recent legislation is not a departure from but a return to the healthy practices of mutual self-help of the early settlers of the Northwest.

Address on popular government, Marietta, Ohio, July 8, 1938

34 / When we see what we know how to do, yet have not done, it is clear that there is need for a coordinated national program of action. Such a [health] program necessarily must take account of the fact that millions of citizens lack the individual means to pay for adequate medical care. The economic loss due to sickness is a very serious matter not only for many families with and without incomes but for the nation as a whole.

Letter to Interdepartmental Committee to Coordinate Health and Welfare Activities of the Federal Government, July 15, 1938

35 / I cannot too strongly urge the wisdom of building upon the principles contained in the present Social Security Act in affording greater protection to our people, rather than turning to untried and demonstrably unsound panaceas. . . .

We shall make the most orderly progress if we look upon social security as a development toward a goal rather than a finished product. We shall make the most lasting progress if we recognize that social security can furnish only a base upon which each one of our citizens may build his individual security through his own individual efforts.

Message to Congress recommending improvements in the Social Security system, Jan. 16, 1939

36 / The health of the people is a public concern; ill health is a major cause of suffering, economic loss and dependency; good health is essential to the security and progress of the nation. . . .

I have been concerned by the evidence of inequalities that exist among the states as to personnel and facilities for health services. There are equally serious inequalities of resources, medical facilities and services in different sections and among different economic groups. These inequalities create handicaps for the parts of our country and the groups of our people which most sorely need the benefits of modern medical science.

Message to Congress recommending improvement of the National Health Program, Jan. 23, 1939

37 / It is still our task to bring to bear on the major problems of child life all the wisdom and the understanding that can be distilled from compilations of facts, from the intuitions of common sense, and from professional skill. . . .

In providing for the health and education of children and for the formation of their minds and characters in ways which are in harmony with the institutions of a free society, democracy is training its future leaders. The safety of democracy therefore depends upon the widespread diffusion of opportunities for developing those qualities of mind and character which are essential to leadership in our modern age. . . .

Democracy must inculcate in its children capacities for living and assure opportunities for the fulfillment of those capacities. The success of democratic institutions is measured, not by extent of territory, financial power, machines or armaments, but by the desires, the hopes and the deep-lying satisfactions of the individual men, women and children who make up its citizenship. . . .

We make the assumption that a happy child should live in a home where he will find warmth and food and affection; that his parents will take care of him should he fall ill; that at school he will find the teachers and tools needed for an education; that when he grows up there will be a job for him and that he will some day be able to establish his own home.

As we consider these essentials of a happy childhood our hearts are necessarily heavy with the knowledge that there are many children who cannot make these assumptions.

We are concerned about the children of the unemployed.

We are concerned about other children who are without adequate shelter or food or clothing because of the poverty of their parents.

We are concerned about the children of migratory families who have no settled place of abode or normal community relationships.

We are concerned about the children of minority groups in our population who, confronted with discrimination and prejudice, must find it difficult to believe in the just ordering of life or the ability of the adults in their world to deal with life's problems.

We are concerned about the children living beyond the reach of medical service or lacking medical service because their parents cannot afford to pay for it.

We are concerned about the children who are not in school or who attend schools poorly equipped to meet their needs.

We are concerned about the children who are outside the reach of religious influences, and are denied help in attaining faith in an ordered universe and in the fatherhood of God.

We are concerned about the future of our democracy when children cannot make the assumptions that mean security and happiness.

Address before the White House Conference on Children in a Democracy, Washington, D.C., April 23, 1939

38 / I am in favor of war. I am very much in favor of the kind of war that we are conducting here at Warm Springs, the kind of war that, aided

and abetted by what we have been doing at Warm Springs now for fourteen or fifteen years, is spreading all over the country—the war against the
crippling of men and women and, especially, of children.

Extemporaneous remarks at Thanksgiving Day dinner, Warm Springs, Ga.,
Nov. 23, 1939

39 / For instance, who a generation ago would have thought that a week
from tomorrow—January 1, 1940—tens of thousands of elderly men and
women in every state and every county and every city of the nation would
begin to receive checks every month for old age retirement insurance—and
not only that but that there would be also insurance benefits for the wife,
the widow, the orphan children and even dependent parents? Who would
have thought a generation ago that people who lost their jobs would, for
an appreciable period, receive unemployment insurance—that the needy,
the blind and the crippled children would receive some measure of protection which will reach down to the millions of Bob Cratchits, the Marthas
and the Tiny Tims of our own "four-room homes."

Radio address on Christmas Eve, Dec. 24, 1939

40 / The unemployment problem today has become very definitely a
problem of youth as well as of age. As each year has gone by hundreds of
thousands of boys and girls have come of working age. They must be an
especial concern of democratic government.

We must continue, above all things, to look for a solution of their
special problem. For they, looking ahead to life, are entitled to action on
our part and not merely to admonitions of optimism or lectures on economic laws.

Some in our midst have sought to instill a feeling of fear and defeatism
in the minds of the American people about this problem.

To face the task of finding jobs faster than invention can take them
away—is not defeatism. To warble easy platitudes that if we will only go
back to ways that have failed, everything will be all right—is not courage.

State of the Union Message, Jan. 3, 1940

41 / It was with far-sighted wisdom that the framers of the Constitution
brought together in one magnificent phrase three great concepts—"common defense," "general welfare" and "domestic tranquility."

More than a century and a half later we still believe with them that
our best defense is the promotion of our general welfare and domestic
tranquility. . . .

I hope that we shall have fewer ostriches in our midst. It is not good for the ultimate health of ostriches to bury their heads in the sand.
Ibid.

42 / In order that at least a beginning may be made I propose for the consideration of the Congress a program for the construction of small hospitals in needy areas of the country, especially in rural areas, not now provided with them. Hospitals are essential to physicians in giving modern medical service to the people. In many areas present hospital facilities are almost non-existent. The most elementary health needs are not being met.

The provision of hospitals in the areas to which I refer will greatly improve existing health services, attract competent doctors and raise the standards of medical care in these communities. The new hospitals should serve the additional purpose of providing laboratory and other diagnostic facilities for the use of local physicians, as well as accommodations for local health departments.

The proposed hospitals should be built only where they are most needed; they should not be constructed in communities where public or private institutions are already available to the people in need of service even if these institutions are not up to the highest standards. To insure proper location and good standards of operation, approval of hospital construction projects should be given by the Surgeon General of the Public Health Service, with the advice of an advisory council consisting of outstanding medical and scientific authorities who are expert in matters relating to hospital and other public health services. . . .

The areas which I have in mind are so poor that they cannot raise their share of the cost of building and equipping a hospital. Yet I believe that many of such communities have enough public-spirited citizens with means, and enough citizens able to pay something for hospital treatment, to care for operating costs of a hospital, provided they do not have to pay for its original construction and equipment, or to pay annual interest and amortization on borrowed money. Treatment in such a hospital would, of course, be available to men, women and children who literally can afford to contribute little or nothing toward their treatment.

Message to Congress recommending the construction of hospitals in needy areas, Jan. 30, 1940

43 / I recommend the continuance in full measure of the social-security programs. This includes not only the payment of old-age benefits as required by law but also aid to youth and continued payments toward the

state aid of old persons not covered by the insurance benefits; aids to children and to the physically handicapped. . . .

Furthermore, I deem it vital that the Congress give consideration to the inclusion in the old-age and survivors insurance system and the unemployment compensation system of workers not now covered.

Annual budget message to Congress, Jan. 3, 1941

44 / Certainly this is no time for any of us to stop thinking about the social and economic problems which are the root cause of the social revolution which is today a supreme factor in the world.

For there is nothing mysterious about the foundations of a healthy and strong democracy. The basic things expected by our people of their political and economic systems are simple. They are:

Equality of opportunity for youth and for others.

Jobs for those who can work.

Security for those who need it.

The ending of special privilege for the few.

The preservation of civil liberties for all.

The enjoyment of the fruits of scientific progress in a wider and constantly rising standard of living.

These are the simple, basic things that must never be lost sight of in the turmoil and unbelievable complexity of our modern world. The inner and abiding strength of our economic and political systems is dependent upon the degree to which they fulfill these expectations.

State of the Union Message ("The Four Freedoms" speech), Jan. 6, 1941

45 / I am convinced that the best solution of the problem [social security] would be a uniform national system of unemployment insurance with adequate benefit provisions.

Letter to Speaker of the House Sam Rayburn on social legislation, Jan. 19, 1942

46 / This is the time to strengthen, not to weaken, the social-security system. It is time now to prepare for the security of workers in the post-war years. . . . This is one case in which social and fiscal objectives, war and post-war aims, are in full accord. Expanded social security, together with other fiscal measures, would set up a bulwark of economic security for the people now and after the war and at the same time would provide anti-inflationary sources for financing the war.

Letter to Senator Walter F. George on strengthening of the Social Security system, Oct. 3, 1942

47 / The people at home and the people at the front—men and women—are wondering about the Third Freedom—Freedom from Want. To them it means that when they are mustered out, when war production is converted to the economy of peace, they will have the right to expect full employment—for themselves and for all able-bodied men and women in America who want to work.

They expect the opportunity to work, to run their farms, their stores, to earn decent wages. They are eager to face the risks inherent in our system of free enterprise.

They do not want a postwar America which suffers from under-nourishment or slums—or the dole. They want no get-rich-quick era of bogus "prosperity" which will end for them in selling applies on a street corner, as happened after the bursting of the boom in 1929. . . .

I have been told that this is no time to speak of a better America after the war. I am told it is a grave error on my part. I dissent.

If the security of the individual citizen, or the family, should become a subject of national debate, the country knows where I stand. . . .

In this war of survival we must keep before our minds not only the evil things we fight against but the good things we are fighting for. We fight to retain a great past—and we fight to gain a greater future.

State of the Union Message, Jan. 7, 1943

48 / We fight today for security for our nation and at the same time we can endeavor to give our citizens and their families security against attacks from without, and against fear of economic distress in old age, in poverty, sickness, involuntary unemployment, and accidental injuries. We need to look forward to the accomplishment of these objectives—world peace, democratic society, and a dynamic economy.

Message to Congress on postwar security for the citizen and the nation, March 10, 1943

49 / The members of the armed forces have been compelled to make greater economic sacrifice and every other kind of sacrifice than the rest of us, and are entitled to definite action to help take care of their special problems.

The least to which they are entitled, it seems to me, is something like this:

1. Mustering-out pay to every member of the armed forces and merchant marine when he or she is honorably discharged, large enough in each case to cover a reasonable period of time between his discharge and the finding of a new job.

2. In case no job is found after diligent search, then unemployment insurance if the individual registers with the United States Employment Service.

3. An opportunity for members of the armed service to get further education or trade training at the cost of their government.

4. Allowance of credit to all members of the armed forces, under unemployment compensation and federal old-age and survivors' insurance, for their period of service. For these purposes they should be treated as if they had continued their employment in private industry.

> Radio address (Fireside Chat) on winning the war and planning for peace, July 28, 1943

50 / That humanitarian law [Social Security Act] made a real beginning toward the abolition of want in this country. More than 60 million workers with their own contributions are building security for their old age and for their families in case of death. Several million are already enjoying benefits. However, in all fairness, and in all equity, we should extend these benefits to farmers, farm laborers, small businessmen, and others working for themselves or in occupations specifically excluded by law. We should extend social security to provide protection against the serious economic hazard of ill health.

> Statement on the anniversary of the Atlantic Charter and the Social Security Act, Aug. 14, 1943

51 / I therefore recommend that the Congress enact legislation to make it possible for members of the armed forces to obtain credit under the federal old-age and survivors' insurance law during their period of military service. The burden of this extension of old-age and survivors' insurance to members of the armed forces should be carried by the federal government, and the federal contributions should be uniform for all members of the armed forces irrespective of their rank.

I have already communicated with the Congress requesting the enactment of legislation to provide educational and training opportunities for the members of the armed forces who desire to pursue their studies after their discharge.

The Congress will agree, I am sure, that, this time, we must have plans and legislation ready for our returning veterans instead of waiting until the last moment. It will give notice to our armed forces that the people back home do not propose to let them down.

> Message to Congress recommending Social Security and educational legislation for veterans, Nov. 23, 1943

"Economic Bill of Rights"

[*Excerpts*]

52 / We have come to a clear realization of the fact that true individual freedom cannot exist without economic security and independence. "Necessitous men are not free men." People who are hungry and out of a job are the stuff of which dictatorships are made.

In our day these economic truths have become accepted as self-evident. We have accepted, so to speak, a second Bill of Rights under which a new basis of security and prosperity can be established for all—regardless of station, race, or creed.

Among these are:

The right to a useful and remunerative job in the industries or shops or farms or mines of the nation;

The right to earn enough to provide adequate food and clothing and recreation;

The right of every farmer to raise and sell his products at a return which will give him and his family a decent living;

The right of every businessman, large and small, to trade in an atmosphere of freedom from unfair competition and domination by monopolies at home or abroad;

The right of every family to a decent home;

The right to adequate medical care and the opportunity to achieve and enjoy good health;

The right to adequate protection from the economic fears of old age, sickness, accident, and unemployment;

The right to a good education.

All of these rights spell security. And after this war is won we must be prepared to move forward, in the implementation of these rights, to new goals of human happiness and well-being.

America's own rightful place in the world depends in large part upon how fully these and similar rights have been carried into practice for our citizens. For unless there is security here at home there cannot be lasting peace in the world.

One of the great American industrialists of our day . . . recently emphasized the grave dangers of "rightist reaction" in this nation. . . . Indeed, if such reaction should develop—if history were to repeat itself and we were to return to the so-called "normalcy" of the 1920's—then it is certain that even though we shall have conquered our enemies on the battlefields abroad, we shall have yielded to the spirit of fascism at home.

State of the Union Message ("Economic Bill of Rights" speech), Jan. 11, 1944

53 / I have already emphasized the need to strengthen our social-security program. With respect to the reconversion period, I am particularly concerned over the fact that broad categories of workers are not covered by present legislation and that present standards for unemployment compensation are not adequate in many states. To promote unemployment opportunities and to assure the proper occupational adjustment of returning veterans and war workers, a strong, integrated system of public employment offices is a basic necessity. We can best accomplish this objective by the establishment, through permanent legislation, of an effective national employment service with adequate coverage throughout the nation. For the reconversion period we should provide assistance for travel and retraining of war workers. . . .

Our program should include provision for extended social security, including medical care, for better education, public health, and nutrition; for the improvement of our homes, cities, and farms; and for development of transportation facilities and river valleys.

Annual budget message to Congress, Jan. 3, 1945

54 / Economic rights of American citizenship, such as the right to a decent home, to a good education, to good medical care, to social security, to reasonable farm income, will, if fulfilled, make major contributions to achieving adequate levels of employment. . . .

An expanded social-security program and adequate health and education programs must play essential roles in a program designed to support individual productivity and mass purchasing power.

State of the Union Message, Jan. 6, 1945

18

Strength and Promise of American Democracy

1 / Let us now and here highly resolve to resume the country's interrupted march along the path of real progress, of real justice, of real equality for all of our citizens, great and small. Our indomitable leader in that interrupted march is no longer with us, but there still survives today his spirit. . . . Let us feel that in everything we do there still lives with us, if not the body, the great indomitable, unquenchable, progressive soul of our Commander-in-chief, Woodrow Wilson.

Acceptance speech, Democratic National Convention, Chicago, Ill., July 2, 1932

2 / I pledge you, I pledge myself, to a new deal for the American people. Let us all here assembled constitute ourselves prophets of a new order of competence and of courage. This is more than a political campaign; it is a call to arms. Give me your help, not to win votes alone, but to win in this crusade to restore America to its own people.

Ibid.

3 / This is preeminently the time to speak the truth, the whole truth, frankly and boldly. Nor need we shrink from honestly facing conditions in our country today. This great nation will endure as it has endured, will revive and will prosper. So, first of all, let me assert my firm belief that the only thing we have to fear is fear itself—nameless, unreasoning, unjustified terror which paralyzes needed efforts to convert retreat into advance. In

every dark hour of our national life a leadership of frankness and vigor has met with that understanding and support of the people themselves which is essential to victory. I am convinced that you will again give that support to leadership in these critical days.

.   .   .   .   .

For the trust reposed in me I will return the courage and the devotion that befit the time. I can do no less.

We face the arduous days that lie before us in the warm courage of the national unity; with the clear consciousness of seeking old and precious moral values; with the clean satisfaction that comes from the stern performance of duty by old and young alike. We aim at the assurance of a rounded and permanent national life.

We do not distrust the future of essential democracy. The people of the United States have not failed. In their need they have registered a mandate that they want direct, vigorous action. They have asked for discipline and direction under leadership. They have made me the present instrument of their wishes. In the spirit of the gift I take it.

First Inaugural Address, March 4, 1933

4 / Democracy is not a static thing. It is an everlasting march.
Address on democratic processes, Los Angeles, Calif., Oct. 1, 1935

5 / The vigor of our history comes, largely, from the fact that, as a comparatively young nation we have gone fearlessly ahead doing things that were never done before.
Address to the Young Democratic Club, Baltimore, Md., April 13, 1936

6 / It will never be possible for any length of time for any group of the American people, either by reason of wealth or learning or inheritance or economic power, to retain any mandate, any permanent authority to arrogate to itself the political control of American public life.
Address on the centennial of Arkansas's admission into the Union, Little Rock, June 10, 1936

7 / There is a mysterious cycle in human events. To some generations much is given. Of other generations much is expected. This generation of Americans has a rendezvous with destiny.

In this world of ours in other lands, there are some people, who, in times past, have lived and fought for freedom, and seem to have grown too weary to carry on the fight. They have sold their heritage of freedom for the illusion of a living. They have yielded their democracy.

I believe in my heart that only our success can stir their ancient hope. They begin to know that here in America we are waging a great and successful war. It is not alone a war against want and destitution and economic demoralization. It is more than that; it is a war for a survival of democracy. We are fighting to save a great and precious form of government for ourselves and for the world.

Acceptance speech, Democratic National Convention, Philadelphia, Pa., June 27, 1936

8 / The realization that we are all bound together by hope of a common future rather than by reverence for a common past has helped us to build upon this continent a unity unapproached in any similar area or population in the whole world. For all our millions of square miles, for all our millions of people, there is a unity in language and speech, in law and in economics, in education and in general purpose, which nowhere finds its match. . . .

Even in times as troubled and uncertain as these, I still hold to the faith that a better civilization than any we have known is in store for America and by our example, perhaps, for the world. Here destiny seems to have taken a long look. Into this continental reservoir there has been poured untold and untapped wealth of human resources. Out of that reservoir, out of the melting pot, the rich promise which the New World held out to those who came to it from many lands is finding fulfillment.

The richness of the promise has not run out. If we keep the faith for our day as those who came before us kept the faith for theirs, then you and I can smile with confidence into the future.

Address on the 50th anniversary of the dedication of the Statue of Liberty, New York City, Oct. 28, 1936

9 / Government is competent when all who compose it work as trustees for the whole people. It can make constant progress when it keeps abreast of all the facts. It can obtain justified support and legitimate criticism when the people receive true information of all that government does. . . .

To maintain a democracy of effort requires a vast amount of patience in dealing with differing methods, a vast amount of humility. But out of the confusion of many voices rises an understanding of dominant public need. Then political leadership can voice common ideals, and aid in their realization.

Second Inaugural Address, Jan. 20, 1937

10 / Among men of good will, science and democracy together offer an ever-richer life and ever-larger satisfaction to the individual. With this change in our moral climate and our rediscovered ability to improve our economic order, we have set our feet upon the road of enduring progress.

Ibid.

11 / Democratic government has innate capacity to protect its people against disasters once considered inevitable, to solve problems once considered unsolvable. We would not admit that we could not find a way to master economic epidemics just as, after centuries of fatalistic suffering, we had found a way to master epidemics of disease. We refused to leave the problems of our common welfare to be solved by the winds of chance and the hurricanes of disaster.

Ibid.

12 / I am very confident of the future of this country as long as we maintain the democracy of our manners and the democracy of our hearts.

Extemporaneous remarks on democracy and government, Mount Marion, N.Y., July 5, 1937

13 / Under democratic government the poorest are no longer necessarily the most ignorant part of society. I agree with the saying of one of our famous statesmen who devoted himself to the principle of majority rule: "I respect the aristocracy of learning; I deplore the plutocracy of wealth; but thank God for the democracy of the heart."

Address on traditional American democracy, Roanoke Island, N.C., Aug. 18, 1937

14 / Democratic processes of government can always meet the problems of an emergency, if the leadership in public life recognizes and has the courage to tackle the problems of the day.

Extemporaneous remarks on solving current problems through democratic processes, Casper, Wyo., Sept. 24, 1937

15 / Civilized man increasingly insists and in the long run will insist on genuine participation in his own government. Our people believe that over the years democracies of the world will survive, and that democracy will be restored or established in those nations which today know it not. In that faith lies the future peace of mankind.

State of the Union Message, Jan. 3, 1938

16 / We, a successful democracy, face a troubled world. Elsewhere schools of thought contend that democracy is doomed to failure. They tell us that free speech and the free exchange of views will destroy democracies. My conviction, on the contrary, is that the United States retaining free speech and a free exchange of views can furnish a dynamic example of successful government: provided the nation can unite in practical measures when the times call for united action. The driving force of a nation lies in its spiritual purpose, made effective by free, tolerant but unremitting national will. . . .

If we accept that high and splendid road this free democracy will give successful answer to the fears and questionings which today trouble the minds and souls of men and women the world over.

Message to Congress recommending legislation to stimulate recovery, April 14, 1938

17 / America needs a government of constant progress along liberal lines. America requires that this progress be sane and that this progress be honest. America calls for government with a soul.

Address on the need for constant progress, Oklahoma City, Okla., July 9, 1938

18 / Whatever convictions I have, none is stronger than my abiding belief that the security and well-being of the American people can best be served by the democratic processes that have made this country strong and great.

The future, however, rests not on chance alone, not on mere conservatism, mere smugness, mere fatalism, but on the affirmative action which we take in America. What America does or fails to do in the next few years has a far greater bearing and influence on the history of the whole human race for centuries to come than most of us who are here today can ever conceive.

We are not only the largest and most powerful democracy in the whole world, but many other democracies look to us for leadership that world democracy may survive. . . .

What I would emphasize is the maintenance of successful democracy at home. Necessarily democratic methods within a nation's life entail change —the kind of change through local processes described by Mr. Justice Cardozo—the kind of change to meet new social and economic needs through recognized processes of government.

Because we live in an era of acceleration, we can no longer trust to the evolution of future decades to meet these new problems. They rise before us today and they must be met today.

Address on American leadership for the survival of democracy, University of North Carolina, Chapel Hill, N.C., Dec. 5, 1938

19 / The success of democratic institutions is measured, not by extent of territory, financial power, machines or armaments, but by the desires, the hopes and the deep-lying satisfactions of the individual men, women and children who make up its citizenship.

Address before the White House Conference on Children in a Democracy, Washington, D.C., April 23, 1939

20 / In these days of ruthless attempts to destroy democratic government, it is baldly asserted that democracies must always be weak in order to be democratic at all; and that, therefore, it will be easy to crush all free states out of existence.

Confident in our republic's 150 years of successful resistance to all subversive attempts upon it, whether from without or within, nevertheless we must be constantly alert to the importance of keeping the tools of American democracy up to date. It is our responsibility to make sure that the people's government is in condition to carry out the people's will, promptly, effectively, without waste or lost motion. . . .

We are not free if our administration is weak. But we are free if we know, and others know, that we are strong; that we can be tough as well as tender-hearted, and that what the American people decide to do can and will be done, capably and effectively, with the best national equipment that modern organizing ability can supply in a country where management and organization is so well understood in private affairs.

Message to Congress on Governmental Reorganization Plan No. 1, April 25, 1939

21 / There are certain freedoms. The first I would call "freedom of information," which is terribly important. It is a much better phrase than "freedom of the press," because there are all kinds of information so that the inhabitants of a country can get news of what is going on in every part of the country and in every part of the world without censorship and through many forms of communication. That, I think, is one of the objectives of peace, because you will never have a completely stable world without freedom of knowledge, freedom of information.

The second, of course, is freedom of religion which, under democracies, has always—not always but almost all the time—been fairly well maintained. It is not maintained in those nations which have adopted other systems of government. You have to take it as it comes, and that, in my mind, is an essential of permanent peace.

Then, a third freedom is the freedom to express one's self as long as you don't advocate the overthrow of government. That is a different thing. In other words, the kind of expression that we certainly have in this country, and that they have in most democracies. That, I think, is an essential of peace —I mean permanent peace.

Fourth, freedom from fear, so that people won't be afraid of being bombed from the air or attacked, one way or the other, by some other nation. And, of course, we have maintained all along that freedom from fear must be based on a removal of the weapons that cause fear—in other words, disarmament. And that is an essential of peace.

Press conference, Hyde Park, N.Y., July 5, 1940

22 / The command of the democratic faith has been ever onward and upward. Never have free men been satisfied with the mere maintenance of any status quo, however comfortable or secure it may have seemed at the moment.

We have always held to the hope, the belief, the conviction, that there is a better life, a better world, beyond the horizon. . . .

On this side of the ocean there is no desire, there will be no effort, on the part of any one race, or people, or nation, to control any other. The only encirclement sought is the encircling bond of good old-fashioned neighborly friendship. So bound together, we are able to withstand any attack from the east or from the west. Together we are able to ward off any infiltration of alien political and economic ideas that would destroy our freedom and our democracy.

The core of our defense is the faith we have in the institutions we defend.

Address on the Defense of the Western Hemisphere, Dayton, Ohio, Oct. 12, 1940

23 / All we have known of the glories of democracy—its freedom, its efficiency as a mode of living, its ability to meet the aspirations of the common man—all these are merely an introduction to the greater story of a more glorious future. . . .

For Americans are determined to retain for themselves the right of free speech, free religion, free assembly and the right which lies at the basis of all of them—the right to choose the officers of their own government in free elections.

We intend to keep our freedom—to defend it from attacks from without and against corruption from within. We shall defend it against the forces of dictatorship, whatever disguises and false faces they may wear.

But we have learned that freedom in itself is not enough.

Freedom of speech is of no use to a man who has nothing to say.

Freedom of worship is of no use to a man who has lost his God.

Democracy, to be dynamic, must provide for its citizens opportunity as well as freedom.

We of this generation have seen a rebirth of dynamic democracy in America in these past few years.

Campaign address, Cleveland, Ohio, Nov. 2, 1940

24 / Democracy is not just a word, to be shouted at political rallies and then put back into the dictionary after election day.

The service of democracy must be something much more than mere lip-service.

It is a living thing—a human thing—compounded of brains and muscles and heart and soul. The service of democracy is the birthright of every citizen, the white and the colored; the Protestant, the Catholic, the Jew; the sons and daughters of every country in the world, who make up the people of this land. Democracy is every man and woman who loves freedom and serves the cause of freedom.

Final campaign radio address, Hyde Park, N.Y., Nov. 4, 1940

25 / I, for one, do not believe that the era in democracy in human affairs can or ever will be snuffed out in our lifetime. I, for one, do not believe that mere force will be successful in sterilizing the seeds which had taken such firm root as a harbinger of better lives for mankind. I, for one, do not believe that the world will revert either to a modern form of ancient slavery or to controls vested in modern feudalism or modern emperors or modern dictators or modern oligarchs in these days. I, for one, do believe that the very people under their iron heels will, themselves, rebel.

Armistice Day address, Arlington National Cemetery, Nov. 11, 1940

"The Four Freedoms"

[*Excerpts*]

26 / In the future days, which we seek to make secure, we look forward to a world founded upon four essential human freedoms.

The first is freedom of speech and expression—everywhere in the world.

The second is freedom of every person to worship God in his own way—everywhere in the world.

The third is freedom from want—which, translated into world terms, means economic understandings which will secure to every nation a healthy peacetime life for its inhabitants—everywhere in the world.

The fourth is freedom from fear—which, translated into world terms, means a world-wide reduction of armaments to such a point and in such a thorough fashion that no nation will be in a position to commit an act of physical aggression against any neighbor—anywhere in the world.

That is no vision of a distant millennium. It is a definite basis for a kind of world attainable in our own time and generation. That kind of world is the very antithesis of the so-called new order of tyranny which the dictators seek to create with the crash of a bomb.

State of the Union Message ("Four Freedoms" speech), Jan. 6, 1941

27 / To us there has come a time, in the midst of swift happenings, to pause for a moment and take stock—to recall what our place in history has been, and to rediscover what we are and what we may be. If we do not, we risk the real peril of inaction.

Lives of nations are determined not by the count of years, but by the lifetime of the human spirit. The life of a man is three-score years and ten—a little more, a little less. The life of a nation is the fullness of the measure of its will to live.

There are men who doubt this. There are men who believe that democracy, as a form of government and a frame of life, is limited or measured by a kind of mystical and artificial fate—that, for some unexplained reason, tyranny and slavery have become the surging wave of the future—and that freedom is an ebbing tide.

But we Americans know that this is not true.

Eight years ago, when the life of this republic seemed frozen by a fatalistic terror, we proved that this is not true. We were in the midst of shock—but we acted. We acted quickly, boldly, decisively.

These later years have been living years—fruitful years for the people of this democracy. For they have brought to us greater security and, I hope, a better understanding that life's ideals are to be measured in other than material things.

Most vital to our present and our future is this experience of a democracy which successfully survived crisis at home; put away many evil things; built new structures on enduring lines; and, through it all, maintained the fact of its democracy. . . .

Democracy is not dying.

We know it because we have seen it revive—and grow.

We know it cannot die—because it is built on the unhampered initiative of individual men and women joined together in a common enterprise —an enterprise undertaken and carried through by the free expression of a free majority.

We know it because democracy alone, of all forms of government, enlists the full force of men's enlightened will.

We know it because democracy alone has constructed an unlimited civilization capable of infinite progress in the improvement of human life.

We know it because, if we look below the surface, we sense it still spreading on every continent—for it is the most humane, the most advanced, and in the end the most unconquerable of all forms of human society. . . .

The democratic aspiration is no mere recent phase in human history. It *is* human history. It permeated the ancient life of early peoples. It blazed anew in the Middle Ages. It was written in the Magna Carta.

In the Americas its impact has been irresistible. America has been the New World in all tongues, to all peoples, not because this continent was a new-found land, but because all those who came here believed they could create upon this continent a new life—a life that should be new in freedom.

Its vitality was written into our own Mayflower Compact, into the Declaration of Independence, into the Constitution of the United States, into the Gettysburg Address. . . .

The hopes of the Republic cannot forever tolerate either undeserved poverty or self-serving wealth. . . .

The destiny of America was proclaimed in words of prophecy spoken by our first President in his first inaugural in 1789—words almost directed, it would seem, to this year of 1941: ". . . the preservation of the sacred fire of liberty and the destiny of the republican model of government are justly considered . . . deeply, . . . finally, staked on the experiment intrusted to the hands of the American people."

If we lose that sacred fire—if we let it be smothered with doubt and fear—then we shall reject the destiny which Washington strove so valiantly and so triumphantly to establish. The preservation of the spirit and faith of the nation does, and will, furnish the highest justification for every sacrifice that we may make in the cause of national defense.

In the face of great perils never before encountered, our strong purpose is to protect and to perpetuate the integrity of democracy.

For this we muster the spirit of America, and the faith of America.

We do not retreat. We are not content to stand still. As Americans, we go forward, in the service of our country, by the will of God.

Third Inaugural Address, Jan. 20, 1941

28 / In our democracy officers of the government are the servants, and never the masters of the people.

Address at the Annual Academy Awards dinner, Hollywood, Calif., Feb. 27, 1941

29 / The enemies of democracy were wrong in their calculations for a very simple reason. They were wrong because they believed that democracy could not adjust itself to the terrible reality of a world at war.

They believed that democracy, because of its profound respect for the rights of men, would never arm itself to fight.

They believed that democracy, because of its will to live at peace with its neighbors, could not mobilize its energies even in its own defense.

They know now that democracy can still remain democracy and speak and reach conclusions and arm itself adequately for defense. . . .

The decisions of our democracy may be slowly arrived at. But when that decision is made, it is proclaimed not with the voice of any one man but with the voice of one hundred and thirty millions. It is binding on all of us. And the world is no longer left in doubt.

Address at the White House Correspondents' Association dinner, Washington, D.C., March 15, 1941

30 / The most significant single fact in recent American history is the ability of the American people to face a tough situation and to take orderly and united action in their own behalf and in behalf of the things in which they believe.

Radio address on the ninth anniversary of the administration's agricultural program, March 9, 1942

31 / The four freedoms of common humanity are as much elements of man's needs as air and sunlight, bread and salt. Deprive him of all these freedoms and he dies—deprive him of a part of them and a part of him withers. Give them to him in full and abundant measure and he will cross the threshold of a new age, the greatest age of man.

These freedoms are the rights of men of every creed and every race, wherever they live. This is their heritage, long withheld. We of the United Nations have the power and the men and the will at last to assure man's heritage.

The belief in the four freedoms of common humanity—the belief in man, created free, in the image of God—is the crucial difference between ourselves and the enemies we face today. In it lies the absolute unity of our alliance, opposed to the oneness of the evil we hate. Here is our strength, the source and promise of victory.

We of the United Nations know that our faith cannot be broken by any man or any force. And we know that there are other millions who in their silent captivity share our belief.

Radio address on United Flag Day, June 14, 1942

32 / Today there are many Americans who sneer at the determination to attain freedom from want and freedom from fear on the ground that these are ideals which can never be realized. They say that it is ordained that we must always have poverty and that we must always have war. They are like the people who harp at the Ten Commandments because some people are in the habit of breaking one or more of them.

Radio address on Washington's Birthday, Feb. 22, 1943

33 / I am everlastingly angry only at those who assert vociferously that the Four Freedoms and the Atlantic Charter are nonsense because they are unattainable. If they had lived a century and a half ago they would have sneered and said that the Declaration of Independence was utter piffle. If they had lived nearly a thousand years ago they would have laughed uproariously at the ideas of the Magna Charta. And if they had lived several thousand years ago they would have derided Moses when he came from the Mountain with the Ten Commandments.

Address before the Canadian Parliament, Ottawa, Aug. 25, 1943

34 / We are fighting this war and we are holding this election—both for the same essential reason: because we have faith in democracy.

And there is no force and there is no combination of forces powerful enough to shake that faith.

Campaign address, Chicago, Ill., Oct. 28, 1944

Part II

The United States
in an
Interdependent World

19

Good Neighbors

1 / In the field of world policy I would dedicate this nation to the policy of the good neighbor—the neighbor who resolutely respects himself and, because he does so, respects the rights of others—the neighbor who respects his obligations and respects the sanctity of his agreements in and with a world of neighbors.

First Inaugural Address, March 4, 1933

2 / Common ideals and a community of interests, together with a spirit of cooperation, have led to the realization that the well-being of one nation depends in large measure upon the well-being of its neighbors. It is upon these foundations that Pan Americanism has been built.

This [Pan American Day] celebration commemorates a movement based upon the policy of fraternal cooperation. In my Inaugural Address I stated that I would "dedicate this nation to the policy of the good neighbor. . . ." Never before has the significance of the words "good neighbor" been so manifest in international relations. Never have the need and benefit of neighborly cooperation in every form of human activity been so evident as they are today.

Friendship among nations, as among individuals, calls for constructive efforts to muster the forces of humanity in order that an atmosphere of close understanding and cooperation may be cultivated. It involves mutual obligations and responsibilities, for it is only by sympathetic respect for the rights of others and a scrupulous fulfillment of the corresponding obligations by each member of the community that a true fraternity can be maintained.

The essential qualities of a true Pan Americanism must be the same as those which constitute a good neighbor, namely, mutual understanding, and, through such understanding, a sympathetic appreciation of the other's point of view. It is only in this manner that we can hope to build up a system of which confidence, friendship and good-will are the cornerstones.

In this spirit the people of every republic on our continent are coming to a deep understanding of the fact that the Monroe Doctrine, of which so much has been written and spoken for more than a century, was and is directed at the maintenance of independence by the peoples of the continent. It was aimed and is aimed against the acquisition in any manner of the control of additional territory in this hemisphere by any non-American power.

Hand in hand with this Pan-American doctrine of continental self-defense, the peoples of the American republics understand more clearly, with the passing years, that the independence of each republic must recognize the independence of every other republic. Each one of us must grow by an advancement of civilization and social well-being and not by the acquisition of territory at the expense of any neighbor. . . .

Your Americanism and mine must be a structure built of confidence, cemented by a sympathy which recognizes only equality and fraternity. It finds its source and being in the hearts of men and dwells in the temple of the intellect.

> Pan American Day address before a special session of the Governing Board of the Pan American Union, April 12, 1933

3 / The United States does not seek to annex Canada or any part thereof, to annex Mexico or any part thereof, or to annex Cuba or any part thereof. It is this attitude of the overwhelming majority of our people toward their neighbors—this complete lack of a national desire for territorial expansion—which makes the rest of the world begin to understand that the United States is opposed to war.

> Radio address to the Women's Conference on Current Problems, Oct. 13, 1933

4 / The simple translation of the peaceful and neighborly purposes of the United States has already given to her sister American republics a greater faith in professions of friendship than they have held since the time, a century ago, when James Monroe encouraged South America and Central America in their struggles for freedom.

> Address on the bicentennial celebration of the founding of Georgia, Savannah, Nov. 18, 1933

5 / "Comprehension must be the soil in which shall grow all the fruits of friendship." Those words, used by President Wilson in the Mobile speech in 1913, can well serve as a statement of policy by the Government of the

United States. That policy applies equally to a comprehension of our internal problems and our international relations. . . .

In that speech in Mobile, President Wilson first enunciated the definite statement "that the United States will never again seek one additional foot of territory by conquest." The United States accepted that declaration of policy. President Wilson went further, pointing out with special reference to our Latin American neighbors that material interests must never be made superior to human liberty.

Nevertheless, we know that largely as a result of the convulsion of the World War and its after effects, the complete fruition of that policy of unselfishness has not in every case been obtained. And in this we, all of us, have to share the responsibility. . . .

It therefore has seemed clear to me as President that the time has come to supplement and to implement the declaration of President Wilson by the further declaration that the definite policy of the United States from now on is one opposed to armed intervention.

The maintenance of constitutional government in other nations is not a sacred obligation devolving upon the United States alone. The maintenance of law and the orderly processes of government in this hemisphere is the concern of each individual nation within its own borders first of all. It is only if and when the failure of orderly processes affects the other nations of the continent that it becomes their concern; and the point to stress is that in such an event it becomes the joint concern of a whole continent in which we are all neighbors.

Address before the Woodrow Wilson Foundation, New York City, Dec. 28, 1933

6 / We, the citizens of all the American republics are, I think, at the threshold of a new era.

It is a new era because of the new spirit of understanding that is best expressed in the phrase, "Let us each and every one of us live and let live." In all of our American nations, there is growing insistence on the peaceful solution of international problems. . . .

We are entering a new era in accepting the plan that no one of our nations must hereafter exploit a neighbor nation at the expense of that neighbor. We shall all of us find methods for the development of the commerce and resources of the Americas, but we shall do this in the spirit of fair play and of justice.

Finally, I hope, my friends, that this new era is bringing a communion of understanding of the life and culture and ideals of the separate nations that make up the Americas. It is right that each country should have its own cultural development, but every one of us can learn greatly from each other.

Remarks, Cartagena, Colombia, July 10, 1934

7 / At home we have preached, and will continue to preach, the gospel of the good neighbor. I hope from the bottom of my heart that as the years go on, in every continent and in every clime, nation will follow nation in proving by deed as well as by word their adherence to the ideal of the Americas—I am a good neighbor.

Address, San Diego Exposition, San Diego, Calif., Oct. 2, 1935

8 / This policy of the good neighbor among the Americas is no longer a hope, no longer an objective remaining to be accomplished. It is a fact, active, present, pertinent and effective. In this achievement, every American nation takes an understanding part. There is neither war, nor rumor of war, nor desire for war. The inhabitants of this vast area, two hundred and fifty million strong, spreading more than eight thousand miles from the Arctic to the Antarctic, believe in, and propose to follow, the policy of the good neighbor. They wish with all their heart that the rest of the world might do likewise.

State of the Union Message, Jan. 3, 1936

9 / The noblest monument to peace and to neighborly economic and social friendship in all the world is not a monument in bronze or stone, but the boundary which unites the United States and Canada—3,000 miles of friendship with no barbed wire, no gun or soldier, and no passport on the whole frontier.

Mutual trust made that frontier. To extend the same sort of mutual trust throughout the Americas was our aim. . . .

We have negotiated a Pan American convention embodying the principle of non-intervention. We have abandoned the Platt Amendment which gave us the right to intervene in the internal affairs of the Republic of Cuba. We have withdrawn American marines from Haiti. We have signed a new treaty which places our relations with Panama on a mutually satisfactory basis. We have undertaken a series of trade agreements with other American countries to our mutual commercial profit. At the request of two neighboring republics, I hope to give assistance in the final settlement of the last serious boundary dispute between any of the American nations.

Throughout the Americas the spirit of the good neighbor is a practical and living fact. The twenty-one American republics are not only living together in friendship and in peace; they are united in the determination so to remain. . . .

Peace, like charity, begins at home; that is why we have begun at home. But peace in the Western world is not all that we seek.

It is our hope that knowledge of the practical application of the good-neighbor policy in this hemisphere will be borne home to our neighbors across the seas. . . .

Of all the nations of the world today we are in many ways most singularly blessed. Our closest neighbors are good neighbors. If there are remoter nations that wish us not good but ill, they know that we are strong; they know that we can and will defend ourselves and defend our neighborhood.

We seek to dominate no other nation. We ask no territorial expansion. We oppose imperialism. We desire reduction in world armaments.

We believe in democracy; we believe in freedom; we believe in peace. We offer to every nation of the world the handclasp of the good neighbor. Let those who wish our friendship look us in the eye and take our hand.

Address on the international situation, Chautauqua, N.Y., Aug. 14, 1936

10 / Peace depends upon the acceptance of the principle and practice of the good neighbor. The practice is founded on the golden rule, and must be fortified by cooperation of every kind between nations.

Campaign address, St. Paul, Minn., Oct. 9, 1936

11 / It is no exaggeration to say that in a world torn by conflicting demands, in a world in which democratic institutions are so seriously threatened, in a world in which freedom and human liberty itself are at stake, the Americans stand forth as a notable example of international solidarity, cooperation and mutual helpfulness.

Radio address to the Latin American republics on the eve of the Inter-American Conference for the Maintenance of Peace, Nov. 7, 1936

12 / All of us have learned that no real, no lasting, prosperity can exist where it is secured at the expense of our neighbors; that among nations, as in our domestic relations, the principle of interdependence is paramount. No nation can live entirely to itself.

Each one of us has learned the glories of independence. Let each one of us learn the glories of interdependence. Economically we supply each other's needs; intellectually we maintain a constant, a growing exchange of culture, of science, and of thought; spiritually the life of each can well enrich the life of all.

We are showing in international relations what we have long known in private relations—that good neighbors make a good community.

In that knowledge we meet today as neighbors. We can discard the dangerous language of rivalry; we can put aside the empty phrases of "diplomatic triumphs" or "shrewd bargains." We can forget all thought of domination, of selfish coalitions, or of balances of power. Those false gods have no place among American neighbors.

Address before the Congress and Supreme Court of Brazil, Rio de Janeiro, Nov. 27, 1936

13 / Peace comes from the spirit and must be grounded in faith. In seeking peace, perhaps we can best begin by proudly affirming the faith of the Americas: the faith in freedom and it fulfillment, which has proved a mighty fortress beyond reach of successful attack in half the world.

That faith arises from a common hope and a common design given us by our fathers in differing form but with a single aim: freedom and security of the individual, which has become the foundation of our peace. . . .

Finally, in expressing our faith of the Western World, let us affirm:

That we maintain and defend the democratic form of constitutional representative government.

That through such government we can more greatly provide a wider distribution of culture, of education, of thought, and of free expression.

That through it we can obtain a greater security of life for our citizens and a more equal opportunity for them to prosper.

That through it we can best foster commerce and the exchange of art and science between nations.

That through it we can avoid the rivalry of armaments, avert hatreds, and encourage good-will and true justice.

That through it we offer hope for peace and a more abundant life to the peoples of the whole world.

But this faith of the Western World will not be complete if we fail to affirm our faith in God. . . .

In the constitution and in the practice of our nations is the right of freedom of religion. But this ideal, these words, presuppose a belief and a trust in God.

The faith of the Americas, therefore, lies in the spirit. The system, the sisterhood, of the Americas is impregnable so long as her nations maintain that spirit.

In that faith and spirit we will have peace over the Western World. In that faith and spirit we will all watch and guard our Hemisphere. In that faith and spirit may we also, with God's help, offer hope to our brethren overseas.

Address before the Inter-American Conference for the Maintenance of Peace, Buenos Aires, Argentina, Dec. 1, 1936

14 / Democracy cannot thrive in an atmosphere of international insecurity. Such insecurity breeds militarism, regimentation and the denial of freedom of speech, of peaceful assemblage and of religion. Such insecurity challenges the ideals of democracy based on the free choice of government by the people themselves. And as the logical development we of the Americas believe that the continued maintenance and improvement of democracy constitute the most important guarantee of international peace.

Moreover, . . . [it is] well understood that peace is something more significant than the mere absence of conflict. A durable peace, one that will resist the onslaught of untoward or temporary circumstance, is something far more positive and constructive. It demands a policy based on positive international cooperation, on mutual confidence, and on united effort in the solution of problems of common concern.

Pan American Day address before the Governing Board of the Pan American Union, Washington, D.C., April 14, 1937

15 / The nations of the Western Hemisphere, as good neighbors, in a spirit of mutual collaboration and sacrifice, have been successful in establishing a machinery for peace.

Letter to the Institute of Public Affairs, University of Virginia, Charlottesville, June 29, 1937

16 / Ours [United States and Canada] is an enviable record of friendship and amity, as witness an unfortified boundary of more than five thousand miles as the outward and visible token of mutual confidence and good will. This friendship between our two peoples is secure from every hazard of destruction or misunderstanding because it is based upon a common aspiration to maintain, to defend, and to perpetuate the democratic form of constitutional, representative government.

Radio congratulations on the 70th anniversary of the Canadian Confederation, July 1, 1937

17 / Civilization, after all, is not national—it is international—even though that observation, trite as it is to most of us, seems to be challenged in some parts of the world today. Ideas are not limited by territorial borders; they are the common inheritance of all free people. Thought is not anchored in any land; and the profit of education redounds to the equal benefit of the whole world. That is one form of free trade to which the leaders of every opposing political party can subscribe.

In a large sense we in the Americas stand charged today with the maintaining of that tradition. When, speaking a little over a year ago in similar veins in the Republic of Brazil, I included the Dominion of Canada in the fellowship of the Americas, our South American neighbors gave hearty acclaim. We in all the Americas know the sorrow and the wreckage which may follow if the ability of men to understand each other is rooted out from among the nations.

Many of us here today know from experience that of all the devastations of war none is more tragic than the destruction which it brings to the processes of men's minds. Truth is denied because emotion pushes it aside. Forbearance is succeeded by bitterness. In that atmosphere human thought cannot advance. . . .

We as good neighbors are true friends because we maintain our own rights with frankness, because we refuse to accept the twists of secret diplomacy, because we settle our disputes by consultation and because we discuss our common problems in the spirit of the common good. We seek to be scrupulously fair and helpful, not only in our relations with each other, but each of us at home in our relations with our own people.

Address at Queen's University, Kingston, Ontario, Canada, Aug. 18, 1938

18 / [The policy of the Good Neighbor] is a policy which can never be merely unilateral. In stressing it the American republics appreciate, I am confident, that it is a bilateral, a multilateral policy, and that the fair dealing which it implies must be reciprocated.

It is a policy which was not in its inception, or subsequently, limited to one hemisphere. It has proven so successful in the Western Hemisphere that the American republics believe that it could succeed in all the rest of the world if the spirit which lies behind it were better understood and more actively striven for in the other parts of the world.

Address at the laying of the cornerstone of the Federal Building, New York World's Fair, June 30, 1938

19 / To show our faith in democracy, we have made the policy of the good neighbor the corner stone of our foreign relations. No other policy would be consistent with our ideas and our ideals. In the fulfillment of this policy we propose to heed the ancient Scriptural admonition not to move our neighbor's landmarks, not to encroach on his metes and bounds.

We desire by every legitimate means to promote freedom in trade and travel and in the exchange of cultural ideas among nations. We seek no territorial expansion, we are not covetous of our neighbor's goods; we shall cooperate in every proposal honestly put forward to limit armaments; we abhor the appeal to physical force except to repulse aggression.

We say to all the world that in the Western Hemisphere—in the three Americas—the institutions of democracy—government with the consent of the governed must and shall be maintained.

Radio greetings to the Pan American Hernando de Soto Exposition, Tampa, Fla., Feb. 18, 1939

20 / Few of us realize that the Pan American organization as we know it, has now attained a longer history and a greater catalogue of achievements than any similar group known to modern history. Justly we can be proud of it. With even more right we can look to it as a symbol of great hope at a time when much of the world finds hope dim and difficult. . . .

What was it that has protected us from the tragic involvements which are today making the Old World a new cockpit of old struggles? The answer is easily found. A new, and powerful ideal—that of the community of nations—sprang up at the same time that the Americas became free and independent. It was nurtured by statesmen, thinkers and plain people for decades. Gradually it brought together the Pan American group of governments; today it has fused the thinking of the peoples, and the desires of their responsible representatives toward a common objective.

The result of this thinking through all these years has been to shape a typically American institution. This is the Pan American group, which works in open conference, by open agreement. We hold our conferences not as a result of wars, but as the result of our will to peace. . . .

The American family of nations may also rightfully claim, now, to speak to the rest of the world. We have an interest, wider than that of the mere defense of our sea-ringed continent. We know now that the development of the next generation will so narrow the oceans separating us from the Old World, that our customs and our actions are necessarily involved with hers, whether we like it or not.

Beyond question, within a scant few years air fleets will cross the ocean as easily as today they cross the closed European seas. Economic functioning of the world becomes therefore necessarily a unit; no interruption of it anywhere can fail, in the future, to disrupt economic life everywhere.

The past generation in Pan American matters was concerned with constructing the principles and the mechanisms through which this hemisphere would work together. But the next generation will be concerned with the methods by which the New World can live together in peace with the Old. . . .

Our will to peace can be as powerful as our will to mutual defense; it can command greater loyalty, greater devotion, greater discipline than that enlisted elsewhere for temporary conquest or equally futile glory. It will have its voice in determining the order of world affairs in the days to come.

This, gentlemen, is the living message which the New World can and does send to the Old. It can be light opening on dark waters. It shows the path of peace.

Pan American Day address before the Governing Board of the Pan American Union, Washington, D.C., April 14, 1939

21 / We of this hemisphere have no need to seek a new international order; we have already found it. This was not won by hysterical outcries, or violent movements of troops. We do not stamp out nations, capture governments, or uproot innocent people from the homes that they have built. We do not invent absurd doctrines of race supremacy, or claim dictatorship through universal revolution.

The inter-American order was not built by hatred and terror. It has been paved by the endless and effective work of men of good will. We have built a foundation for the lives of hundreds of millions. We have unified these lives by a common devotion to a moral order.

This cooperative peace in the Western Hemisphere was not created by mere wishing; and it will require more than mere words to maintain. In this association of nations, whoever touches any one of us touches us all. We have only asked that the world go with us in the path of peace. But we shall be able to keep that way open only if we are prepared to meet force with force if challenge is ever made against us. . . .

We know that what happens in the Old World directly and powerfully affects the peace and well-being of the New. It was for this very reason that we have adopted procedures that enable us to meet any eventuality. At Buenos Aires [1936] we agreed that we could consult, should our peace be threatened. At Lima [1938] we agreed to stand together to defend and maintain the absolute integrity of every American nation from any attack, direct or indirect, from beyond the seas. At Panama [1939] we worked out means for keeping war away from our hemisphere. I pray God that we shall have to do no more than that; but should it be necessary, I am convinced that we should be wholly successful. For the inner strength of a group of free people is irresistible when they are prepared to act. . . .

Pan American Day address before the Governing Board of the Pan American Union, Washington, D.C., April 15, 1940

22 / Wherever men and women of good will gather together to serve their community, there is America. It was true in the first little town meet-

ings in the Massachusetts Bay Colony, when the good folk assembled to decide measures of defense against the Indians, and how to build their first school, and how to care for their aged and sick. It is still true. . . .

When we join together in serving our local community, we add strength to our national community, we help to fortify the structure of our whole Union. That form of fortification—that spiritual fortification—is not to be dismissed lightly by those in other lands who believe that nations can live by force alone.

Human kindness has never weakened the stamina or softened the fiber of a free people. A nation does not have to be cruel in order to be tough. The vigorous expression of our American community spirit is truly important.

The ancient injunction to love thy neighbor as thyself is still the force that animates our faith—a faith that we are determined shall live and conquer in a world poisoned by hatred and ravaged by war.

Radio address on Mobilization for Human Needs, Oct. 13, 1940

23 / It is time that every citizen in every one of the American republics recognizes that the Good Neighbor policy means that harm to one republic means harm to every republic. We have all of us recognized the principle of independence. It is time that we recognize also the *privilege* of interdependence—one upon another.

Address at Monterrey during short trip to Mexico, April 20, 1943

24 / Finally, as the war progresses, we seek a national cooperation with other nations toward the end that world aggression be ended and that fair international relationships be established on a permanent basis. The policy of the Good Neighbor has shown such success in the Hemisphere of the Americas that its extension to the whole world seems to keep faith with our sons and daughters who are fighting for freedom and justice and security at home and abroad.

Message to Congress on progress of the war, Sept. 17, 1943

25 / That [Good Neighbor] policy not only has long-term implications of incalculable importance; it has also enabled the American republics in a time of serious peril and grave threat to their independence to concert measures and take steps in unison for their common defense. I am confident that the people of the United States have adopted this policy as a part of their permanent political philosophy.

Remarks to the new Argentine ambassador, Washington, D.C., Feb. 15, 1944

26 / The Good Neighbor Policy . . . should most certainly not be uni-lateral; it depends for its strength and effectiveness upon the participation and joint efforts of the American nations.

Remarks to the new Chilean ambassador, Washington, D.C., Oct. 5, 1944

27 / The bonds that unite the American republics into a community of good neighbors must remain strong. We have not labored long and faith-fully to build in this New World a system of international security and cooperation—merely to let it be dissipated in any period of postwar in-difference. Within the framework of the world organization of the United Nations, which the governments and people of the American republics are helping to establish, the inter-American system can and must play a strong and vital role.

Address to the chiefs of diplomatic missions from the other American republics, Washington, D.C., Oct. 12, 1944

28 / We and the other American republics have made the Good Neighbor policy real in this hemisphere. It is my conviction that this policy can be, and should be, made universal.

Address before the Foreign Policy Association, New York City, Oct. 21, 1944

29 / It is our purpose to help the peace-loving peoples of Europe to live together as good neighbors, to recognize their common interests and not to nurse their traditional grievances against one another.

State of the Union Message, Jan. 6, 1945

20

Reciprocal Trade Program

1 / It is time for this nation to use a little horse sense about the objective we seek and the results of our present tariff law. It is time for us to sit down with other nations and say to them: "This tariff fence business, on our part and on yours, is preventing world trade. Let us see if we can work out reciprocal methods by which we can start the actual interchange of goods. We do not ask you to buy our goods for cash because we know you do not have the cash, but we do suggest that it would be good for us and for you if we could send to you each year a large volume of American products in exchange for your products. We recognize the fact that we can probably use many of your articles and at the same time we can start our own wheels of industry going in manufacturing the things you need and want—all with adequate safeguards for the American standards of labor."

Address before the N.Y. State Grange, Albany, Feb. 2, 1932

2 / I have advocated and continue to advocate a tariff policy based on reason, on the same old-fashioned horse sense that you and I would use in dealing in our own business with our own neighbor. It is a tariff policy based in large part upon the simple principle of profitable exchange, arrived at through negotiated tariff, with benefit to each nation. . . .

This principle of tariff by negotiation means to deal with each country concerned, on a basis of fair barter; if it has something we need, and we have something it needs, a tariff agreement can and should be made that is satisfactory to both countries. That, of course, avoids a violent and a general shake-up in business. It is a just method of dealing with our foreign customers. It keeps the general structure of international trade, stable and sound. And it makes for world peace. It is practical, it is American! Let us lead the way!

Campaign address, Seattle, Wash., Sept. 20, 1932

3 / For romantic adventurings in foreign markets we expect and hope to substitute realistic study and actual exchange of goods. . . .

More realistic mutual arrangements for trade, substituted for the present system in which each nation attempts to exploit the markets of every other, giving nothing in return, will do more for the peace of the world and will contribute more to supplement the eventual reduction of armament burdens, than any other policy which could be devised. At the same time it will make possible the approach to a national economic policy at home which will have as its central feature the fittings of production programs to the actual probabilities of consumption.

Radio address to the Business and Professional Men's League throughout the nation, Oct. 6, 1932

4 / I am requesting the Congress to authorize the Executive to enter into executive commercial agreements with foreign nations; and in pursuance thereof, within carefully guarded limits, to modify existing duties and import restrictions in such a way as will benefit American agriculture and industry. This action seems opportune and necessary at this time for several reasons.

First, world trade has declined with startling rapidity. . . . This has meant idle hands, still machines, ships tied to their docks, despairing farm households, and hungry industrial families. It has made infinitely more difficult the planning for economic readjustment in which the government is now engaged. . . .

Second, other governments are to an ever-increasing extent winning their share of international trade by negotiated reciprocal trade agreements. If American agricultural and industrial interests are to retain their deserved place in this trade, the American government must be in a position to bargain for that place with other governments by rapid and decisive negotiation based upon a carefully considered program, and to grant with discernment corresponding opportunities in the American market for foreign products supplementary to our own.

If the American government is not in a position to make fair offers for fair opportunities, its trade will be superseded. If it is not in a position at a given moment rapidly to alter the terms on which it is willing to deal with other countries, it cannot adequately protect its trade against discriminations and against bargains injurious to its interests. Furthermore a promise to which prompt effect cannot be given is not an inducement which can pass current at par in commercial negotiations.

For this reason, any smaller degree of authority in the hands of the Executive would be ineffective. The executive branches of virtually all other important trading countries already possess some such power.

Message to Congress requesting authority to make executive commercial agreements, March 2, 1934

5 / If we would build constructively for peace, we must build upon economic foundations which are sound; and sound economics requires liberalized trade. America stands ready to go forward with other nations in this great movement.

Letter to the National Foreign Trade Council, Houston, Tex., Nov. 19, 1935

6 / In the belief that there is an intimate relationship between domestic prosperity, the untrammeled movement of goods between nations and the preservation of peace, this government has promoted widely and successfully a trade agreements program. Economic armaments and military armaments go hand in hand and since the problems are interdependent they must be attacked in a comprehensive manner, by the concerted effort of all peoples and in international agreement. Only this way may we find the way which will lead from the morass of international misunderstanding to the haven of enduring peace.

Letter to the Institute of Public Affairs, University of Virginia, Charlottesville, June 29, 1937

7 / The importance of the trade agreements program as a movement for peace perhaps transcends the importance of the material benefits to be gained from it.

Letter to the convention of the National Foreign Trade Council, New York City, Oct. 30, 1937

8 / The trade agreements that we have concluded with seventeen foreign countries . . . attest to the progress that has been made. With patient persistence we are thus gradually building more secure foundations for our own national economic well-being. At the same time, we are strengthening

the foundations of enduring world peace, which is so essential to the continued progress of civilization and to the well-being of the people of every land.

Statement on the observance of Foreign Trade Week, May 20, 1938

9 / For many years after the World War, blind economic selfishness in most countries, including our own, resulted in a destructive mine-field of trade restrictions which blocked the channels of commerce among nations. Indeed, this policy was one of the contributing causes of existing wars. . . .

To point the way to break up that log-jam our Trade Agreements Act [1934] was passed—based upon a policy of equality of treatment among nations and of mutually profitable arrangements of trade. . . .

But what is more important, the Trade Agreements Act should be extended as an indispensable part of the foundation of any stable and enduring peace.

The old conditions of world trade made for no enduring influence to open up the trade channels of the world, in all nations, in order that no one nation need feel compelled in later days to seek by force of arms what it can well gain by peaceful conference. For that purpose, too, we need the Trade Agreements Act even more today than when it was passed.

I emphasize the leadership which this nation can take when the time comes for a renewal of world peace. Such an influence will be greatly weakened if this government becomes a dog in the manger of trade selfishness. . . .

Even as through these trade agreements we prepare to cooperate in a world that wants peace, we must likewise be prepared to take care of ourselves if the world cannot attain peace.

State of the Union Message, Jan. 3, 1940

2 I

Uneasy Peace—
Impending War

1 / [The hope of the American people] is that peace may be assured through practical measures of disarmament. . . .

If we ask what are the reasons for armaments, which, in spite of the lessons and tragedies of the World War, are today a greater burden on the peoples of the earth than ever before, it becomes clear that they are two-fold: first, the desire, disclosed or hidden, on the part of governments to enlarge their territories at the expense of a sister nation and I believe that only a small minority of governments or of peoples harbor such a purpose; second, the fear of nations that they will be invaded. I believe that the overwhelming majority of peoples feel obliged to retain excessive arma-ments because they fear some act of aggression against them and not because they themselves seek to be aggressors.

There is justification for this fear. Modern weapons of offense are vastly stronger than modern weapons of defense. Frontier forts, trenches, wire entanglements, coast defenses—in a word, fixed fortifications—are no longer impregnable to the attack of war planes, heavy mobile artillery, land battleships called tanks, and poison gas.

If all nations will agree wholly to eliminate from possession and use the weapons which make possible a successful attack, defenses automatically will become impregnable, and the frontiers and independence of every nation will become secure.

The ultimate objective of the Disarmament Conference [1932–1934] must be the complete elimination of all offensive weapons. The immediate objective is a substantial reduction of some of these weapons and the elimination of many others. . . .

But the peace of the world must be assured during the whole period of disarmament and I, therefore, propose . . . :

That all the nations of the world should enter into a solemn and definite pact of non-aggression; that they should solemnly reaffirm the obligations they have assumed to limit and reduce their armaments, and, provided these obligations are faithfully executed by all signatory powers, individually agree that they will send no armed force of whatsoever nature across their frontiers.

Common sense points out that if any strong nation refuses to join with genuine sincerity in these concerted efforts for political and economic peace, the one at Geneva and the other at London, progress can be obstructed and ultimately blocked. In such event the civilized world, seeking both forms of peace, will know where the responsibility for failure lies. I urge that no nation assume such a responsibility, and that all the nations joined in these great conferences translate their professed policies into action. This is the way to political and economic peace.

> Message to the nations of the world appealing for peace by disarmament, May 16, 1933

2 / I have made it clear that the United States cannot take part in political arrangements in Europe, but that we stand ready to cooperate at any time in practicable measures on a world basis looking to immediate reduction of armaments and the lowering of the barriers against commerce.

> State of the Union Message, Jan. 3, 1934

3 / A deep love of peace is the common heritage of the people of both our countries [the Soviet Union and the United States] and I fully agree . . . that the cooperation of our great nations will inevitably be of the highest importance in the preservation of world peace. The successful accomplishment of this mutual task will be of immediate and lasting benefit not only to the peoples of our countries but to all peace-loving peoples everywhere.

> Remarks to the first ambassador of the U.S.S.R. on presentation of credentials, Jan. 8, 1934

4 / The peoples of many countries are being taxed to the point of poverty and starvation in order to enable governments to engage in a mad race in armament which, if permitted to continue, may well result in war.

> Message to Congress on the menace of uncontrolled manufacture and sale of arms and munitions, May 18, 1934

5 / I cannot with candor tell you that general international relationships outside the borders of the United States are improved. . . .

I believe, however, that our own peaceful and neighborly attitude toward other nations is coming to be understood and appreciated. The maintenance of international peace is a matter in which we are deeply and unselfishly concerned. . . .

There is no ground for apprehension that our relations with any nation will be otherwise than peaceful. Nor is there ground for doubt that the people of most nations seek relief from the threat and burden attaching to the false theory that extravagant armament cannot be reduced and limited by international accord.

State of the Union Message, Jan. 4, 1935

6 / It is the policy of this government to avoid being drawn into wars between other nations, but it is a fact that no Congress and no Executive can foresee all possible future situations. History is filled with unforeseeable situations that call for some flexibility of action. It is conceivable that situations may arise in which the wholly inflexible provisions of Section I of this [Neutrality] Act might have exactly the opposite effect from that which was intended. In other words, the inflexible provisions might drag us into war instead of keeping us out. The policy of the government is definitely committed to the maintenance of peace and the avoidance of any entanglement which would lead us into conflict. At the same time it is the policy of the government by every peaceful means and without entanglement to cooperate with other similarly minded governments to promote peace.

Statement on approval of neutrality legislation, Aug. 31, 1935

7 / [Foreign war is a] potent danger at this moment to the future of civilization. It is not surprising that many of our citizens feel a deep sense of apprehension lest some of the nations of the world repeat the folly of twenty years ago and drag civilization to a level from which world-wide recovery may be all but impossible.

In the face of this apprehension the American people can have but one concern—the American people can speak but one sentiment: despite what happens in continents overseas, the United States of America shall and must remain, as long ago the Father of our Country prayed that it might remain—unentangled and free.

Address, San Diego Exposition, San Diego, Calif., Oct. 2, 1935

8 / The primary purpose of the United States of America is to avoid being drawn into war. We seek also in every practicable way to promote peace and to discourage war. Except for those few who have placed or who place temporary, selfish gain ahead of national and world peace, the overwhelming mass of American citizens are in hearty accord with these basic policies of our Government, as they are also entirely sympathetic with the efforts of other nations to avoid and to end war.

That is why we too have striven with great consistency to approve steps to remove the causes of war and to disapprove steps taken by others to commit acts of aggression. We have either led or performed our full part in every important attempt to limit and to reduce world armaments. We have sought by definite act and solemn commitment to establish the United States as a good neighbor among Nations. We are acting to simplify definitions and facts by calling war "War" when armed invasion and a resulting killing of human beings take place.

But though our course is consistent and clear, it is with disappointment and sorrow that most Americans confess that the world's gain thus far has been small.

I would not be frank with you if I did not tell you that the dangers that confront the future of mankind as a whole are greater to the world and therefore to us than the dangers which confront the people of the United States by and in themselves alone.

Jealousies between nations continue, armaments increase; national ambitions that disturb the world's peace are thrust forward. Most serious of all, international confidence in the sacredness of international contracts is on the wane. . . .

While, therefore, we cannot and must not hide our concern for grave world dangers, and while, at the same time, we cannot and must not build walls around ourselves and hide our heads in the sand, we must go forward with all our strength to stress and strive for international peace.

In this effort America must and will protect herself. Under no circumstances will this policy of self-protection go to lengths beyond self-protection. Aggression on the part of the United States is an impossibility in so far as the present administration of your government is concerned. Defense against aggression by others—adequate defense on land, on sea and in air—is our accepted policy; and the measure of that defense is and will be solely the amount necessary to safeguard us against the armaments of others. The more greatly they decrease their armaments, the more quickly and surely shall we decrease ours.

Armistice Day address, Arlington National Cemetery, Nov. 11, 1935

9 / Since the summer of . . . 1933, the temper and the purposes of the rulers of many of the great populations in Europe and in Asia have not

pointed the way either to peace or to good-will among men. Not only have peace and good-will among men grown more remote in those areas of the earth during this period, but a point has been reached where the people of the Americas must take cognizance of growing ill-will, of marked trends toward aggression, of increasing armaments, of shortening tempers—a situation which has in it many of the elements that lead to the tragedy of general war. . . .

Nations seeking expansion, seeking the rectification of injustice springing from former wars, or seeking outlets for trade, for population, or even for their own peaceful contributions to the progress of civilization, fail to demonstrate that patience necessary to attain reasonable and legitimate objectives by peaceful negotiation or by an appeal to the finer instincts of world justice.

They have therefore impatiently reverted to the old belief in the law of the sword, or to the fantastic conception that they, and they alone, are chosen to fulfill a mission and that all the others among the billion and a half of human beings in the world must and shall learn from and be subject to them.

State of the Union Message, Jan. 3, 1936

10 / We confront the question of disarmament. On that issue our policy is clear. That policy has two elements in it. First, we propose to press, continually, for a limitation of armaments by international agreement. Second, failing to get that, we will make no increase of our own armaments unless other powers by increasing their armaments make increase by us necessary to our national safety.

Letter to the Daughters of the American Revolution on disarmament and national defense, Washington, D.C., April 20, 1936

11 / We have a disinterested, consistent and successful foreign policy. In it we give no thought to a war of aggression on the part of the United States. We stand firmly by our solemn treaty obligations renouncing war as an instrument of national policy.

Ibid.

12 / We are not isolationists except in so far as we seek to isolate ourselves completely from war. Yet we must remember that so long as war exists on earth there will be some danger that even the nation which most ardently desires peace may be drawn into war.

I have seen war. I have seen war on land and sea. I have seen blood running from the wounded. I have seen men coughing out their gassed lungs. I have seen the dead in the mud. I have seen cities destroyed. I have seen two hundred limping, exhausted men come out of line—the survivors of a regiment of one thousand that went forward forty-eight hours before. I have seen children starving. I have seen the agony of mothers and wives. I hate war.

I have passed unnumbered hours, I shall pass unnumbered hours, thinking and planning how war may be kept from this nation.

I wish I could keep war from all nations; but that is beyond my power. I can at least make certain that no act of the United States helps to produce or to promote war. I can at least make clear that the conscience of America revolts against war and that any Nation which provokes war forfeits the sympathy of the people of the United States.

Address on the international situation, Chautauqua, N.Y., Aug. 14, 1936

13 / We have sought steadfastly to assist international movements to prevent war. We cooperated to the bitter end—and it was a bitter end— in the work of the General Disarmament Conference [1932–1934]. When it failed we sought a separate treaty to deal with the manufacture of arms and the international traffic in arms. That proposal also came to nothing. We participated—again to the bitter end—in a conference to continue naval limitations [1935], and when it became evident that no general treaty could be signed because of the objections of other nations, we concluded with Great Britain and France a conditional treaty of qualitative limitation which, much to my regret, already shows signs of ineffectiveness.

Ibid.

14 / A prosperous world has no permanent room in it . . . for war. In striving for peace, I am confident that the American people seek it with their hearts and with their heads as well. Enlightened self-interest is justification for what we do.

Campaign address, St. Paul, Minn., Oct. 9, 1936

15 / We in America do not build monuments to war. We do not build monuments to conquest. We build monuments to commemorate the spirit of sacrifice in war—reminders of our desire for peace.

The memory of those whom the War called to the beyond urges us to consecrate the best that is in us to the service of country in times of peace.

We best honor the memory of those dead by striving for peace, that the terror of the days of war will be with us no more.

> Address at dedication of a site for a World War memorial, St. Louis, Mo., Oct. 14, 1936

16 / The men, women, and children of the Americas know that warfare in this day and age means more than the mere clash of armies: they see the destruction of cities and of farms; they foresee that children and grand-children, if they survive, will stagger for long years not only under the burden of poverty but also amid the threat of broken society and the destruction of constitutional governments.

I am profoundly convinced that the plain people everywhere in the civilized world today wish to live in peace one with another. And still leaders and governments resort to war. Truly, if the genius of mankind that has invented the weapons of death cannot discover the means of preserving peace, civilization as we know it lives in an evil day. . . .

Let no man or woman forget that there is no profit in war. Sacrifices in the cause of peace are infinitesimal compared with the holocaust of war.

> Address before the Inter-American Conference for the Maintenance of Peace, Buenos Aires, Argentina, Dec. 1, 1936

17 / Peace comes from the spirit and must be grounded in faith.
> *Ibid.*

18 / The motto of war is: "Let the strong survive; let the weak die." The motto of peace is: "Let the strong help the weak to survive."

> Address before the Congress and Supreme Court of Brazil, Rio de Janeiro, Nov. 27, 1936

19 / Peace may not be won with asking, but it can be won with striving, and I was never more convinced than now that the plain people everywhere in the civilized world today wish to live in peace, one with another.

> Greeting to *The Christian Science Monitor* on its efforts to preserve peace, April 10, 1937

20 / Some people think of military training in terms of acute pacifism. You and I do not. We think of it in terms of the preservation of the Nation.

When you come down to it, we are not paying a high price for national defense.

We know another thing—that our preparation is honestly made for defense and not for aggression. We devoutly hope that other nations in the world are going to get our point of view in the days to come in order that they may spend less of their national income in preparation for war and more of it for the arts of peace.

Informal remarks at Texas A. & M. College, College Station, May 11, 1937

The "Quarantine" Speech
[Excerpts]

21 / Innocent peoples, innocent nations, are being cruelly sacrificed to a greed for power and supremacy which is devoid of all sense of justice and humane considerations.

To paraphrase a recent author "[Old Perrault] foresaw a time when men, exultant in the technique of homicide, would rage so hotly over the world that every precious thing would be in danger, every book and picture and harmony, every treasure garnered through two millenniums, the small, the delicate, the defenseless—all would be lost like the lost books of Livy, or wrecked as the English wrecked the Summer Palace in Pekin. . . ."[1]

If those things come to pass in other parts of the world, let no one imagine that America will escape, that America may expect mercy, that this Western Hemisphere will not be attacked and that it will continue tranquilly and peacefully to carry on the ethics and the arts of civilization.

If those days come, "It will be such a one [storm], my son, as the world has not seen before. There will be no safety by arms, no help from authority, no answer in science. It will rage till every flower of culture is trampled, and all human things are leveled in a vast chaos."[2]

If those days are not to come to pass—if we are to have a world in which we can breathe freely and live in amity without fear—the peace-loving nations must make a concerted effort to uphold laws and principles on which alone peace can rest secure.

The peace-loving nations must make a concerted effort in opposition to those violations of treaties and those ignorings of humane instincts which today are creating a state of international anarchy and instability from which there is no escape through mere isolation or neutrality.

[1] James Hilton, *Lost Horizon* (William Morrow and Company, Inc.).
[2] *Ibid.*

Those who cherish their freedom and recognize and respect the equal right of their neighbors to be free and live in peace, must work together for the triumph of law and moral principles in order that peace, justice and confidence may prevail in the world. There must be a return to a belief in the pledged word, in the value of a signed treaty. There must be recognition of the fact that national morality is as vital as private morality. . . .

There is a solidarity and interdependence about the modern world, both technically and morally, which makes it impossible for any nation completely to isolate itself from economic and political upheavals in the rest of the world, especially when such upheavals appear to be spreading and not declining. There can be no stability or peace either within nations or between nations except under laws and moral standards adhered to by all. International anarchy destroys every foundation for peace. It jeopardizes either the immediate or the future security of every nation, large or small. It is, therefore, a matter of vital interest and concern to the people of the United States that the sanctity of international treaties and the maintenance of international morality be restored. . . .

The situation is definitely of universal concern. The questions involved relate not merely to violations of specific provisions of particular treaties; they are questions of war and of peace, of international law and especially of principles of humanity. It is true that they involve definite violations of agreements, and especially of the Covenant of the League of Nations, the Briand-Kellogg Pact and the Nine Power Treaty. But they also involve problems of world economy, world security and world humanity.

It is true that the moral consciousness of the world must recognize the importance of removing injustices and well-founded grievances; but at the same time it must be aroused to the cardinal necessity of honoring sanctity of treaties, of respecting the rights and liberties of others and of putting an end to acts of international aggression.

It seems to be unfortunately true that the epidemic of world lawlessness is spreading.

When an epidemic of physical disease starts to spread, the community approves and joins in a quarantine of the patients in order to protect the health of the community against the spread of the disease. . . .

War is a contagion, whether it be declared or undeclared. It can engulf states and peoples remote from the original scene of hostilities. We are determined to keep out of war, yet we cannot insure ourselves against the disastrous effects of war and the dangers of involvement. We are adopting such measures as will minimize our risk of involvement, but we cannot have complete protection in a world of disorder in which confidence and security have broken down.

If civilization is to survive the principles of the Prince of Peace must be restored. Trust between nations must be revived.

Most important of all, the will for peace on the part of peace-loving nations must express itself to the end that nations that may be tempted to violate their agreements and the rights of others will desist from such a course. There must be positive endeavors to preserve peace.

America hates war. America hopes for peace. Therefore, America actively engages in the search for peace.

Address on the worsening world situation ("Quarantine" speech), Chicago, Ill., Oct. 5, 1937

22 / Aloofness from war is not promoted by unawareness of war. In a world of mutual suspicions, peace must be affirmatively reached for . . . it cannot just be wished for. It cannot just be waited for. . . .

Radio address (Fireside Chat) announcing a call for a special session of Congress, Oct. 12, 1937

23 / Resolute in our determination to respect the rights of others, and to command respect for the rights of ourselves, we must keep ourselves adequately strong in self-defense.

State of the Union Message, Jan. 3, 1938

24 / Armaments increase today at an unprecedented and alarming rate. It is an ominous fact that at least one-fourth of the world's population is involved in merciless devastating conflict in spite of the fact that most people in most countries, including those where conflict rages, wish to live at peace. Armies are fighting in the Far East and Europe; thousands of civilians are being driven from their homes and bombed from the air. Tension throughout the world is high. . . .

It is our clear duty to further every effort toward peace but at the same time to protect our nation. . . . Such protection is and will be based not on aggression but on defense.

Message to Congress recommending increased armaments, Jan. 28, 1938

25 / Every right-thinking man and woman in our country wishes that it were safe for the nation to spend less of our national budget on our armed forces. All know that we are faced with a condition and not a theory—and that the condition is not of our choosing.

Address on National Defense, San Francisco, Calif., July 14, 1938

26 / The fabric of peace on the continent of Europe, if not throughout the rest of the world, is in immediate danger. The consequences of its rupture are incalculable. Should hostilities break out the lives of millions of men,

women and children in every country involved will most certainly be lost under circumstances of unspeakable horror.

The economic system of every country involved is certain to be shattered. The social structure of every country involved may well be completely wrecked.

The United States has no political entanglements. It is caught in no mesh of hatred. Elements of all Europe have formed its civilization.

The supreme desire of the American people is to live in peace. But in the event of a general war they face the fact that no nation can escape some measure of the consequences of such a world catastrophe.

The traditional policy of the United States has been the furtherance of the settlement of international disputes by pacific means. It is my conviction that all people under the threat of war today pray that peace may be made before, rather than after, war.

It is imperative that peoples everywhere recall that every civilized nation of the world voluntarily assumed the solemn obligations of the Kellogg-Briand Pact of 1928 to solve controversies only by pacific methods. In addition, most nations are parties to other binding treaties obligating them to preserve peace. Furthermore, all countries have today available for such peaceful solution of difficulties which may arise, treaties of arbitration and conciliation to which they are parties.

Whatever may be the differences in the controversies at issue and however difficult of pacific settlement they may be, I am persuaded that there is no problem so difficult or so pressing for solution that it cannot be justly solved by the resort to reason rather than by the resort to force.

During the present crisis the people of the United States and their Government have earnestly hoped that the negotiations for the adjustment of the controversy which has now arisen in Europe might reach a successful conclusion.

So long as these negotiations continue, so long will there remain the hope that reason and the spirit of equity may prevail and that the world may thereby escape the madness of a new resort to war.

On behalf of the 130 millions of people of the United States of America and for the sake of humanity everywhere I most earnestly appeal to you not to break off negotiations looking to a peaceful, fair, and constructive settlement of the questions at issue.

I earnestly repeat that so long as negotiations continue, differences may be reconciled. Once they are broken off reason is banished and force asserts itself.

And force produces no solution for the future good of humanity.

First peace appeal to Czechoslovakia, Germany, Great Britain, and France during Munich Crisis, Sept. 26, 1938

27 / The question before the world today, Mr. Chancellor, is not the question of errors of judgment or of injustices committed in the past. It is the question of the fate of the world today and tomorrow. The world asks of us who at this moment are heads of nations the supreme capacity to achieve the destinies of nations without forcing upon them, as a price, the mutilation and death of millions of citizens.

Resort to force in the Great War failed to bring tranquillity. Victory and defeat were alike sterile. That lesson the world should have learned. . . .

In my considered judgment, and in the light of the experience of this century, continued negotiations remain the only way by which the immediate problem can be disposed of upon any lasting basis.

Should you agree to a solution in this peaceful manner I am convinced that hundreds of millions throughout the world would recognize your action as an outstanding historic service to all humanity.

Allow me to state my unqualified conviction that history, and the souls of every man, woman, and child whose lives will be lost in the threatened war, will hold us and all of us accountable should we omit any appeal for its prevention.

The government of the United States has no political involvements in Europe, and will assume no obligations in the conduct of the present negotiations. Yet in our own right we recognize our responsibilities as a part of a world of neighbors.

The conscience and the impelling desire of the people of my country demand that the voice of their government be raised again and yet again to avert and to avoid war.

Second peace appeal to Germany during Munich Crisis, Sept. 27, 1938

28 / It is becoming increasingly clear that peace by fear has no higher or more enduring quality than peace by the sword.

There can be no peace if the reign of law is to be replaced by a recurrent sanctification of sheer force.

There can be no peace if national policy adopts as a deliberate instrument the threat of war.

There can be no peace if national policy adopts as a deliberate instrument the dispersion all over the world of millions of helpless and persecuted wanderers with no place to lay their heads.

There can be no peace if humble men and women are not free to think their own thoughts, to express their own feelings, to worship God.

There can be no peace if economic resources that ought to be devoted to social and economic reconstruction are to be diverted to an intensified competition in armaments which will merely heighten the suspicions and fears and threaten the economic prosperity of each and every nation.

Radio address to the New York *Herald Tribune* Forum, Oct. 26, 1938

29 / You cannot organize civilization around the core of militarism and at the same time expect reason to control human destinies.

    Ibid.

30 / We do not expect a new Heaven and a new Earth overnight, but in our own land, and other lands—wherever men of good will listen to our appeal—we shall work as best we can with the instruments at hand to banish hatred, greed and covetousness from the heart of mankind.

    And so the pledge I have so often given to my own countrymen I renew before all the world on this glad Christmas Eve, that I shall do whatever lies within my own power to hasten the day foretold by Isaiah, when men "shall beat their swords into ploughshares and their spears into pruning hooks; nation shall not lift up sword against nation, neither shall they learn war any more."

    Radio address on Christmas Eve, Washington, D.C., Dec. 24, 1938

31 / When we deliberately try to legislate neutrality, our neutrality laws may operate unevenly and unfairly—may actually give aid to an aggressor and deny it to the victim. The instinct of self-preservation should warn us that we ought not to let that happen anymore.

    State of the Union Message, Jan. 4, 1939

32 / No. 1: We are against any entangling alliances, obviously. No. 2: We are in favor of the maintenance of world trade for everybody—all nations—including ourselves. No. 3: We are in complete sympathy with any and every effort made to reduce or limit armaments. No. 4: As a nation —as American people—we are sympathetic with the peaceful maintenance of political, economic and social independence of all nations in the world.

    Press conference, Feb. 3, 1939

33 / . . . the statement that the American frontier is on the Rhine. Some "boob" "got that off"; I don't think it was a member of the Press. . . . the attack and the applause are again based on a misstatement of fact.

    Ibid.

34 / I have had a fine holiday here with you all. I'll be back in the fall if we do not have a war.

    Extemporaneous remarks on leaving Warm Springs, Ga., April 9, 1939

35 / You have repeatedly asserted that you and the German people have no desire for war. If this is true there need be no war.

Nothing can persuade the peoples of the earth that any governing power has any right or need to inflict the consequences of war on its own or any other people save in the cause of self-evident home defense.

In making this statement we as Americans speak not through selfishness or fear or weakness. If we speak now it is with the voice of strength and with friendship for mankind. It is still clear to me that international problems can be solved at the council table.

It is therefore no answer to the plea for peaceful discussion for one side to plead that unless they receive assurances beforehand that the verdict will be theirs, they will not lay aside their arms. In conference rooms, as in courts, it is necessary that both sides enter upon the discussion in good faith, assuming that substantial justice will accrue to both; and it is customary and necessary that they leave their arms outside the room where they confer.

I am convinced that the cause of world peace would be greatly advanced if the nations of the world were to obtain a frank statement relating to the present and future policy of governments.

Because the United States, as one of the nations of the Western Hemisphere, is not involved in the immediate controversies which have arisen in Europe, I trust that you may be willing to make such a statement of policy to me as head of a nation far removed from Europe in order that I, acting only with the responsibility and obligation of a friendly intermediary, may communicate such declaration to other nations now apprehensive as to the course which the policy of your government may take.

Are you willing to give assurance that your armed forces will not attack or invade the territory or possessions of the following independent nations: Finland, Estonia, Latvia, Lithuania, Sweden, Norway, Denmark, The Netherlands, Belgium, Great Britain and Ireland, France, Portugal, Spain, Switzerland, Liechtenstein, Luxemburg, Poland, Hungary, Rumania, Yugoslavia, Russia, Bulgaria, Greece, Turkey, Iraq, the Arabias, Syria, Palestine, Egypt and Iran?

Peace appeal to Chancellor Adolf Hitler and Premier Benito Mussolini, April 14, 1939

36 / During recent months international political considerations have required still greater emphasis upon the vitalization of our defense, for we have had dramatic illustrations of the fate of undefended nations. . . . We seek peace by honorable and pacific conduct of our international relations; but that desire for peace must never be mistaken for weakness.

Commencement address, U.S. Military Academy, West Point, N.Y., June 12, 1939

37 / I therefore urge with all earnestness—and I am likewise urging the President of the Republic of Poland—that the governments of Germany and of Poland agree by common accord to refrain from any positive act of hostility for a reasonable and stipulated period, and that they agree likewise by common accord to solve the controversies which have arisen between them by one of the three following methods: first, by direct negotiation; second, by submission of these controversies to an impartial arbitration in which they can both have confidence; or, third, that they agree to the solution of these controversies through the procedure of conciliation, selecting as conciliator or moderator a national of one of the traditionally neutral states of Europe, or a national of one of the American republics which are all of them free from any connection with or participation in European political affairs. . . .

I appeal to you in the name of the people of the United States, and I believe in the name of peace-loving men and women everywhere, to agree to the solution of the controversies existing between your government and that of Poland through the adoption of one of the alternative methods I have proposed. I need hardly reiterate that should the governments of Germany and of Poland be willing to solve their differences in the peaceful manner suggested, the government of the United States still stands prepared to contribute its share to the solution of the problems which are endangering world peace in the form set forth in my message of April 14.

Peace appeal to Chancellor Adolf Hitler on the eve of World War II [similar messages sent to King Victor Emmanuel of Italy and President Ignace Moszicki of Poland], Aug. 24, 1939

38 / I have this hour received from the President of Poland a reply to the message which I addressed to Your Excellency and to him last night. . . .

Your Excellency has repeated and publicly stated that the ends and the objectives sought by the German Reich were just and reasonable. In this reply to my message the President of Poland has made it plain that the Polish Government is willing, upon the basis set forth in my messages, to agree to solve the controversy which has arisen between the Republic of Poland and the German Reich by direct negotiation or through the process of conciliation.

Countless human lives can yet be saved and hope may still be restored that the nations of the modern world may even now construct a foundation for a peaceful and happier relationship if you and the government of the German Reich will agree to the pacific means of settlement accepted by the government of Poland.

All the world prays that Germany, too, will accept.

Second peace appeal to Chancellor Adolf Hitler on the eve of World War II, Aug. 25, 1939

39 / [In answer to request for comment on question about war—"Can we stay out?"]: Only this, that I not only sincerely hope so, but I believe we can; and that every effort will be made by the administration so to do.

Press conference, Sept. 1, 1939

40 / You must master at the outset a simple but unalterable fact in modern foreign relations between nations. When peace has been broken anywhere, the peace of all countries everywhere is in danger. . . .

Passionately though we may desire detachment, we are forced to realize that every word that comes through the air, every ship that sails the sea, every battle that is fought, does affect the American future.

Radio Address (Fireside Chat) on the outbreak of war in Europe, Sept. 3, 1939

41 / I should like to be able to offer the hope that the shadow over the world might swiftly pass. I cannot. The facts compel my stating, with candor, that darker periods may lie ahead. The disaster is not of our making; no act of ours engendered the forces which assault the foundations of civilization. Yet we find ourselves affected to the core; our currents of commerce are changing, our minds are filled with new problems, our position in world affairs has already been altered.

In such circumstances our policy must be to appreciate in the deepest sense the true American interest. Rightly considered, this interest is not selfish. Destiny first made us, with our sister nations on this hemisphere, joint heirs of European culture. Fate seems now to compel us to assume the task of helping to maintain in the Western world a citadel wherein that civilization may be kept alive. The peace, the integrity, and the safety of the Americas—these must be kept firm and serene.

In a period when it is sometimes said that free discussion is no longer compatible with national safety, may you by your deeds show the world that we of the United States are one people, of one mind, one spirit, one clear resolution, walking before God in the light of the living.

Message to Congress urging repeal of arms embargo, Sept. 21, 1939

42 / While we, as a nation, are neutral in the present tragic war in Europe, I am sure we cannot be indifferent to the suffering inflicted upon the peoples of the war-torn countries, particularly upon the helpless women and children. It is traditional that the American people should wish, after providing in full measure for the support of our necessary charitable endeavors at home, to extend material aid to the helpless victims of war abroad.

Appeal for cooperation and coordination of war relief agencies, Oct. 12, 1939

43 / That we can be neutral in thought as well as in act is impossible of fulfillment because again, the people of this country, thinking things through calmly and without prejudice, have been and are making up their minds about the relative merits of current events on other continents.

It is a fact increasingly manifest that presentation of real news has sharpened the minds and the judgment of men and women everywhere in these days of real public discussion. We Americans begin to know the difference between the truth on the one side and the falsehood on the other, no matter how often the falsehood is iterated and reiterated. Repetition does not transform a lie into a truth.

Radio address to the New York *Herald Tribune* Forum, Oct. 26, 1939

44 / In this season we have been used to celebrating the anniversary of the Armistice of the World War. Now we need a new and better peace: a peace which shall cause men at length to lay down weapons of hatred which have been used to divide them; and to forego purposeless ambitions which have created fear—ambitions which in the long run serve no useful end. We seek a language in which neighbor can talk to neighbor; in which men can talk to men; and by which the common and homely and human instincts which are found everywhere may reach expression through the elimination of fear.

Address on the 100th anniversary of the Virginia Military Institute, Lexington, Va., Nov. 11, 1939

45 / We have never had the illusion that peace and freedom could be based on weakness.

Ibid.

46 / It is tragic to see the policy of force spreading, and to realize that wanton disregard for law is still on the march.

Statement on the Russo-Finnish War, Dec. 1, 1939

47 / The American government and the American people have for some time pursued a policy of wholeheartedly condemning the unprovoked bombing and machine gunning of civilian populations from the air.

This government hopes, to the end that such unprovoked bombing shall not be given material encouragement in the light of recent recurrence of such acts, that American manufacturers and exporters of airplanes, aeronautical equipment and materials essential to airplane manufacture will bear this fact in mind before negotiating contracts for the exportation of these articles to nations obviously guilty of such unprovoked bombing.

Request to manufacturers not to sell war equipment to belligerents who bomb civilians, Dec. 2, 1939

48 / The world has created for itself a civilization capable of giving to mankind security and peace firmly set in the foundations of religious teachings. Yet, though it has conquered the earth, the sea, and even the air, civilization today passes through war and travail. . . .

In their hearts men decline to accept, for long, the law of destruction forced upon them by wielders of brute force. Always they seek, sometimes in silence, to find again the faith without which the welfare of nations and the peace of the world cannot be rebuilt. . . .

I believe that while statesmen are considering a new order of things, the new order may well be at hand. I believe that it is even now being built, silently but inevitably, in the hearts of masses whose voices are not heard, but whose common faith will write the final history of our time. They know that unless there is belief in some guiding principle and some trust in a divine plan, nations are without light, and peoples perish. They know that the civilization handed down to us by our fathers was built by men and women who knew in their hearts that all were brothers because they were children of God. They believe that by His will enmities can be healed; that in His mercy the weak can find deliverance, and the strong can find grace in helping the weak.

In the grief and terror of the hour, these quiet voices, if they can be heard, may yet tell of the rebuilding of the world.

Christmas message to Pope Pius XII, Dec. 23, 1939

49 / Force and military aggression are once more on the march against small nations, in this instance through the invasion of Denmark and Norway. These two nations have won and maintained during a period of many generations the respect and regard not only of the American people, but of all peoples, because of their observance of the highest standards of national and international conduct.

The government of the United States has on the occasion of recent invasions strongly expressed its disapprobation of such unlawful exercise of force. It here reiterates, with undiminished emphasis, its point of view as expressed on those occasions. If civilization is to survive, the rights of the smaller nations to independence, to their territorial integrity, and to the unimpeded opportunity for self-government must be respected by their more powerful neighbors.

Statement on the Nazi invasion of Denmark and Norway, April 13, 1940

50 / The almost incredible events . . . in the European conflict, particularly as a result of the use of aviation and mechanized equipment, together with the possible consequence of further developments, necessitate another enlargement of our military program. . . .

The problem of defending our national institutions and territorial integrity is no longer a problem for men equipped simply with an indomitable determination. Modern defense requires that this determination be supported by the highly developed machinery of our industrial productive capacity.

Message to Congress requesting additional funds for national defense, May 31, 1940

51 / The Government of Italy has now chosen to preserve what it terms its "freedom of action" and to fulfill what it states are its promises to Germany. In so doing it has manifested disregard for the rights and security of other nations, disregard for the lives of the peoples of those nations which are directly threatened by this spread of the war; and has evidenced its unwillingness to find the means through pacific negotiations for the satisfaction of what it believes are legitimate aspirations.

On this tenth day of June, 1940, the hand that held the dagger has struck it into the back of its neighbor.

On this tenth day of June, 1940, in this University founded by the first great American teacher of democracy, we send forth our prayers and our hopes to those beyond the seas who are maintaining with magnificent valor their battle for freedom.

In our American unity, we will pursue two obvious and simultaneous courses; we will extend to the opponents of force the material resources of this nation and, at the same time, we will harness and speed up the use of those resources in order that we ourselves in the Americas may have equipment and training equal to the task of any emergency and every defense.

Address as Italy entered the war against France, University of Virginia, Charlottesville, June 10, 1940

52 / I am distinctly in favor of a selective training bill and I consider it necessary to the national defense.

Press conference, Aug. 2, 1940

53 / We must prepare in a thousand ways. Men are not enough. They must have arms. They must learn how to use those arms. They must have skilled leaders—who must be trained. New bases must be established . . . to en-

able our fleet to defend our shores. Men and women must be taught to create the supplies that we need. And we must counter the agents of the dictators within our nation. . . .

It is not a change from the American way of life to advocate or legislate a greater and a speedier preparedness. It is a positive protection to the American way of life.

Address at the dedication of the Great Smoky Mountains National Park, Sept. 2, 1940

54 / We will not participate in foreign wars, and we will not send our Army, naval or air forces to fight in foreign lands outside of the Americas, except in case of attack.

Address before the Teamsters' Union convention, Washington, D.C., Sept. 11, 1940

55 / We arm. Because, I repeat, this nation wants to keep war away from these two continents. . . . Because great strength of arms is the practical way of fulfilling our hopes for peace and for staying out of this war or any other war.

Address on the defense of the Western Hemisphere, Dayton, Ohio, Oct. 12, 1940

56 / I give to you and to the people of this country this most solemn assurance: There is no secret treaty, no secret obligation, no secret commitment, no secret understanding in any shape or form, direct or indirect, with any other government, or any other nation in any part of the world, to involve this nation in any war or for any other purpose.

Campaign address, Philadelphia, Pa., Oct. 23, 1940

57 / I have said this before, but I shall say it again and again and again:
Your boys are not going to be sent into any foreign wars.
They are going into training to form a force so strong that, by its very existence, it will keep the threat of war far away from our shores.
The purpose of our defense is defense.

Campaign address, Boston, Mass., Oct. 30, 1940

58 / The experience of the past two years [1939–1940] has proven beyond doubt that no nation can appease the Nazis. No man can tame a tiger into a kitten by stroking it. There can be no appeasement with ruthlessness. There

can be no reasoning with an incendiary bomb. We know now that a nation can have peace with the Nazis only at the price of total surrender.

Radio address (Fireside Chat) on national security, Dec. 29, 1940

59 / When the dictators, if the dictators, are ready to make war upon us, they will not wait for an act of war on our part.

State of the Union Message ("Four Freedoms" speech), Jan. 6, 1941

60 / If we sit down now we may get run over later. And if our kind of civilization gets run over, the kind of peace we seek will become an unattainable hope.

Radio address to Jackson Day dinners, from Fort Lauderdale, Fla., March 29, 1941

61 / It is, indeed, a fallacy, based on no logic at all, for any Americans to suggest that the rule of force can defeat human freedom in all the other parts of the world and permit it to survive in the United States alone. . . .

We know too that we cannot save freedom in our own midst, in our own land, if all around us—our neighbor nations—have lost their freedom. . . .

I tell the American people solemnly that the United States will never survive as a happy and fertile oasis of liberty surrounded by a cruel desert of dictatorship.

Radio address on Independence Day, Hyde Park, N.Y., July 4, 1941

62 / And I am sure that even now the Nazis are waiting to see whether the United States will by silence give them the green light to go ahead on this path of destruction.

The Nazi danger to our Western World has long ceased to be a mere possibility. The danger is here now—not only from a military enemy but from an enemy of all law, all liberty, all morality, all religion.

There has now come a time when you and I must see the cold, inexorable necessity of saying to these inhuman, unrestrained seekers of world conquest and permanent world domination by the sword, "You seek to throw our children and our children's children into your form of terrorism and slavery. You have now attacked our own safety. You shall go no further."

Normal practices of diplomacy—note writing—are of no possible use in dealing with international outlaws who sink our ships and kill our citizens.

One peaceful nation after another has met disaster because each refused to look the Nazi danger squarely in the eye until it actually had them by the throat.

The United States will not make that fatal mistake.

Radio address (Fireside Chat) on the sinking of the *U.S.S. Greer* by the Germans, Sept. 11, 1941

63 / Hitler has offered a challenge which we as Americans cannot and will not tolerate.

We will not let Hitler prescribe the waters of the world on which our ships may travel. The American flag is not going to be driven from the seas either by his submarines, his airplanes, or his threats.

We cannot permit the affirmative defense of our rights to be annulled and diluted by sections of the Neutrality Act which have no realism in the light of unscrupulous ambition of madmen.

We Americans have determined our course.

We intend to maintain the security and the integrity and the honor of our country.

We intend to maintain the policy of protecting the freedom of the seas against domination by any foreign power which has become crazed with a desire to control the world.

Message to Congress recommending the arming of merchant vessels and the revision of neutrality legislation, Oct. 9, 1941

64 / Every school child knows what our foreign policy is. It is to defend the honor, the freedom, the rights, the interests and the well-being of the American people. We seek no gain at the expense of others. We threaten no one, nor do we tolerate threats from others. No nation is more deeply dedicated to the ways of peace; no nation is fundamentally stronger to resist aggression.

Message to the Foreign Policy Association, New York City, Oct. 25, 1941

65 / Hitler has attacked shipping in areas close to the Americas in the North and South Atlantic.

Many American-owned merchant ships have been sunk on the high seas. One American destroyer was attacked on September fourth. Another destroyer was attacked and hit on October seventeenth. Eleven brave and loyal men of our Navy were killed by the Nazis.

We have wished to avoid shooting. But the shooting has started. And history has recorded who fired the first shot. In the long run, however, all that will matter is who fired the last shot.

America has been attacked. The *U.S.S. Kearny* is not just a Navy ship. She belongs to every man, woman and child in this nation. . . .

The purpose of Hitler's attack was to frighten the American people off the high seas—to force us to make a trembling retreat. This is not the first time he has misjudged the American spirit. That spirit is now aroused.

If our national policy were to be dominated by the fear of shooting, then all of our ships and those of our sister republics would have to be tied up in home harbors. Our Navy would have to remain respectfully—ab-jectly—behind any line which Hitler might decree on any ocean as his own dictated version of his own war zone.

Naturally we reject that absurd and insulting suggestion. We reject it because of our own self-interest, because of our own self-respect, because, most of all, of our own good faith. Freedom of the seas is now, as it has always been, a fundamental policy of your generation and mine.

Address on Navy Day concerning the German attack on the *U.S.S. Kearny*, Oct. 27, 1941

66 / The people of the United States, believing in peace and in the right of nations to live and let live, have eagerly watched the conversations be-tween our two governments during these past months. We have hoped for a termination of the present conflict between Japan and China. We have hoped that a peace of the Pacific could be consummated in such a way that nationalities of many diverse peoples could exist side by side without fear of invasion; that unbearable burdens of armaments could be lifted for them all; and that all peoples would resume commerce without discrimination against or in favor of any nation. . . .

During the past few weeks it has become clear to the world that Japanese military, naval, and air forces have been sent to southern Indo-China in such large numbers as to create a reasonable doubt on the part of other nations that this continuing concentration in Southern Indo-China is not defensive in its character. . . .

It is clear that a continuance of such a situation is unthinkable.

None of the peoples whom I have spoken of above can sit either in-definitely or permanently on a keg of dynamite. . . .

A withdrawal of the Japanese forces from Indo-China would result in the assurance of peace throughout the whole of the South Pacific area.

I address myself to Your Majesty at this moment in the fervent hope that Your Majesty may, as I am doing, give thought in this definite emer-gency to ways of dispelling the dark clouds. I am confident that both of us, for the sake of the peoples not only of our own great countries but for the sake of humanity in neighboring territories, have a sacred duty to restore traditional amity and prevent further death and destruction in the world.

Message to the Emperor of Japan, Dec. 6, 1941

The "Day of Infamy" Speech

[Excerpts]

67 / Yesterday, December 7, 1941—a date which will live in infamy—the United States of America was suddenly and deliberately attacked by naval and air forces of the Empire of Japan.

The United States was at peace with that nation and, at the solicitation of Japan, was still in conversation with its government and its Emperor looking toward the maintenance of peace in the Pacific. Indeed, one hour after Japanese air squadrons had commenced bombing in Oahu, the Japanese Ambassador to the United States and his colleague delivered to the Secretary of State a formal reply to a recent American message. While this reply stated that it seemed useless to continue the existing diplomatic negotiations, it contained no threat or hint of war or armed attack.

It will be recorded that the distance of Hawaii from Japan makes it obvious that the attack was deliberately planned many days or even weeks ago. During the intervening time the Japanese government has deliberately sought to deceive the United States by false statements and expressions of hope for continued peace. . . .

Always will we remember the character of the onslaught against us.

No matter how long it may take us to overcome this premeditated invasion, the American people, in their righteous might, will win through to absolute victory.

I believe I interpret the will of the Congress and of the people when I assert that we will not only defend ourselves to the uttermost but will make very certain that this form of treachery shall never endanger us again.

Hostilities exist. There is no blinking at the fact that our people, our territory, and our interests are in grave danger.

With confidence in our armed forces—with the unbounded determination of our people—we will gain the inevitable triumph—so help us God.

I ask that the Congress declare that since the unprovoked and dastardly attack by Japan on Sunday, December 7, a state of war has existed between the United States and the Japanese Empire.

Message to Congress asking for declaration of the existence of war between the U.S. and Japan, Dec. 8, 1941

68 / On the morning of December 11 the government of Germany, pursuing its course of world conquest, declared war against the United States.

The long known and the long expected has thus taken place. The forces endeavoring to enslave the entire world now are moving toward this hemisphere.

Never before has there been a greater challenge to life, liberty, and civilization.

Delay invites greater danger. Rapid and united effort by all the peoples of the world who are determined to remain free will insure a world victory of the forces of justice and of righteousness over the forces of savagery and of barbarism.

Italy also has declared war against the United States.

I therefore request the Congress to recognize a state of war between the United States and Germany and between the United States and Italy.

Message to Congress requesting recognition of a state of war between the U.S. and Germany and the U.S. and Italy, Dec. 11, 1941

22

Challenge to Democracy

1 / We heard a great deal during the late war about the challenge to democracy and I think it was a good thing for our complacency to learn that democracy was being challenged. But I think, too, that democracy is being challenged today just as forcibly if not as clamorously. The challenge is heard right here among us from all who complain about the inefficiency, the stupidity and the expense of government. It may be read in the statistics of crime and seen in the ugliness of many of our committees. It is expressed in all the newspaper accounts of official graft and blundering. It is written on our tax rolls and even in the patriotic-seeming text books that our children study in their schools. It looms large on election day when voters see before them long lists of names of men and women of whom they have never heard to be voted upon as candidates for salaried offices of whose duties and functions the voter has but the haziest impression.

> Address on the finances and responsibilities of local government, University of Virginia, Charlottesville, July 6, 1931

2 / Our national determination to keep free of foreign wars and foreign entanglements cannot prevent us from feeling deep concern when ideals and principles that we have cherished are challenged.

> Address, San Diego Exposition, San Diego, Calif., Oct. 2, 1935

3 / Here is the challenge to our democracy: In this nation I see tens of millions of its citizens—a substantial part of its whole population—who at this very moment are denied the greater part of what the very lowest standards of today call the necessities of life.

I see millions of families trying to live on incomes so meager that the pall of family disaster hangs over them day by day.

I see millions whose daily lives in city and on farm continue under conditions labeled indecent by a so-called polite society half a century ago.

I see millions denied education, recreation, and the opportunity to better their lot and the lot of their children.

I see millions lacking the means to buy the products of farm and factory and by their poverty denying work and productiveness to many other millions.

I see one-third of a nation ill-housed, ill-clad, ill-nourished.

The test of our progress is not whether we add more to the abundance of those who have much; it is whether we provide enough for those who have too little.

Second Inaugural Address, Jan. 30, 1937

4 / There are among us some who are a little too complacent these days in the assertion that democracy as a system of government is challenged abroad. Can we be too sure that it is not distrusted right here within our own gates by a small minority, powerful and articulate, which, paying lip service to democracy, seeks by every means within its power to thwart the will of the majority? Let us not forget that eternal vigilance is the price of liberty.

Letter to the Institute of Human Relations, National Conference of Jews and Christians, Aug. 20, 1937

5 / We do not deny that the methods of the challengers—whether they be called "communistic" or "dictatorial" or "military"—have obtained for many who live under them material things they did not obtain under democracies which they had failed to make function. Unemployment has been lessened—even though the cause is a mad manufacturing of armaments. Order prevails—even though maintained by fear, at the expense of liberty and individual rights.

So their leaders laugh at all constitutions, predict the copying of their own methods, and prophesy the early end of democracy throughout the world.

Both that attitude and that prediction are denied by those of us who still believe in democracy—that is, by the overwhelming majority of the nations of the world and by the overwhelming majority of the people of the world.

And the denial is based on two reasons eternally right.

The first reason is that modern men and women will not tamely commit to one man or one group the permanent conduct of their government. Eventually they will insist not only on the right to choose who shall govern them but also upon the periodic reconsideration of that choice by the free exercise of the ballot.

And the second reason is that the state of world affairs brought about by those new forms of government threatens civilization. Armaments and deficits pile up together. Trade barriers multiply and merchant ships are threatened on the high seas. Fear spreads throughout the world—fear of aggression, fear of invasion, fear of revolution, fear of death.

The people of America are rightly determined to keep that growing menace from our shores.

The known and measurable danger of becoming involved in war we face confidently. As to that, your government knows your mind, and you know your government's mind.

But it takes even more foresight, intelligence and patience to meet the subtle attack which spreading dictatorship makes upon the morale of a democracy.

Radio address on the 150th anniversary of the Constitution, Washington, D.C., Sept. 17, 1937

6 / In many countries democracy is under attack by those who charge that democracy fails to provide its people with the needs of modern civilization. I do not, you do not, subscribe to that charge. You and I . . . believe that democracy today is succeeding, but that an absolute necessity for its future success is the fighting spirit of the American people—their insistence that we go forward and not back.

Address on democratic principles and social objectives, Barnesville, Ga., Aug. 11, 1938

7 / In other lands across the water the flares of militarism and conquest, terrorism and intolerance, have vividly revealed to Americans for the first time since the Revolution how precious and extraordinary it is to be allowed this free choice of free leaders for free men.

No one will order us how to vote, and the only watchers we shall find at the polls are the watchers who guarantee that our ballot is secret. Think how few places are left where this can happen.

But we cannot carelessly assume that a nation is strong and great merely because it has a democratic form of government. We have learned that a democracy weakened by internal dissension, by mutual suspicion born of social injustice, is no match for autocracies which are ruthless enough to repress internal dissension.

Democracy in order to live must become a positive force in the daily lives of its people. It must make men and women whose devotion it seeks, feel that it really cares for the security of every individual; that it is tolerant enough to inspire an essential unity among its citizens; and that it is militant enough to maintain liberty against social oppression at home and against military aggression abroad. . . .

As of today, Fascism and Communism . . . are not threats to the continuation of our form of government. But I venture the challenging statement that if American democracy ceases to move forward as a living force, seeking day and night by peaceful means to better the lot of our citizens, Fascism and Communism . . . will grow in strength in our land.

Radio address on social justice and economic democracy, Hyde Park, N.Y., Nov. 4, 1938

8 / Storms from abroad directly challenge three institutions indispensable to Americans, now as always. The first is religion. It is the source of the other two—democracy and international good faith.

Religion, by teaching man his relationship to God, gives the individual a sense of his own dignity and teaches him to respect himself by respecting his neighbors.

Democracy, the practice of self-government, is a covenant among free men to respect the rights and liberties of their fellows.

International good faith, a sister of democracy, springs from the will of civilized nations of men to respect the rights and liberties of other nations of men.

In a modern civilization, all three—religion, democracy and international good faith—complement and support each other.

Where freedom of religion has been attacked, the attack has come from sources opposed to democracy. Where democracy has been overthrown, the spirit of free worship has disappeared. And where religion and democracy have vanished, good faith and reason in international affairs have given way to strident ambition and brute force.

An ordering of society which relegates religion, democracy and good faith among nations to the background can find no place within it for the ideals of the Prince of Peace. The United States rejects such an ordering, and retains its ancient faith.

State of the Union Message, Jan. 4, 1939

9 / During the past few years you and I have seen event follow event, each and every one of them a shock to our hopes for the peaceful development of modern civilization as we know it. . . .

In some kinds of human affairs the mind of man becomes accustomed to unusual actions if those actions are often repeated. But that is not so in the world happenings of today—and I am proud that it is not so. . . .

The overwhelmingly greater part of the population of the world abhors conquest and war and bloodshed—prays that the hand of neighbor shall not be lifted against neighbor. The whole world has seen attack follow threat on so many occasions and in so many places during these later years. We have come, therefore, to the reluctant conclusion that a continuance of these processes of arms presents a definite challenge to the continuance of the type of civilization to which all of us in the three Americas have been accustomed for so many generations. . . .

We, and most of the people in the world, still believe in a civilization of construction and not of destruction. We, and most of the people in the world, still believe that men and women have an inherent right to hew out the patterns of their own individual lives, just so long as they as individuals do not harm their fellow beings. We call this ideal by many terms which are synonymous—we call it individual liberty, we call it civil liberty and, I think, best of all, we call it democracy.

Address before the Eighth Pan American Scientific Conference, Washington, D.C., May 10, 1940

10 / It is natural and understandable that the younger generation should first ask itself what the extension of the philosophy of force to all the world would lead to ultimately. We see today in stark reality some of the consequences of what we call the machine age.

Where control of machines has been retained in the hands of mankind as a whole, untold benefits have accrued to mankind. For mankind was then the master; and the machine was the servant.

But in this new system of force the mastery of the machine is not in the hands of mankind. It is in the control of infinitely small groups of individuals who rule without a single one of the democratic sanctions that we have known. The machine in hands of irresponsible conquerors becomes the master; mankind is not only the servant; it is the victim, too. Such mastery abandons with deliberate contempt all the moral values to which even this young country for more than three hundred years has been accustomed and dedicated. . . .

Let us not hesitate—all of us—to proclaim certain truths. Overwhelmingly we, as a nation—and this applies to all the other American nations—are convinced that military and naval victory for the gods of force and hate would endanger the institutions of democracy in the western world, and that equally, therefore, the whole of our sympathies lies with those nations that are giving their life blood in combat against these forces.

Address as Italy entered the war against France, University of Virginia, Charlottesville, June 10, 1940

11 / The fact which dominates our world is the fact of armed aggression, the fact of successful armed aggression, aimed at the form of government, the kind of society that we in the United States have chosen and established for ourselves. It is a fact which no one longer doubts—which no one is longer able to ignore.

It is not an ordinary war. It is a revolution imposed by force of arms, which threatens all men everywhere. It is a revolution which proposes not to set men free but to reduce them to slavery—to reduce them to slavery in the interest of a dictatorship which has already shown the nature and the extent of the advantage which it hopes to obtain.

Acceptance speech, Democratic National Convention, Chicago, Ill., July 19, 1940

12 / We face one of the great choices of history.

It is not alone a choice of government by the people versus dictatorship.

It is not alone a choice of freedom versus slavery.

It is not alone a choice between moving forward or falling back.

It is all of these rolled into one.

It is the continuance of civilization as we know it versus the ultimate destruction of all that we have held dear—religion against godlessness; the ideal of justice against the practice of force; moral decency versus the firing squad; courage to speak out, and to act, versus the false lullaby of appeasement.

Ibid.

13 / The Nazi masters of Germany have made it clear that they intend not only to dominate all life and thought in their own country, but also to enslave the whole of Europe, and then to use the resources of Europe to dominate the rest of the world.

It was only three weeks ago their leader stated this: "There are two worlds that stand opposed to each other." And then in defiant reply to his opponents, he said this: "Others are correct when they say: With this world we cannot ever reconcile ourselves. . . . I can beat any other power in the world." So said the leader of the Nazis.

In other words, the Axis not merely admits but *proclaims* that there can be no ultimate peace between their philosophy of government and our philosophy of government.

In view of the nature of this undeniable threat, it can be asserted, properly and categorically, that the United States has no right or reason to encourage talk of peace, until the day shall come when there is a clear intention on the part of the aggressor nations to abandon all thought of dominating or conquering the world. . . .

The history of recent years proves that shootings and chains and concentration camps are not simply the transient tools but the very altars of modern dictatorships. They may talk of a "new order" in the world, but what they have in mind is only a revival of the oldest and the worst tyranny. In that there is no liberty, no religion, no hope.

The proposed "new order" is the very opposite of a United States of Europe or a United States of Asia. It is not a government based upon the consent of the governed. It is not a union of ordinary, self-respecting men and women to protect themselves and their freedom and their dignity from oppression. It is an unholy alliance of power and pelf to dominate and enslave the human race.

Radio address (Fireside Chat) on national security, Dec. 29, 1940

14 / Every realist knows that the democratic way of life is at this moment being directly assailed in every part of the world— assailed either by arms or by secret spreading of poisonous propaganda by those who seek to destroy unity and promote discord in nations still at peace. . . .

No realistic American can expect from a dictator's peace international generosity, or return of true independence, or world disarmament, or freedom of religion—or even good business.

Such a peace would bring no security for us or for our neighbors. "Those who would give up essential liberty to purchase a little temporary safety deserve neither liberty nor safety." [1]

State of the Union Message ("Four Freedoms" speech), Jan. 6, 1941

15 / Nazi forces are not seeking mere modifications in colonial maps or in minor European boundaries. They openly seek the destruction of all elective systems of government on every continent—including our own; they seek to establish systems of government based on the regimentation of all human beings by a handful of individual rulers who have seized power by force.

[1] Benjamin Franklin.

These men and their hypnotized followers call this a new order. It is not new. It is not order. For order among nations presupposes something enduring—some system of justice under which individuals, over a long period of time, are willing to live. Humanity will never permanently accept a system imposed by conquest and based on slavery.

These modern tyrants find it necessary to their plans to eliminate all democracies—eliminate them one by one. . . .

They know now that democracy can still remain democracy and speak and reach conclusions and arm itself adequately for defense.

From the bureaus of propaganda of the Axis powers came the confident prophecy that the conquest of our country would be "an inside job" —a job accomplished not by overpowering invasion from without, but by disrupting confusion and disunion and moral disintegration from within.

Those who believed that knew little of our history. America is not a country which can be confounded by the appeasers, the defeatists, the backstairs manufacturers of panic. It is a country which talks out its problems in the open, where any man can hear them.

Address at the White House Correspondents' Association dinner, Washington, D.C., March 15, 1941

16 / The enemies of democracy are now trying, by every means, to destroy our unity. The chief weapon they now use against us is propaganda.

The propaganda comes in ever increasing quantities, with ever increasing violence, from across the seas. And it is disseminated within our own borders by agents or innocent dupes of foreign powers.

It is directed against all Americans—Republican and Democratic— farmers and bankers—employers and employees.

Propagandists, defeatists and dupes, protected as they are by our fundamental civil liberties, have been preaching, and are still preaching, the ungodly gospel of fear. They use insinuation and falsehood. They have tried to shatter the confidence of Americans in their government and in one another.

Radio address to Jackson Day dinners, from Fort Lauderdale, Fla., March 29, 1941

17 / Totalitarian aggression is now reaching out into nearly every quarter of the globe. It has become clear that this aggression menaces not only our foreign trade and our national business prosperity, but also the very social and spiritual framework of our democratic way of life.

Statement on the observance of National Foreign Trade Week, May 17, 1941

18 / Even our right to worship would be threatened. The Nazi world does not recognize any god except Hitler, for the Nazis are as ruthless as the Communists in the denial of God. What place has religion which preaches the dignity of the human being, the majesty of the human soul, in a world where moral standards are measured by treachery and bribery and "fifth columnists"? Will our children, too, wander off, goose-stepping in search of new gods?

We do not accept, and will not permit, this Nazi "shape of things to come." It will never be forced upon us, if we act in this present crisis with the wisdom and the courage which has distinguished our country in all the crises of the past.

Today the whole world is divided between human slavery and human freedom—between pagan brutality and the Christian ideal.

We choose human freedom—which is the Christian ideal.

Radio address announcing an unlimited national emergency, White House, May 27, 1941

19 / Hitler has often protested that his plans for conquest do not extend across the Atlantic Ocean. But his submarines and raiders prove otherwise. So does the entire design of his new world order.

For example, I have in my possession a secret map made in Germany by Hitler's government—by the planners of the new world order. It is a map of South America and a part of Central America, as Hitler proposes to reorganize it. Today in this area there are fourteen separate countries. The geographical experts of Berlin, however, have ruthlessly obliterated all existing boundary lines; and have divided South America into five vassal states, bringing the whole continent under their domination. And they have also so arranged it that the territory of one of these new puppet states includes the Republic of Panama and our great life line—the Panama Canal.

That is his plan. It will never go into effect.

This map makes clear the Nazi design not only against South America but against the United States itself.

Your government has in its possession another document made in Germany by Hitler's government. It is a detailed plan, which, for obvious reasons, the Nazis did not wish and do not wish to publicize just yet, but which they are ready to impose a little later on a dominated world—if Hitler wins. It is a plan to abolish all existing religions—Protestant, Catholic, Mohammedan, Hindu, Buddhist, and Jewish alike. The property of all churches will be seized by the Reich and its puppets. The cross and all other symbols of religion are to be forbidden. The clergy are to be forever silenced under penalty of the concentration camps, where even now so many fearless men are being tortured because they have placed God above Hitler.

In the place of the churches of our civilization, there is to be set up an international Nazi church—a church which will be served by orators sent out by the Nazi government. In the place of the Bible, the words of *Mein Kampf* will be imposed and enforced as Holy Writ. And in place of the cross of Christ will be put two symbols—the swastika and the naked sword.

A god of Blood and Iron will take the place of the God of Love and Mercy. Let us well ponder that statement which I have made tonight.

Address on Navy Day concerning the German attack on the *U.S.S. Kearny*, Oct. 27, 1941

20 / I say to you solemnly that if Hitler's present military plans are brought to successful fulfillment, we Americans shall be forced to fight in defense of our own homes and our own freedom in a war as costly and as devastating as that which now rages on the Russian front.

Hitler has offered a challenge which we as Americans cannot and will not tolerate.

Message to Congress recommending the arming of merchant vessels and the revision of neutrality legislation, Oct. 9, 1941

21 / In the year 1933, there came to power in Germany a political clique which did not accept the declarations of the American bill of human rights as valid; a small clique of ambitious and unscrupulous politicians whose announced and admitted platform was precisely the destruction of the rights that instrument declared. Indeed the entire program and goal of these political and moral tigers was nothing more than the overthrow, throughout the earth, of the great revolution of human liberty of which our American Bill of Rights is the mother charter.

The truths which were self-evident to Thomas Jefferson—which have been self-evident to the six generations of Americans who followed him—were to these men hateful. The rights to life, liberty, and the pursuit of happiness which seemed to Jefferson, and which seem to us, inalienable, were, to Hitler and his fellows, empty words which they proposed to cancel forever.

The propositions they advanced to take the place of Jefferson's inalienable rights were these:

That the individual human being has no rights whatever in himself and by virtue of his humanity;

That the individual human being has no right to a soul of his own, or a mind of his own, or a tongue of his own, or a trade of his own; or even to live where he pleases or to marry the woman he loves;

That his only duty is the duty of obedience, not to his God, and not to his conscience, but to Adolf Hitler; and that his only value is his value not as a man, but as a unit of the Nazi state.

To Hitler, the ideal of the people, as we conceive it—the free, self-governing, and responsible people—is incomprehensible. The people, to Hitler, are "the masses" and the highest human idealism is, in his own words, that a man should wish to become "a dust particle" of the order "of force" which is to shape the universe.

To Hitler, the government, as we conceive it, is an impossible conception. The government to him is not the servant and the instrument of the people, but their absolute master and the dictator of their every act.

To Hitler, the church, as we conceive it, is a monstrosity to be destroyed by every means at his command. The Nazi church is to be the national church, absolutely and exclusively in the service of but one doctrine, race, and nation.

To Hitler, the freedom of men to think as they please and speak as they please and worship as they please is, of all things imaginable, most hateful and most desperately to be feared.

The issue of our time, the issue of the war in which we are engaged, is the issue forced upon the decent, self-respecting peoples of the earth by the aggressive dogmas of this attempted revival of barbarism, this proposed return to tyranny, this effort to impose again upon the peoples of the world doctrines of absolute obedience, and of dictatorial rule, and of the suppression of truth, and of the oppression of conscience, which the free nations of the earth have long ago rejected.

What we face is nothing more nor less than an attempt to overthrow and to cancel out the great upsurge of human liberty of which the American Bill of Rights is the fundamental document; to force the peoples of the earth, and among them the peoples of this continent, to accept again the absolute authority and despotic rule from which the courage and the resolution and the sacrifices of their ancestors liberated them many, many years ago.

Radio address on the 150th anniversary of the adoption of the American Bill of Rights, Dec. 15, 1941

23

Defense of Democracy

1 / In expressing our faith of the Western World, let us affirm:

That we maintain and defend the democratic form of constitutional representative government.

<small>Address before the Inter-American Conference for the maintenance of peace, Buenos Aires, Argentina, Dec. 1, 1936</small>

2 / There comes a time in the affairs of men when they must prepare to defend, not their homes alone, but the tenets of faith and humanity on which their churches, their governments and their very civilization are founded. The defense of religion, of democracy and of good faith among nations is all the same fight. To save one we must now make up our minds to save all.

We know what might happen to us of the United States if the new philosophies of force were to encompass the other continents and invade our own. We, no more than other nations, can afford to be surrounded by the enemies of our faith and our humanity. Fortunate it is, therefore, that in this Western Hemisphere we have, under a common ideal of democratic government, a rich diversity of resources and of peoples functioning together in mutual respect and peace.

That hemisphere, that peace, and that ideal we propose to do our share in protecting against storms from any quarter. Our people and our resources are pledged to secure that protection. From that determination no American flinches. . . .

We have learned that God-fearing democracies of the world which observe the sanctity of treaties and good faith in their dealings with other nations cannot safely be indifferent to international lawlessness anywhere.

They cannot forever let pass, without effective protest, acts of aggression against sister nations—acts which automatically undermine all of us.

Obviously they must proceed along practical, peaceful lines. But the mere fact that we rightly decline to intervene with arms to prevent acts of aggression does not mean that we must act as if there were no aggression at all. Words may be futile, but war is not the only means of commanding a decent respect for the opinions of mankind. There are many methods short of war, but stronger and more effective than mere words, of bringing home to aggressor governments the aggregate sentiments of our own people.

At the very least, we can and should avoid any action, or any lack of action, which will encourage, assist or build up an aggressor.

State of the Union Message, Jan. 4, 1939

3 / The American peace . . . has no quality of weakness in it. We are prepared to maintain it, and to defend it to the fullest extent of our strength, matching force to force if any attempt is made to subvert our institutions, or to impair the independence of any one of our [Pan American] group. . . .

Our will to peace can be as powerful as our will to mutual defense; it can command greater loyalty, greater devotion, greater discipline than that enlisted elsewhere for temporary conquest of equally futile glory.

Pan American Day address before the Governing Board of the Pan American Union, Washington, D.C., April 14, 1939

4 / The permanent security of America in the present crisis does not lie in armed force alone. What we face is a set of world-wide forces of disintegration—vicious, ruthless, destructive of all the moral, religious and political standards which mankind, after centuries of struggle, has come to cherish most.

In these moral values, in these forces which have made our nation great, we must actively and practically reassert our faith.

These words—"national unity"—must not be allowed to become merely a high sounding phrase, a vague generality, a pious hope, to which everyone can give lip-service. They must be made to have real meaning in terms of the daily thoughts and acts of every man, woman and child in our land during the coming year and the years that lie ahead.

For national unity is, in a very real and deep sense, the fundamental safeguard of all democracy. . . .

We must as a united people keep ablaze on this continent the flames of human liberty, of reason, of democracy and of fair play as living things to be preserved for the better world that is to come.

State of the Union Message, Jan. 3, 1940

5 / I am a pacifist. You, my fellow citizens of twenty-one American republics, are pacifists too.

But I believe that by overwhelming majorities in all the Americas you and I, in the long run if it be necessary, will act together to protect and defend by every means at our command our science, our culture, our American freedom and our civilization.

Address before the Eighth Pan American Scientific Conference, Washington, D.C., May 10, 1940

6 / New powers of destruction, incredibly swift and deadly, have been developed; and those who wield them are ruthless and daring.

No old defense is so strong that it requires no further strengthening and no attack is so unlikely or impossible that it may be ignored.

Let us examine, without self-deception, the dangers which confront us. Let us measure our strength and our defense without self-delusion.

The clear fact is that the American people must recast their thinking about national protection. . . .

The Atlantic and Pacific oceans were reasonably adequate defensive barriers when fleets under sail could move at an average speed of five miles an hour. Even in those days by a sudden foray, it was possible for an opponent actually to burn our national capital. Later, the oceans still gave strength to our defense when fleets and convoys propelled by steam could sail the oceans at fifteen or twenty miles an hour.

But the new element—air navigation—steps up the speed of possible attack to 200, to 300 miles an hour.

Furthermore, it brings the new possibilities of the use of nearer bases from which an attack or attacks on the American continents could be made. . . .

For the permanent record, I ask the Congress not to take any action which would in any way hamper or delay the delivery of American-made planes to foreign nations which have ordered them, or seek to purchase new planes. That, from the point of view of our own national defense, would be extremely shortsighted. . . .

Our task is plain. The road we must take is clearly indicated. Our defenses must be invulnerable, our security absolute. But our defense as it was yesterday, or even as it is today, does not provide security against potential developments and dangers of the future.

Defense cannot be static. Defense must grow and change from day to day. Defense must be dynamic and flexible, an expession of the vital forces of the nation and of its resolute will to meet whatever challenge the future may hold. . . .

Our ideal, yours and mine, the ideal of every man, woman and child in the country—our objective is still peace—peace at home and peace abroad. Nevertheless we stand ready not only to spend millions for defense but to give our service and even our lives for the maintenance of our American liberties.

Our security is not a matter of weapons alone. The arm that wields them must be strong, the eye that guides them clear, the will that directs them indomitable.

Message to Congress requesting additional funds for national defense, May 16, 1940

7 / While our Navy and our airplanes and our guns and our ships may be our first lines of defense, it is still clear that way down at the bottom, underlying them all, giving them their strength, sustenance and power, are the spirit and the morale of a free people.

For that reason, we must make sure, in all that we do, that there be no breakdown or cancellation of any of the great social gains which we have made in these past years. We have carried on an offensive on a broad front against social and economic inequalities, against abuses which had made our society weak. That offensive should not now be broken down by the pincers movement of those who would use the present needs of physical military defense to destroy it.

Radio address (Fireside Chat) on social gains and national defense, May 26, 1940

8 / It is necessary now that the people of this nation and their representatives in Congress look at the problem of the national defense with utterly dispassionate realism. Never have we as a nation attempted to define the word "defense" in terms of a specific attack at a certain place at a certain time or with specified land and sea forces. In the long sweep of the century and a half since our defenses have been concentrated and unified under the Constitution, it has been a prime obligation of the President and Commander-in-Chief promptly to advise the Congress with respect to any world circumstances calling for either increased or diminished defense needs.

From time to time during the last seven years, I have not failed to advise the people and their representatives of grave dangers threatening the United States and its people, and the institutions of democracy everywhere.

From time to time I have availed myself of opportunities to reassert and to implement the right of all nations of the American hemisphere to freedom from attack or control by any non-American power. . . .

We, the free men and women of the United States, with memories of our fathers to inspire us and the hopes of our children to sustain us are determined to be strong as well as free. The apologists for despotism and those who aid them by whispering defeatism or appeasement, assert that because we have not devoted our full energies to arms and to preparation for war that we are now incapable of defense.

I refute that imputation.

We fully understand the threat of the new enslavement in which men may not speak, may not listen, may not think. As these threats become more numerous and their dire meaning more clear, it deepens the determination of the American people to meet them with wholly adequate defense.

We have seen nation after nation, some of them weakened by treachery from within, succumb to the force of the aggressor. We see great nations still gallantly fighting against aggression, encouraged by high hope of ultimate victory.

That we are opposed to war is known not only to every American, but to every government in the world. We will not use our arms in a war of aggression; we will not send our men to take part in European wars.

But, we will repel aggression against the United States or the Western Hemisphere. The people and their representatives in the Congress know that the threats to our liberties, the threats to our security, the threats against our way of life, the threats to our institutions of religion, of democracy, and of international good faith, have increased in number and gravity from month to month, from week to week, and almost from day to day. . . .

The principal lesson of the war up to the present time is that partial defense is inadequate defense.

If the United States is to have any defense, it must have total defense.

We cannot defend ourselves a little here and a little there. We must be able to defend ourselves wholly and at any time.

Our plans for national security, therefore, should cover total defense. I believe that the people of this country are willing to make any sacrifice to attain that end.

Message to Congress requesting additional funds for national defense, July 10, 1940

9 / It has been well said that a selfish and greedy people cannot be free.

The American people must decide whether these things are worth making sacrifices of money, of energy, and of self. They will not decide by listening to mere words or by reading mere pledges, interpretations and claims. They will decide on the record—the record as it has been made—the record of things as they are.

The American people will sustain the progress of a representative democracy, asking the Divine Blessing as they face the future with courage and with faith.

Acceptance speech, Democratic National Convention, Chicago, Ill., July 19, 1940

10 / Only the seasoned and highly trained troops can hope for success in combat. Our citizen soldiery, no matter how willing and earnest, cannot possibly attain the necessary degree of efficiency through their normal training activities. Even our professional soldiers require months of intensive training to bring them to their present satisfactory state. We know too well the tragedy that ensues when inadequately trained men are assailed by a more skillful adversary. . . .

I cannot, and with clear conscience, longer postpone this vitally essential step in our progress toward adequate preparedness, and I am therefore transmitting herewith legislation that, if enacted, will enable me to order the National Guard of the United States to active service for such period of intensive training as may be necessary to raise its efficiency to a point comparable with that of our small regular establishment.

Message to Congress requesting authority to order the National Guard into active service, July 29, 1940

11 / If we are to survive, we cannot be soft in a world in which there are dangers that threaten Americans—dangers far more deadly than were those the frontiersmen had to face.

The earth has been so shrunk by the airplane and the radio that Europe is closer to America today than one side of these mountains to the other when the pioneers toiled through the primeval forest. The arrow, the tomahawk and the scalping knife have been replaced by the airplane, the bomb, the tank and the machine gun. Their threat is as close to us today as was the threat to the frontiersmen when hostile Indians were lurking on the other side of the gap. . . .

It is not a change from the American way of life to advocate or legislate a greater and a speedier preparedness. It is a positive protection to the American way of life. We know that in the process of preparing against danger we shall not have to abandon and we will not abandon the great social improvements that have come to the American people in these later years. We need not swap the gain of better living for the gain of better defense. I propose to retain the one and gain the other. . . .

What shall we be defending? The good earth of this land, our homes, our families—and far more. We shall be defending a way of life which has given more freedom to the soul and body of man than ever has been realized in the world before, a way of life that has let men scale whatever heights they could scale without hurting their fellows, a way of life that has let men hold up their heads and admit no master but God. . . .

It is our pride that in our country men are free to differ with each other and with their government, and to follow their own thoughts and express them. We believe that the only whole man is a free man. And we believe that, in the face of danger, the old spirit of the frontiersmen which is in our blood will give us the courage and unity that we must have.

Address at the dedication of the Great Smoky Mountains National Park, Sept. 2, 1940

12 / America has adopted selective service in time of peace, and, in doing so, has broadened and enriched our basic concept of citizenship. Beside the clear democratic ideals of equal rights, equal privileges and equal opportunities, we have set forth the underlying other duties, obligations and responsibilities of equal service. . . .

Universal service will bring not only greater preparedness to meet the threat of war, but a wider distribution of tolerance and understanding to enjoy the blessings of peace.

Statement on the adoption of peace-time universal selective service, Sept. 16, 1940

13 / Great Britain and a lot of other nations would never have received one ounce of help from us—if the decision had been left to [Joseph] Martin, [Bruce] Barton, and [Hamilton] Fish.

Campaign address, New York City, Oct. 28, 1940

14 / The duty of this day has been imposed upon us from without. Those who have dared to threaten the whole world with war—those who have created the name and deed of total war—have imposed upon us and upon all free peoples the necessity of preparation for total defense.

But this day not only imposes a duty; it provides also an opportunity —an opportunity for united action in the cause of liberty—an opportunity for the continuing creation on this continent of a country where the people alone shall be master, where the people shall be truly free.

To the sixteen million young men who register today, I say that democracy is your cause—the cause of youth.

Democracy is the one form of society which guarantees to every new generation of men the right to imagine and to attempt to bring to pass a better world. Under the despotisms the imagination of a better world and its achievement are alike forbidden.

Your act today affirms not only your loyalty to your country, but your will to build your future for yourselves.

We of today, with God's help, can bequeath to Americans of tomorrow a nation in which the ways of liberty and justice will survive and be secure. Such a nation must be devoted to the cause of peace. And it is for that cause that America arms itself.

It is to that cause—the cause of peace—that we Americans today devote our national will and our national spirit and our national strength.

Radio address on Selective Service registration day, Oct. 16, 1940

15 / We must be the great arsenal of democracy. For us this is an emergency as serious as war itself. We must apply ourselves to our task with the same resolution, the same sense of urgency, the same spirit of patriotism and sacrifice as we would show were we at war.

We have furnished the British great material support and we will furnish far more in the future.

There will be no "bottlenecks" in our determination to aid Great Britain. No dictator, no combination of dictators, will weaken that determination by threats of how they will construe that determination.

The British have received invaluable military support from the heroic Greek army, and from the forces of all the governments in exile. Their strength is growing. It is the strength of men and woman who value their freedom more highly than they value their lives.

I believe that the Axis powers are not going to win this war. I base that belief on the latest and best information.

We have no excuse for defeatism. We have every good reason for hope—hope for peace, hope for the defense of our civilization and for the building of a better civilization in the future.

Radio address (Fireside Chat) on national security, Dec. 29, 1940

16 / Let us say to the democracies: "We Americans are vitally concerned in your defense of freedom. We are putting forth our energies, our resources and our organizing powers to give you the strength to regain and maintain a free world. We shall send you, in ever-increasing numbers, ships, planes, tanks, guns. This is our purpose and our pledge."

In fulfillment of this purpose we will not be intimidated by the threats of dictators that they will regard as a breach of international law or as an act of war our aid to the democracies which dare to resist their aggression. Such aid is not an act of war, even if a dictator should unilaterally proclaim it so to be.

When the dictators, if the dictators, are ready to make war upon us, they will not wait for an act of war on our part. They did not wait for Norway or Belgium or The Netherlands to commit an act of war. . . .

The happiness of future generations of Americans may well depend upon how effective and how immediate we can make our aid felt. No one can tell the exact character of the emergency situations that we may be called upon to meet. The nation's hands must not be tied when the nation's life is in danger. . . .

As men do not live by bread alone, they do not fight by armaments alone. Those who man our defenses, and those behind them who build our defenses, must have the stamina and the courage which come from unshakable belief in the manner of life which they are defending. The mighty action that we are calling for cannot be based on a disregard of all things worth fighting for.

State of the Union Message ("Four Freedoms" speech), Jan. 6, 1941

17 / In the assault on the democratic form of government which imperils world civilization today, our problem of national defense has become one of defending the entire Western Hemisphere—all three of the Americas— North, Central and South. We can no longer consider our own problem of defense as a separate interest. It involves the defense of all the democracies of all the Americas—and therefore, in fact, it involves the future of democracy wherever it is imperiled by force or terror.

Address at the annual Academy Awards dinner, Hollywood, Calif., Feb. 27, 1941

18 / It is the fate of this common life that weighs upon all our hearts . . . only a few hours ago the Senate passed, by a vote of about two to one, the Lend-Lease bill for aid to the democracies of the world that are trying to save their democracy. . . .

Democracy over large areas of the Old World is threatend with extinction. And no democratic farm program in the United States, nor the democratic way of life here, can hope to survive the death of democracy over the rest of the earth.

Radio address on the eighth anniversary of the administration's agricultural program, March 8, 1941

19 / The light of democracy must be kept burning. To the perpetuation of this light, each of us must do his own share. . . . It is not enough for us merely to trim the wick, or polish the glass. The time has come when we must provide the fuel in ever-increasing amounts to keep the flame alight.

There will be no divisions of party or section or race or nationality or religion. There is not one among us who does not have a stake in the outcome of the effort in which we are now engaged.

A few weeks ago I spoke of four freedoms—freedom of speech and expression, freedom of every person to worship God in his own way, freedom from want, freedom from fear. They are the ultimate stake. They may not be immediately attainable throughout the world but humanity does move toward those ideals through democratic processes. If we fail— if democracy is superseded by slavery—then those four freedoms, or even the mention of them, will become forbidden things. Centuries will pass before they can be revived.

By winning now, we strengthen their meaning, we increase the stature of mankind and the dignity of human life.

I have often thought that there is a vast difference between the word "loyalty" and the word "obedience." Obedience can be obtained and enforced in a dictatorship by the use of threat or extortion or blackmail or it can be obtained by a failure on the part of government to tell the truth to its citizens.

Loyalty is different. It springs from the mind that is given the facts, that retains ancient ideals and proceeds without coercion to give support to its own government. . . .

The essence of . . . morale is in the masses of plain people who are completely clear in their own minds about one essential fact—that they would rather die as free men than live as slaves. . . .

And so our country is going to be what our people have proclaimed it must be—the arsenal of democracy.

Our country is going to play its full part.

And when dictatorships disintegrate—and pray God that will be sooner than any of us now dares to hope—then our country must continue to play its great part in the period of world reconstruction. . . .

Never in all our history have Americans faced a job so well worth while. May it be said of us in the days to come that our children and our children's children rise up and call us blessed.

Address at the White House Correspondents' Association dinner, Washington, D.C., March 15, 1941

20 / We are engaged in an all-out effort to perpetuate democracy in the New World by aiding embattled democracy in the Old World.

Radio address on purchasing the first Savings Bond and Stamps, April 30, 1941

21 / When your enemy comes at you in a tank or a bombing plane, if you hold your fire until you see the whites of his eyes, you will never know what hit you. Our Bunker Hill of tomorrow may be several thousand miles from Boston. . . .

There are some timid ones among us who say that we must preserve peace at any price—lest we lose our liberties forever. To them I say this: never in the history of the world has a nation lost its democracy by a successful struggle to defend its democracy. . . .

We have pledged material support to the other democracies of the world—and we will fulfill that pledge.

We in the Americas will decide for ourselves whether, and when, and where, our American interests are attacked or our security threatened.

We are placing our armed forces in strategic military position.

We will not hesitate to use our armed forces to repel attack.

We reassert our abiding faith in the vitality of our constitutional republic as a perpetual home of freedom, of tolerance, and of devotion to the word of God.

Therefore, with profound consciousness of my responsibilities to my countrymen and to my country's cause, I have tonight issued a proclamation that an unlimited national emergency exists and requires the strengthening of our defense to the extreme limit of our national power and authority.

The nation will expect all individuals and all groups to play their full parts without stint, and without selfishness, and without doubt that our democracy will triumphantly survive.

I repeat the words of the signers of the Declaration of Independence —that little band of patriots, fighting long ago against overwhelming odds, but certain, as are we, of ultimate victory: "With a firm reliance on the protection of Divine Providence, we mutually pledge to each other our lives, our fortunes, and our sacred honor."

Radio address announcing an unlimited national emergency, White House, May 27, 1941

22 / We, too, born to freedom, and believing in freedom, are willing to fight to maintain freedom.

We, and all others who believe as deeply as we do, would rather die on our feet than live on our knees.

Message to the Special Convocation of Oxford University, held at Harvard University, on the awarding of the degree of Doctor of Civil Law, Cambridge, Mass., June 19, 1941

23 / Against naked force the only possible defense is naked force. The aggressor makes the rules for such a war; the defenders have no alternative but matching destruction with more destruction, slaughter with greater slaughter.

Message to the National Convention of Young Democrats, Louisville, Ky., Aug. 21, 1941

24 / It is clear to all Americans that the time has come when the Americas themselves must now be defended. A continuation of attacks in our own waters, or in waters which could be used for further and greater attacks on us, will inevitably weaken American ability to repel Hitlerism.

Do not let us be hair-splitters. Let us not ask ourselves whether the Americas should begin to defend themselves after the fifth attack, or the tenth attack, or the twentieth attack.

The time for active defense is now.

Do not let us split hairs. Let us not say: "We will only defend ourselves if the torpedo succeeds in getting home, or if the crew and the passengers are drowned."

This is the time for prevention of attack. . . .

It is no act of war on our part when we decide to protect the seas which are vital to American defense. The aggression is not ours. Ours is solely defense.

But let this warning be clear. From now on, if German or Italian vessels of war enter the waters, the protection of which is necessary for American defense, they do so at their own peril.

The orders which I have given as Commander-in-Chief to the United States Army and Navy are to carry out that policy—at once.

The sole responsibility rests upon Germany. There will be no shooting unless Germany continues to seek it.

That is my obvious duty in this crisis. That is the clear right of this sovereign nation. That is the only step possible, if we would keep tight the wall of defense which we are pledged to maintain around this Western Hemisphere.

I have no illusions about the gravity of this step. I have not taken it hurriedly or lightly. It is the result of months and months of constant thought and anxiety and prayer. In the protection of your nation and mine it cannot be avoided. . . .

And with that inner strength that comes to a free people conscious of their duty and of the righteousness of what they do, they will—with Divine help and guidance—stand their ground against this latest assault upon their democracy, their sovereignty, and their freedom.

Radio address (Fireside Chat) on the sinking of the *U.S.S. Greer* by the Germans, Sept. 11, 1941

25 / And it is the nation's will that these vital arms and supplies of all kinds shall neither be locked up in American harbors nor sent to the bottom of the sea. It is the nation's will that America shall deliver the goods. In open defiance of that will, our ships have been sunk and our sailors have been killed.

I say that we do not propose to take this lying down.

Our determination not to take it lying down has been expressed in the orders to the American Navy to shoot on sight. Those orders stand.

Furthermore, the House of Representatives has already voted to amend part of the Neutrality Act of 1937, today outmoded by force of violent circumstances. The Senate Committee on Foreign Relations has also recommended elimination of other hamstringing provisions in that act. That is the course of honesty and of realism.

Our American merchant ships must be armed to defend themselves against the rattlesnakes of the sea.

Our American merchant ships must be free to carry our American goods into the harbors of our friends.

Our American merchant ships must be protected by our American Navy. . . .

It can never be doubted that the goods will be delivered by this nation, whose Navy believes in the tradition of "Damn the torpedoes; full speed ahead!"

Our nation will and must speak from every assembly line, from every coal mine—the all-inclusive whole of our vast industrial machine. Our factories and our shipyards are constantly expanding. Our output must be multiplied. . . .

The lines of our essential defense now cover all the seas; and to meet the extraordinary demands of today and tomorrow our Navy grows to unprecedented size. Our Navy is ready for action. Indeed, units of it in the Atlantic patrol are in action. Its officers and men need no praise from me.

Our new Army is steadily developing the strength needed to withstand the aggressors. Our soldiers of today are worthy of the proudest traditions of the United States Army. But traditions cannot shoot down dive bombers or destroy tanks. That is why we must and shall provide, for every one of our soldiers, equipment and weapons—not merely as good but better than that of any other army on earth. And we are doing that right now.

For this—and all of this—is what we mean by total national defense. . . .

Today in the face of this newest and greatest challenge of them all we Americans have cleared our decks and taken our battle stations. We stand ready in the defense of our nation and the faith of our fathers to do what God has given us the power to see as our full duty.

Address on Navy Day concerning the German attack on the *U.S.S. Kearny*, Oct. 27, 1941

26 / We will not, under any threat, or in the face of any danger, surrender the guarantees of liberty our forefathers framed for us in our Bill of Rights.

We hold with all the passion of our hearts and minds to those commitments of the human spirit.

We are solemnly determined that no power or combination of powers of this earth shall shake our hold upon them.

We covenant with each other before all the world that, having taken up arms in the defense of liberty, we will not lay them down before liberty is once again secure in the world we live in. For that security we pray; for that security we act—now and evermore.

Radio address on the 150th anniversary of the adoption of the American Bill of Rights, Dec. 15, 1941

27 / For the first time since the Japanese and the Fascists and the Nazis started along their blood-stained course of conquest they now face the fact that superior forces are assembling against them. Gone forever are the days when the aggressors could attack and destroy their victims one by one without unity of resistance. We of the United Nations will so dispose our forces that we can strike at the common enemy wherever the greatest damage can be done him.

The militarists in Berlin and Tokyo started this war. But the massed, angered forces of common humanity will finish it. . . .

Our own objectives are clear; the objective of smashing the militarism imposed by war lords upon their enslaved peoples—the objective of liberating the subjugated nations—the objective of establishing and securing freedom of speech, freedom of religion, freedom from want and freedom from fear everywhere in the world.

We shall not stop short of these objectives—nor shall we be satisfied merely to gain them and then call it a day. I know that I speak for the American people—and I have good reason to believe I speak also for all the other peoples who fight with us—when I say that this time we are determined not only to win the war, but also to maintain the security of the peace which will follow. . . .

We cannot wage this war in a defensive spirit. As our power and our resources are fully mobilized, we shall carry the attack against the enemy—we shall hit him and hit him again wherever and whenever we can reach him.

We must keep him far from our shores, for we intend to bring this battle to him on his own home grounds. . . .

Many people ask, "When will this war end?" There is only one answer to that. It will end just as soon as we make it end, by our combined efforts, our combined strength, our combined determination to fight through and work through until the end—the end of militarism in Germany and Italy and Japan. Most certainly we shall not settle for less. . . .

But we of the United Nations are not making all this sacrifice of human effort and human lives to return to the kind of world we had after the last world war.

We are fighting today for security, for progress, and for peace, not only for ourselves but for all men, not only for one generation but for all generations. We are fighting to cleanse the world of ancient evils, ancient ills. . . .

We are inspired by a faith which goes back through all the years to the first chapter of the Book of Genesis: "God created man in His own image."

We . . . are striving to be true to that divine heritage. We are fighting, as our fathers have fought, to uphold the doctrine that all men are equal in the sight of God. . . .

That is the conflict that day and night now pervades our lives. No compromise can end that conflict. There never has been—there never can be—successful compromise between good and evil. Only total victory can reward the champions of tolerance, and decency, and freedom, and faith.

   State of the Union Message, Jan. 6, 1942

28 / Those Americans who believed that we could live under the illusion of isolationism wanted the American eagle to imitate the tactics of the ostrich. Now, many of those same people, afraid that we may be sticking our necks out, want our national bird to be turned into a turtle. But we prefer to retain the eagle as it is—flying high and striking hard. . . .

The task that we Americans now face will test us to the uttermost.

Never before have we been called upon for such a prodigious effort. Never before have we had so little time in which to do so much.

"These are the times that try men's souls."

   Radio address (Fireside Chat) on the progress of the war, Feb. 23, 1942

29 / So I am looking for a word . . . I want a name for the war. I haven't had any very good suggestions. Most of them are too long. My own thought is that perhaps there is one word that we could use for this war, the word "survival." The Survival War. That is what it comes pretty close to being —the survival of our civilization, the survival of democracy, the survival of a hemisphere—the newest hemisphere of all of them—which has developed in its own ways.

   Pan American Day address before the Governing Board of the Pan American
   Union, Washington, D.C., April 14, 1942

30 / Thomas Jefferson believed, as we believe, in Man. He believed, as we believe, that men are capable of their own government, and that no king,

no tyrant, no dictator can govern for them as wisely as they can govern for themselves.

He believed, as we believe, in certain inalienable rights. He, as we, saw those principles and freedoms challenged. He fought for them, as we fight for them.

He proved that the seeming eclipse of liberty can well become the dawn of more liberty. Those who fight the tyranny of our own time will come to learn that old lesson. Among all the peoples of the earth, the cruelties and oppressions of its would-be masters have taught this generation what its liberties can mean. This lesson, so bitterly learned, will never be forgotten while this generation lives.

Address on the dedication of the Thomas Jefferson Memorial, Washington, D.C., April 13, 1943

31 / May this country never forget that its power in this war has come from the efforts of its citizens, living in freedom and equality.

May this country hold in piety and steadfast faith those who have battled and died to give it new opportunities for service and growth.

May it reserve its contempt for those who see in it only an instrument for their own selfish interests.

May it marshal its righteous wrath against those who would divide it by racial struggles.

May it lavish its scorn upon the faint-hearted.

And may this country always give its support to those who have engaged with us in the war against oppression and who will continue with us in the struggle for a vital, creative peace.

God bless the United States of America.

Campaign address, Philadelphia, Pa., Oct. 27, 1944

24

Victory—Punishment of War Criminals

1 / The Nazis might have learned from the last war the impossibility of breaking men's spirit by terrorism. Instead they develop their "*lebensraum*" and "new order" by depths of frightfulness which even they have never approached before. These are the acts of desperate men who know in their hearts that they cannot win.

Statement denouncing German practice of killing hostages, Oct. 25, 1941

2 / The United States can accept no result save victory, final and complete. Not only must the shame of Japanese treachery be wiped out, but the sources of international brutality, wherever they exist, must be absolutely and finally broken. . . .

We will make very certain that this form of treachery shall never endanger us again. In order to achieve that certainty, we must begin the great task that is before us by abandoning once and for all the illusion that we can ever again isolate ourselves from the rest of humanity. . . .

We may acknowledge that our enemies have performed a brilliant feat of deception, perfectly timed and executed with great skill. It was a thoroughly dishonorable deed, but we must face the fact that modern warfare as conducted in the Nazi manner is a dirty business. We don't like it —we didn't want to get in it—but we are in it and we're going to fight it with everything we've got.

I do not think any American has any doubt of our ability to administer proper punishment to the perpetrators of these crimes.

Radio address (Fireside Chat) on the American will to win the war and the peace, Dec. 9, 1941

3 / Looking into the days to come, I have set aside a Day of Prayer, and in that Proclamation I have said:

"The year 1941 has brought upon our nation a war of aggression by powers dominated by arrogant rulers whose selfish purpose is to destroy free institutions. They would thereby take from the freedom-loving peoples of the earth the hard-won liberties gained over many centuries.

"The new year of 1942 calls for the courage and the resolution of old and young to help to win a world struggle in order that we may preserve all we hold dear.

"We are confident in our devotion to country, in our love of freedom, in our inheritance of courage. But our strength, as the strength of all men everywhere, is of greater avail as God upholds us.

"Therefore, I . . . do hereby appoint the first day of the year 1942 as a day of prayer, of asking forgiveness for our shortcomings of the past, of consecration to the tasks of the present, of asking God's help in days to come.

"We need His guidance that this people may be humble in spirit but strong in conviction of the right; steadfast to endure sacrifice, and brave to achieve a victory of liberty and peace."

Radio address on Christmas Eve, Dec. 24, 1941

4 / Our soldiers and sailors are members of well-disciplined units. But they are still and forever individuals, free individuals. They are farmers, workers, businessmen, professional men, artists, clerks.

They are the United States of America.

That is why they fight.

We, too, are the United States of America.

This is why we must work and sacrifice.

It is for them. It is for us. It is for victory.

Radio address (Fireside Chat) on cooperation and sacrifice for victory, April 28, 1942

5 / Citizens, regardless of religious allegiance, will share in the sorrow of our Jewish fellow citizens over the savagery of the Nazis against their helpless victims. The Nazis will not succeed in exterminating their victims any more than they will succeed in enslaving mankind. The American people not only sympathize with all victims of Nazi crimes but will hold the perpetrators of these crimes to strict accountability in a day of reckoning which will surely come.

Letter to Dr. Stephen S. Wise, Rabbi of Free Synagogue, New York City, July 17, 1942

6 / The United Nations are going to win this war. When victory has been achieved, it is the purpose of the government of the United States, as I know it is the purpose of each of the United Nations, to make appropriate use of the information and evidence in respect to these barbaric crimes of the invaders, in Europe and in Asia. It seems only fair that they should have this warning that the time will come when they shall have to stand in courts of law in the very countries which they are now oppressing and answer for their acts.

Statement warning the Axis Powers against their crimes in occupied countries, Aug. 21, 1942

7 / The number of persons eventually found guilty will undoubtedly be extremely small compared to the total enemy populations. It is not the intention of this government or of the governments associated with us to resort to mass reprisals. It is our intention that just and sure punishment shall be meted out to the ringleaders responsible for the organized murder of thousands of innocent persons and the commission of atrocities which have violated every tenet of the Christian faith.

Statement on punishment of war criminals, Oct. 7, 1942

8 / The United Nations have decided to establish the identity of those Nazi leaders who are responsible for the innumerable acts of savagery. As each of these criminal deeds is committed, it is being carefully investigated; and the evidence is being relentlessly piled up for the future purposes of justice.

We have made it entirely clear that the United Nations seek no mass reprisals against the populations of Germany or Italy or Japan. But the ringleaders and their brutal henchmen must be named, and apprehended and tried in accordance with the judicial processes of criminal law.

Radio address (Fireside Chat) on progress of the war, Oct. 12, 1942

9 / Americans, with the assistance of the United Nations, are striving for their own safe future as well as the restoration of the ideals, the liberties, and the democracy of all those who have lived under the tricolor.

We come among you [the French people] to repulse the cruel invaders who would remove forever your rights of self-government, your rights to religious freedom, and your rights to live your own lives in peace and security.

We come among you solely to defeat and rout your enemies. Have faith in our words. We do not want to cause you any harm.

We assure you that once the menace of Germany and Italy is removed from you, we shall quit your territory at once.

Message to the French people on the Allied invasion of North Africa, Nov. 7, 1942

10 / The people have now gathered their strength. They are moving forward in their might and power—and no force, no combination of forces, no trickery, deceit or violence, can stop them now. They see before them the hope of the world—a decent, secure, peaceful life for all men everywhere. . . .

But, as we face that continuing task, we may know that the state of this nation is good—the heart of this nation is sound—the spirit of this nation is strong—the faith of this nation is eternal.

State of the Union Message, Jan. 7, 1943

11 / [President Roosevelt stated]: The elimination of German, Japanese, and Italian war power means the unconditional surrender of Germany, Italy, and Japan. That means a reasonable assurance of future world peace. It does not mean the destruction of the population . . . , but it does mean the destruction of the philosophies of these countries. . . .

Joint Roosevelt-Churchill press conference, Casablanca, Morocco, Jan. 24, 1943

12 / President Lincoln said in 1862, "Fellow citizens, we cannot escape history. We of this Congress and this administration will be remembered in spite of ourselves. No personal significance or insignificance can spare one or another of us. The fiery trial through which we pass will light us . . . in honor or dishonor, to the latest generation."

Today, eighty years after Lincoln delivered that message, the fires of war are blazing across the whole horizon of mankind—from Kharkov to Kunming—from the Mediterranean to the Coral Sea—from Berlin to Tokyo.

Again—we cannot escape history. We have supreme confidence that with the help of God honor will prevail. We have faith that future generations will know that here, in the middle of the twentieth century, there came the time when men of good-will found a way to unite and produce and fight to destroy the forces of ignorance, intolerance, slavery, and war.

Address at the White House Correspondents' Association dinner, Washington, D.C., Feb. 12, 1943

13 / To these panicky attempts to escape the consequences of their crimes we say—all the United Nations say—that the only terms on which we shall

deal with any Axis government or any Axis factions are the terms proclaimed at Casablanca: "unconditional surrender." . . . in our uncompromising policy we mean no harm to the common people of the Axis nations. But we do mean to impose punishment and retribution in full upon their guilty, barbaric leaders. . . . Our policy toward our Japanese enemies is precisely the same as our policy toward our Nazi enemies: it is a policy of fighting hard on all fronts, and ending the war as quickly as we can on the uncompromising terms of unconditional surrender.

Ibid.

14 / As we strike again and again, lend-lease and reciprocal aid will contribute increasingly to the inevitable defeat of the Axis.

And this mutual aid has become more than a joint weapon of war. In the smoke of battle, lend-lease is helping to forge the unity that will be required to make a just and lasting peace.

Statement on the second anniversary of the Lend-Lease Act, March 11, 1943

15 / I can only say that the government of the United States would regard the action by a neutral government in affording asylum to Axis leaders or their tools as inconsistent with the principles for which the United Nations are fighting and that the United States government hopes that no neutral government will permit its territory to be used as a place of refuge or otherwise assist such persons in any effort to escape their just deserts.

Statement warning neutral nations against giving refuge to war criminals, July 30, 1943

16 / The United Nations are growing stronger because each of them is contributing to the common struggle in full measure—whether in men, in weapons, or in materials. Each is contributing in accordance with its ability and its resources. Everything that all of us have is dedicated to victory over the Axis powers. . . .

The power of the United Nations is great. The will of the United Nations is fixed. In this common war we fight as one man, for one victory—and we shall have it.

Report to Congress on Lend-Lease, Aug. 25, 1943

17 / Except for the responsible fascist leaders, the people of the Axis need not fear unconditional surrender to the United Nations. . . . The people of Axis-controlled areas may be assured that when they agree to uncondi-

tional surrender they will not be trading Axis despotism for ruin under the United Nations. The goal of the United Nations is to permit liberated peoples to create a free political life of their own choosing and to attain economic security. These are two of the great objectives of the Atlantic Charter.

Ibid.

18 / The American people will never stop to reckon the cost of redeeming civilization. They know there can never be any economic justification for failing to save freedom.

Radio address (Fireside Chat) on War Loan Drive, Sept. 8, 1943

19 / In the genius of the American people—for freedom, and decency, and friendliness among neighbors—lies one of our best weapons for . . . victory, and certainly our greatest insurance for a peace that will be just and lasting.

Radio address on the National War Fund Drive, Oct. 5, 1943

20 / The three great Allies are fighting this war to restrain and punish the aggression of Japan. They covet no gain for themselves and have no thought of territorial expansion. It is their purpose that Japan shall be stripped of all the islands in the Pacific which she has seized or occupied since the beginning of the first World War in 1914, and that all the territories Japan has stolen from the Chinese, such as Manchuria, Formosa, and the Pescadores, shall be restored to the Republic of China. Japan will also be expelled from all other territories which she has taken by violence and greed. The aforesaid three great powers, mindful of the enslavement of the people of Korea, are determined that in due course Korea shall become free and independent.

With these objects in view the three Allies, in harmony with those of the United Nations at war with Japan, will continue to persevere in the serious and prolonged operations necessary to procure the unconditional surrender of Japan.

Roosevelt–Churchill–Chiang Kai-shek statement on cooperative prosecution of the war in the Pacific until the "unconditional surrender of Japan," Cairo, Egypt, Dec. 1, 1943

21 / No power on earth can prevent our destroying the German armies by land, their U-boats by sea, and their war plants from the air.

Our attack will be relentless and increasing.

Emerging from these cordial conferences [Cairo and Teheran] we look with confidence to the day when all peoples of the world may live free lives, untouched by tyranny, and according to their varying desires and their own consciences.

We came here with hope and determination. We leave here, friends in fact, in spirit and in purpose.

> Roosevelt–Churchill–Stalin declaration on cooperation to win the war and the peace, Teheran, Iran, Dec. 1, 1943

22 / It is . . . fitting that we should again proclaim our determination that none who participate in these acts of savagery shall go unpunished. The United Nations have made it clear that they will pursue the guilty and deliver them up in order that justice be done. That warning applies not only to the leaders but also to their functionaries and subordinates in Germany and in the satellite countries. All who knowingly take part in the deportation of Jews to their death in Poland or Norwegians and French to their death in Germany are equally guilty with the executioner. All who share the guilt shall share the punishment.

> Statement on punishment of war criminals, March 24, 1944

23 / Yesterday, June 4, 1944, Rome fell to American and Allied troops. The first of the Axis capitals is now in our hands. One up and two to go.

> Radio address (Fireside Chat) on the fall of Rome to the Allies, June 5, 1944

24 / Last night, when I spoke with you about the fall of Rome, I knew at that moment that troops of the United States and our Allies were crossing the Channel in another and greater operation. It has come to pass with success thus far.

And so, in this poignant hour, I ask you to join me in prayer:

ALMIGHTY GOD: Our sons, pride of our nation, this day have set upon a mighty endeavor, a struggle to preserve our republic, our religion, and our civilization, and to set free a suffering humanity.

Lead them straight and true; give strength to their arms, stoutness to their hearts, steadfastness to their faith.

They will need Thy blessings. Their road will be long and hard. For the enemy is strong. He may hurl back our forces. Success may not come with rushing speed, but we shall return again and again; and we know that by Thy grace, and by the righteousness of our cause, our sons will triumph.

They will be sore tried, by night and by day, without rest—till the victory is won. The darkness will be rent by noise and flame. Men's souls will be shaken with the violences of war.

For these are men lately drawn from the ways of peace. They fight not for the lust of conquest. They fight to end conquest. They fight to liberate. They fight to let justice arise, and tolerance and goodwill among all Thy people. They yearn but for the end of battle, for their return to the haven of home.

Some will never return. Embrace these, Father, and receive them, Thy heroic servants, into Thy kingdom.

And for us at home—fathers, mothers, children, wives, sisters, and brothers of brave men overseas—whose thoughts and prayers are ever with them—help us, Almighty God, to rededicate ourselves in renewed faith in Thee in this hour of great sacrifice.

Many people have urged that I call the nation into a single day of special prayer. But because the road is long and the desire is great, I ask that our people devote themselves in continuance of prayer. As we rise to each new day, and again when each day is spent, let words of prayer be on our lips, invoking Thy help to our efforts.

Give us strength, too—strength in our daily tasks, to redouble the contributions we make in the physical and material support of our armed forces.

And let our hearts be stout, to wait out the long travail, to bear sorrows that may come, to impart our courage unto our sons wheresoever they may be.

And, O Lord, give us Faith. Give us Faith in Thee; Faith in our sons; Faith in each other; Faith in our united crusade. Let not the keenness of our spirit ever be dulled. Let not the impacts of temporary events, of temporal matters of but fleeting moment—let not these deter us in our unconquerable purpose.

With Thy blessing, we shall prevail over the unholy forces of our enemy. Help us to conquer the apostles of greed and racial arrogancies. Lead us to the saving of our country, and with our sister nations into a world unity that will spell a sure peace—a peace invulnerable to the schemings of unworthy men. And a peace that will let all men live in freedom, reaping the just rewards of their honest toil.

Thy will be done, Almighty God. AMEN.

Prayer on the occasion of the Allied invasion of Europe (Normandy), June 6, 1944

25 / To the Hitlerites, their subordinates and functionaries and satellites, to the German people and to all other peoples under the Nazi yoke, we have

made clear our determination to punish all participants in these acts of savagery.

Message to Congress on refugee policy, June 12, 1944

26 / The joy that entered the hearts of all civilized men and women at the news of the liberation of Paris can only be measured by the gloom which settled there one June day four years ago when German troops occupied the French capital. Through the rising tide of Allied successes that patch of gloom remained and has only today been dispelled. For Paris is a precious symbol of that civilization which it was the aim of Hitler and his armed hordes to destroy. We rejoice with the gallant French people at the liberation of their capital and join in the chorus of congratulation to the commanders and fighting men, French and Allied, who have made possible this brilliant presage of total victory.

Statement on the liberation of Paris, Aug. 24, 1944

27 / Brussels, the capital of another freedom-loving people, has been delivered from four terrible years of tyranny—the second such period in a generation. The American people are filled with admiration for the imperturbable conduct of the Belgian people toward the hated invaders and their unswerving devotion to the ideals which they share with the people of the United States and the other United Nations.

Statement on the liberation of Brussels, Sept. 4, 1944

28 / To no people who have borne the Nazi yoke can liberation mean more than to those of the Grand Duchy of Luxembourg. Ruthlessly attacked and occupied by the German military in May, 1940, their country was not only incorporated into the Third Reich and German citizenship thrust upon them, but their sons were forced to serve in the ranks and wear the hated uniform of their oppressors. With unparalleled sacrifice and fortitude the heroic Luxembourgers have resisted every Nazi effort to break their spirit. On the occasion of their release from tyranny and their return to the free institutions which they hold so dear, the American people salute the brave people of Luxembourg.

Statement on the liberation of Luxembourg, Sept. 11, 1944

29 / For four long years The Netherlands has suffered under the heel of German oppression. For four long years its liberties have been crushed, its homes destroyed, its people enslaved. But the spark of freedom could never

be extinguished. It has always glowed in the hearts of the Netherlands people. It now emerges as an avenging flame.

The armies of liberation are flowing across the borders of Holland. A gallant Queen is returning to her gallant people. The Netherlands again stands on the threshold of her ancient liberties.

But the fight will not end with the restoration of freedom to Holland. It will not end with the inevitable defeat of Germany. The people of The Netherlands know as the people of the United States know that final victory cannot be achieved until Japan has likewise been vanquished.

Only then can peace and freedom return to the world.

Statement on the liberation of The Netherlands, Sept. 18, 1944

30 / I am deeply moved at the news that the liberation of Greece has begun. In a truer sense, its enslavement has never been a fact. For nearly four years an indomitable Greek nation has suffered the terrifying effects of aggression on an unprecedented scale. When many men—even stout-hearted men of good-will—had almost lost hope, the Greek people challenged the invincibility of the mechanized Nazi monster, pitting against inhuman engines of war and cold-blooded calculating strategy little more than the fierce spirit of freedom.

Four years is a long time to starve and die, to see children massacred, to watch villages burn to rubble and ashes. But it is not a long enough time to extinguish the clear flame of the Hellenic heritage which throughout centuries has taught the dignity of man. It is more than fitting, it is inevitable, that as hopeless darkness is engulfing the ideals of Nazi barbarism the clear Greek air will once more be breathed by free men without fear of oppression, and that the Acropolis, for twenty-five centuries a symbol of man's accomplishment in an environment of human liberty, will again be a beacon of faith for the future.

Statement on the liberation of Greece, Oct. 6, 1944

31 / This anniversary of the independence of Czechoslovakia is of especial significance.

The people and armed forces inside Czechoslovakia have joined actively and gloriously with their countrymen abroad in the ranks of the nations united against tyranny, and can look forward confidently to the celebration of future anniversaries in the full enjoyment of unsuppressed freedom.

We Americans salute our Czechoslovak comrades-in-arms who are today so bravely contributing to the liberation of their homeland and the rest of Europe.

The close ties and deep sympathy between the democratic peoples of Czechoslovakia and the United States have never ceased to find concrete expression since the days of President Masaryk and President Wilson.

I look forward to the day when, victorious after a second great war for freedom, they can continue to work in harmony for their mutual security and welfare in a peaceful world.

Message to Dr. Eduard Beneš, President of Czechoslovakia, Oct. 28, 1944

32 / There is going to be stern punishment for all those in Germany directly responsible for this agony of mankind.

The German people are not going to be enslaved—because the United Nations do not traffic in human slavery. But it will be necessary for them to earn their way back into the fellowship of peace-loving and law-abiding nations. And, in their climb up that steep road, we shall certainly see to it that they are not encumbered by having to carry guns. They will be relieved of that burden—we hope, forever.

Address before the Foreign Policy Association, New York City, Oct. 21, 1944

33 / The victory of the American people and their Allies in this war will be far more than a victory against fascism and reaction and the dead hand of despotism and of the past. The victory of the American people and their Allies in this war will be a victory for democracy. It will constitute such an affirmation of the strength and power and vitality of government by the people as history has never before witnessed.

With that affirmation of the vitality of democratic government behind us, that demonstration of its resilience and its capacity for decision and for action—with that knowledge of our own strength and power—we move forward with God's help to the greatest epoch of free achievement by free men the world has ever known or imagined possible.

Address before the International Brotherhood of Teamsters, Washington, D.C., Sept. 23, 1944

34 / This war must be waged—it is being waged—with the greatest and most persistent intensity. . . . Everything we are and have will be given. American men, fighting far from home, have already won victories which the world will never forget.

We have no question of the ultimate victory. We have no question of the cost. Our losses will be heavy.

We and our Allies will go on fighting together to ultimate total victory.

State of the Union Message, Jan. 6, 1945

35 / The American people rejoice with me in the liberation of your capital [Manila].

After long years of planning, our hearts have quickened at the magnificent strides toward freedom that have been made in the last months—at Leyte, Mindoro, Lingayen Gulf, and now Manila.

We are proud of the mighty blows struck by General MacArthur, our sailors, soldiers, and airmen; and in their comradeship-in-arms with your loyal and valiant people who in the darkest days have not ceased to fight for their independence. You may be sure that this pride will strengthen our determination to drive the Jap invader from your islands.

We will join you in that effort—with our armed forces, as rapidly and fully as our efforts against our enemies and our responsibilities to other liberated peoples permit. With God's help we will complete the fulfillment of the pledge we renewed when our men returned to Leyte.

Let the Japanese and other enemies of peaceful nations take warning from these great events in your country; their world of treachery, aggression, and enslavement cannot survive in the struggle against our world of freedom and peace.

Message to the Philippine President on the liberation of Manila, Feb. 4, 1945

36 / It is our inflexible purpose to destroy German militarism and Nazism and to ensure that Germany will never again be able to disturb the peace of the world. We are determined to disarm and disband all German armed forces; break up for all time the German General Staff that has repeatedly contrived the resurgence of German militarism; remove or destroy all German military equipment; eliminate or control all German industry that could be used for military production; bring all war criminals to just and swift punishment and exact reparation in kind for the destruction wrought by the Germans; wipe out the Nazi party, Nazi laws, organizations and institutions, remove all Nazi and militarist influences from public office and from the cultural and economic life of the German people; and take in harmony such other measures in Germany as may be necessary to the future peace and safety of the world. It is not our purpose to destroy the people of Germany, but only when Nazism and militarism have been extirpated will there be hope for a decent life for Germans, and a place for them in the comity of nations.

Roosevelt–Churchill–Stalin statement on "The Occupation and Control of Germany," Yalta (Crimea) Conference, Feb. 11, 1945

37 / Unconditional surrender does not mean the destruction or enslavement of the German people. . . .

It means the temporary control of Germany by Great Britain, Russia, France, and the United States. Each of these nations will occupy and control a separate zone of Germany—and the administration of the four zones will be coordinated in Berlin by a Control Council composed of representatives of the four nations.

Unconditional surrender means something else. It means the end of Nazism. It means the end of the Nazi party—and all of its barbaric laws and institutions.

It means the termination of all militaristic influence in the public, private, and cultural life of Germany. It means for the Nazi war criminals a punishment that is speedy and just—and severe.

It means the complete disarmament of Germany. . . .

It means that Germany will have to make reparations in kind for the damage which it has done to the innocent victims of its aggression.

Report to Congress on the Yalta (Crimea) Conference, March 1, 1945

25

Design for Peace

1 / I am not afraid of the League of Nations. I believe it is the old guard reactionary . . . leaders who are trying to befuddle this issue. It is natural for them as reactionaries in home affairs to be reactionary also in international affairs. In the same way, progressives, whether they are Republicans or Democrats, will, if truly progressive, wish to see international affairs continue to reach higher levels instead of going back to the method of old fashioned diplomacy. . . .

The League of Nations is but an expression of the new law of nations. . . .

There can be no neutrality as between right and wrong. We in the United States honestly tried to walk the path of neutrality because it was then the law of nations, but finally and at an enormous cost the whole American nation joined in condemning that law.

Shall we then not learn by experience? Must we continue a policy which men and women of courage and sanity have rejected, regardless of party?

The old policy has broken down. The world is crying for an extension of the law of the individual and of the state to the law of international relations.

Vice-presidential campaign address, Milwaukee, Wisc., Aug. 12, 1920

2 / I am not wholly convinced that the country is quite ready for a definite stand on our part in favor of immediate entry into the League of Nations. That will come in time, but I am convinced that we should stand firmly against the isolation policy of Harding's administration.

Letter to James M. Cox [Democratic nominee for the Presidency in 1920, with F.D.R. as his running mate], Dec. 8, 1922

3 / We believe that the participation of the United States with other nations in a serious and continuing effort to eliminate the causes of war, is not only justified but is called for by the record of our history, by our own best interests, and chiefly by our high purpose to help mankind to better things.

Foreword to "A Plan to Preserve World Peace," prepared for presentation for the American Peace Award established by Edward W. Bok, 1923

4 / The League of Nations today is not the League conceived by Woodrow Wilson. It might have been had the United States joined. Too often, through these years, its major function has been not the broad overwhelming purpose of world peace, but rather a mere meeting place for the political discussion of strictly European political national difficulties. In these the United States should have no part.

Address before the N.Y. State Grange, Albany, Feb. 2, 1932

5 / We are not members [League of Nations] and we do not contemplate membership. We are giving cooperation to the League in every matter which is not primarily political and in every matter which obviously represents the views and the good of the peoples of the world as distinguished from the views and the good of political leaders, of privileged classes or of imperialistic aims.

Address before the Woodrow Wilson Foundation, New York City, Dec. 28, 1933

6 / I hope that at an early date the Senate will advise and consent to the adherence by the United States to the Protocol of Signature of the Statute of the Permanent Court of International Justice. . . .

The sovereignty of the United States will be in no way diminished or jeopardized by such action. At this period in international relationships, when every act is of moment to the future of world peace, the United States has an opportunity once more to throw its weight into the scale in favor of peace.

Message to Senate recommending adherence to the Statute of the World Court, Jan. 16, 1935

7 / We shun political commitments which might entangle us in foreign wars; we avoid political connection with the political activities of the League of Nations; but I am glad to say that we have cooperated wholeheartedly in the social and humanitarian work of Geneva.

Address on the international situation, Chautauqua, N.Y., Aug. 14, 1936

8 / The development of civilization and of human welfare is based on the acceptance by individuals of certain fundamental decencies in their relations with each other. The development of peace in the world is dependent similarly on the acceptance by nations of certain fundamental decencies in their relations with each other.

Ultimately I hope *each* nation will accept the fact that violations of these rules of conduct are an injury to the well-being of *all* nations.

Radio address (Fireside Chat) announcing a call for a special session of Congress, Oct. 12, 1937

9 / Today we seek a moral basis for peace. It cannot be a real peace if it fails to recognize brotherhood. It cannot be a lasting peace if the fruit of it is oppression, or starvation, or cruelty, or human life dominated by armed camps. It cannot be a sound peace if small nations must live in fear of powerful neighbors. It cannot be a moral peace if freedom from invasion is sold for tribute. It cannot be an intelligent peace if it denies free passage to that knowledge of those ideals which permit men to find common ground. It cannot be a righteous peace if worship of God is denied.

Radio address to the Christian Foreign Service Convocation, New York City, March 16, 1940

10 / If the human race as a whole is to survive, the world must find the way by which men and nations can live together in peace. We cannot accept the doctrine that war must be forever a part of man's destiny.

Campaign address, Cleveland, Ohio, Nov. 2, 1940

11 / We cannot escape our collective responsibility for the kind of life that is going to emerge from the ordeal through which the world is passing today. We cannot be an island. We may discharge that responsibility unwisely, but we cannot escape the consequences of our choice. We would have it a world in which we may live in peace, freedom and security—that kind of world our farmer forefathers dreamed of and worked for as they settled the Atlantic seaboard and pushed their way to the West.

Radio address on the eighth anniversary of the administration's agricultural program, March 8, 1941

12 / Of Woodrow Wilson this can be said, that in a time when world councils were dominated by material considerations of greed and gain and revenge he beheld the vision splendid. That selfish men could not share his

vision of a world emancipated from the shackles of force and the arbitrament of the sword in no wise detracts from its splendor. Rather does the indifference of hostile contemporaries enhance the beauty of the vision which he saw and enlarge the glory of the world he sought to rebuild.

He will be held in everlasting remembrance as a statesman who, when other men sought revenge and material gain, strove to bring nearer the day which should see the emancipation of conscience from power and the substitution of freedom for force in the government of the world.

Address at the dedication of Woodrow Wilson's birthplace, Staunton, Va., May 4, 1941

The Atlantic Charter

13 / The President of the United States of America and the Prime Minister, Mr. Churchill, representing His Majesty's Government in the United Kingdom, being met together, deem it right to make known certain common principles in the national policies of their respective countries on which they base their hopes for a better future for the world.

First, their countries seek no aggrandizement, territorial or other;

Second, they desire to see no territorial changes that do not accord with the freely expressed wishes of the peoples concerned;

Third, they respect the right of all peoples to choose the form of government under which they will live; and they wish to see sovereign rights and self-government restored to those who have been forcibly deprived of them;

Fourth, they will endeavor, with due respect for their existing obligations, to further the enjoyment by all states, great or small, victor or vanquished, of access, on equal terms, to the trade and to the raw materials of the world which are needed for their economic prosperity;

Fifth, they desire to bring about the fullest collaboration between all nations in the economic field with the object of securing, for all, improved labor standards, economic advancement, and social security;

Sixth, after the final destruction of the Nazi tyranny, they hope to see established a peace which will afford to all nations the means of dwelling in safety within their own boundaries, and which will afford assurance that all the men in all the lands may live out their lives in freedom from fear and want;

Seventh, such a peace should enable all men to traverse the high seas and oceans without hindrance;

Eighth, they believe that all of the nations of the world, for realistic as well as spiritual reasons, must come to the abandonment of the use of force. Since no future peace can be maintained if land, sea, or air armaments continue to be employed by nations which threaten, or may threaten, aggression outside of their frontiers, they believe, pending the establishment of a wider and permanent system of general security, that the disarmament of such nations is essential. They will likewise aid and encourage all other practicable measures which will lighten for peace-loving peoples the crushing burden of armaments.

The Atlantic Charter: Joint Roosevelt–Churchill Declaration, Aug. 14, 1941

Declaration by the United Nations

14 / The governments signatory hereto,

Having subscribed to a common program of purposes and principles embodied in the Joint Declaration of the President of the United States of America and the Prime Minister of the United Kingdom of Great Britain and Northern Ireland, dated August 14, 1941, known as the Atlantic Charter,

Being convinced that complete victory over their enemies is essential to defend life, liberty, independence, and religious freedom, and to preserve human rights and justice in their own lands as well as in other lands, and that they are now engaged in a common struggle against savage and brutal forces seeking to subjugate the world, DECLARE:

1. Each government pledges itself to employ its full resources, military or economic, against those members of the Tripartite Pact and its adherents with which such government is at war.

2. Each government pledges itself to cooperate with the governments signatory hereto and not make a separate armistice or peace with the enemies.

The foregoing declaration may be adhered to by other nations which are, or which may be, rendering material assistance and contributions in the struggle for victory over Hitlerism.

Declaration by the United Nations (nations pledged to cooperation in winning the war against the Axis Powers), Washington, D.C., Jan. 1, 1942

15 / A year ago today the nations resisting a common, barbaric foe were units or small groups, fighting for their existence.

Now, these nations and groups of nations in all the continents of the earth have united. They have formed a great union of humanity, dedicated to the realization of that common program of purposes and principles set forth in the Atlantic Charter, through world-wide victory over their common enemies. Their faith in life, liberty, independence and religious freedom, and in the preservation of human rights and justice in their own lands as well as in other lands, has been given form and substance and power through a great gathering of peoples now know as the United Nations. . . .

When victory comes, we shall stand shoulder to shoulder in seeking to nourish the great ideals for which we fight. It is a worthwhile battle. It will be so recognized through all the ages, even amid the unfortunate peoples who follow false gods today.

We reaffirm our principles. They will bring us to a happier world.

Message to Prime Minister Winston Churchill on the first anniversary of the Atlantic Charter, Aug. 14, 1942

16 / The cause of the United Nations is the cause of youth itself. It is the hope of the new generation—and the generations that are to come—hope for a new life that can be lived in freedom, and justice, and decency. . . .

We of the United Nations have the technical means, the physical resources, and, most of all, the adventurous courage and the vision and the will that are needed to build and sustain the kind of world order which alone can justify the tremendous sacrifices now being made by our youth.

Address to the International Student Assembly, Washington, D.C., Sept. 3, 1942

17 / The unity achieved on the battle line is being earnestly sought in the not less complex problems on a different front. In this as in no previous war men are conscious of the supreme necessity of planning what is to come after—and of carrying forward into peace the common effort which will have brought them victory in the war. They have come to see that the maintenance and safeguarding of peace is the most vital single necessity in the lives of each and all of us.

Our task on this New Year's Day is threefold: first, to press on with the massed forces of free humanity till the present bandit assault upon civilization is completely crushed; second, so to organize relations among nations that forces of barbarism can never again break loose; third, to cooperate to the end that mankind may enjoy in peace and in freedom the unprecedented blessings which Divine Providence through the progress of civilization has put within our reach.

Statement on the maintenance and safeguarding of peace, Jan. 1, 1943

18 / After the first World War we tried to achieve a formula for permanent peace, based on a magnificent idealism. We failed. But, by our failure, we have learned that we cannot maintain peace at this stage of human development by good intentions alone.

Today the United Nations are the mightiest military coalition in history. They represent an overwhelming majority of the population of the world. Bound together in solemn agreement that they themselves will not commit acts of aggression or conquest against any of their neighbors, the United Nations can and must remain united for the maintenance of peace by preventing any attempt to rearm in Germany, in Japan, in Italy, or in any other nation which seeks to violate the Tenth Commandment—"Thou shalt not covet."

There are cynics and skeptics who say it cannot be done. The American people and all the freedom-loving peoples of this earth are now demanding that it must be done. And the will of these people shall prevail.

State of the Union Message, Jan. 7, 1943

19 / Today . . . the whole world is one neighborhood. That is why this war that had its beginnings in seemingly remote areas . . . has spread to every continent, and most of the islands of the sea, involving the lives and liberties of the entire human race. And unless the peace that follows recognizes that the whole world is one neighborhood and does justice to the whole human race, the germs of another world war will remain as a constant threat to mankind.

Address at the White House Correspondents' Association dinner, Washington, D.C., Feb. 12, 1943

20 / Our ultimate objective can be simply stated: It is to build for ourselves, for all men, a world in which each individual human being shall have the opportunity to live out his life in peace; to work productively, earning at least enough for his actual needs and those of his family; to associate with the friends of his choice; to think and worship freely; and to die secure in the knowledge that his children, and their children, shall have the same opportunities.

That objective, as men know from long and bitter experience, will not be easy to achieve. But you and I know, also, that throughout history there has been no more worthwhile, no more inspiring challenge.

That challenge will be met.

You have demonstrated beyond question that free peoples all over the world can agree upon a common course of action and upon common machinery for action. You have brought new hope to the world that, through the establishment of orderly international procedures for the solution of international problems, there will be attained freedom from want and freedom from fear. The United Nations are united in the war against fear and want as solidly and effectively as they are united on the battle front in this world-wide war against aggression.

And we are winning by action and unity.

Address to the delegates to the United Nations Conference on Food and Agriculture, White House, June 7, 1943

21 / There is a longing in the air. It is not a longing to go back to what they call "the good old days." I have distinct reservations as to how good "the good old days" were. I would rather believe that we can achieve new and better days.

Address before the Canadian Parliament, Ottawa, Aug. 25, 1943

22 / It has long been the policy of the government of the United States progressively to reinforce the machinery of self-government in its territories and island possessions. The principles for which we are now fighting require that we should recognize the right of all our citizens—whether continental or overseas—to the greatest possible degree of home rule and also of participation in the benefits and responsibilities of our federal system.

Message to Congress recommending self-government for Puerto Rico, Sept. 28, 1943

23 / When victory comes there can certainly be no secure peace until there is a return of law and order in the oppressed countries, until the peoples of these countries have been restored to a normal, healthy, self-sustaining existence. This means that the more quickly and effectually we apply measures of relief and rehabilitation, the more quickly will our own boys overseas be able to come home.

We have acted together with the other United Nations in harnessing our raw materials, our production, and our other resources to defeat the common enemy. We have worked together with the United Nations in full agreement and action in the fighting on land, on the sea and in the air. We are now about to take an additional step in the combined actions which are necessary to win the war and to build the foundations for a secure peace. . . .

As in most of the difficult and complex things in life, nations will learn to work together only by actually working together. Why not? They have common objectives. It is, therefore, with a lift of hope that we look on the signing of this agreement by all of the United Nations as a means of joining them together still more firmly.

Such is the spirit and such is the positive action of the United Nations at the time when our military power is becoming predominant, when our enemies are being pushed back—all over the world.

In defeat or in victory, the United Nations have never deviated from adherence to the basic principles of freedom, tolerance, independence, and security.

> Address on the signing of the agreement setting up the United Nations Relief and Rehabilitation Administration, Washington, D.C., Nov. 9, 1943

24 / On the threshold of the New Year, as we look toward the tremendous tasks ahead, let us pledge ourselves that this cooperation shall continue both for winning the final victory on the battlefield and for establishing an international organization of all peace-loving nations to maintain peace and security in generations to come.

> Statement on the second anniversary of the Declaration by the United Nations, Jan. 1, 1944

25 / The best interests of each nation, large and small, demand that all freedom-loving nations shall join together in a just and durable system of peace.

> State of the Union Message ("Economic Bill of Rights" speech), Jan. 11, 1944

26 / The maintenance of peace and security must be the joint task of all peace-loving nations. We have, therefore, sought to develop plans for an international organization comprising all such nations. The purpose of the organization would be to maintain peace and security and to assist the creation, through international cooperation, of conditions of stability and well-being necessary for peaceful and friendly relations among nations.

Accordingly, it is our thought that the organization would be a fully representative body with broad responsibilities for promoting and facilitating international cooperation, through such agencies as may be found necessary, to consider and deal with the problems of world relations. It is our further thought that the organization would provide for a council, elected annually by the fully representative body of all nations, which would include the four major nations and a suitable number of other nations. The council would concern itself with peaceful settlement of international disputes and with the prevention of threats to the peace or breaches of the peace.

There would also be an international court of justice to deal primarily with justiciable disputes.

We are not thinking of a superstate with its own police forces and other paraphernalia of coercive power. We are seeking effective agreement and arrangements through which the nations would maintain, according to their capacities, adequate forces to meet the needs of preventing war and of making impossible deliberate preparation for war, and to have such forces available for joint action when necessary.

All this, of course, will become possible once our present enemies are defeated and effective arrangements are made to prevent them from making war again.

Beyond that, the hope of a peaceful and advancing world will rest upon the willingness and ability of the peace-loving nations, large and small, bearing responsibility commensurate with their individual capacities, to work together for the maintenance of peace and security.

Statement regarding plans for an international organization, June 15, 1944

27 / Not until this generation . . . have people here and elsewhere been compelled more and more to widen the orbit of their vision to include every part of the world. It has been a wrench perhaps—but a very necessary one.

It is good that we are all getting that broader vision. For we shall need it after the war. The isolationists and ostriches who plagued our thinking before Pearl Harbor are becoming extinct. The American people now know that all nations of the world—large and small—will have to play their appropriate part in keeping the peace by force, and in deciding peacefully the disputes which might lead to war.

We all know how truly the world has become one.

Acceptance speech by radio to the Democratic National Convention in Chicago from a naval base on the Pacific Coast, July 20, 1944

28 / The principle of the sovereign equality of peace-loving nations, irrespective of size and power, should indeed constitute the foundation of any future international organization for the maintenance of peace and security.

Remarks to the new Chilean Ambassador, Washington, D.C., Oct. 5, 1944

29 / What is now being won in battle must not be lost by lack of vision or by lack of faith or by division among ourselves and our Allies.

We must and we will continue to be united with our Allies in a powerful world organization which is ready and able to keep the peace— if necessary by force.

To provide that assurance of international security is the policy, the effort, and the obligation of this administration.

We owe it to our posterity, we owe it to our heritage of freedom, we owe it to our God, to devote the rest of our lives and all of our capabilities to the building of a solid durable structure of world peace.

Campaign radio address, White House, Oct. 5, 1944

30 / The projected international organization has for its primary purpose the maintenance of international peace and security and the creation of the conditions that make for peace. . . .

It represents, therefore, a major objective for which this war is being fought, and as such, it inspires the highest hopes of the millions of fathers and mothers whose sons and daughters are engaged in the terrible struggle and suffering of war.

The projected general organization may be regarded as the keystone of the arch and will include within its framework a number of specialized economic and social agencies now existing or to be established.

The task of planning the great design of security and peace has been well begun. It now remains for the nations to complete the structure in a spirit of constructive purpose and mutual confidence.

Statement on the completion of the Dumbarton Oaks conversations on international organization, Oct. 9, 1944

31 / When the first World War was ended . . . I believed—I believe now —that enduring peace in the world has not a chance unless this nation . . . is willing to cooperate in winning it and maintaining it. I thought back in those days of 1918 and 1919—and I know now—that we have to back our American words with American deeds.

A quarter of a century ago we helped to save our freedom, but we failed to organize the kind of world in which future generations could live in freedom. Opportunity knocks again. There is no guarantee that it will knock a third time. . . .

The leaders of this nation have always held that concern for our national security does not end at our borders. President Monroe and every American President following him were prepared to use force, if necessary, to assure the independence of other American nations threatened by aggressors from across the seas.

The principle has not changed, though the world has. Wars are no longer fought from horseback, or from the decks of sailing ships.

It was with recognition of that fact that in 1933 we took, as the basis for our foreign relations, the Good Neighbor policy—the principle of the neighbor who, resolutely respecting himself, equally respects the rights of others.

We and the other American republics have made the Good Neighbor policy real in this hemisphere. It is my conviction that this policy can be, and should be, made universal. . . .

The power which this nation has attained—the moral, the political, the economic, and the military power—has brought to us the responsibility, and with it the opportunity, for leadership in the community of nations. In our own best interest, and in the name of peace and humanity, this nation cannot, must not, and will not shirk that responsibility. . . .

Our objective . . . is to complete the organization of the United Nations without delay and before hostilities actually cease.

Peace, like war, can succeed only where there is a will to enforce it, and where there is available power to enforce it.

The Council of the United Nations must have the power to act quickly and decisively to keep the peace by force, if necessary. A policeman would not be a very effective policeman if, when he saw a felon break into a house, he had to go to the Town Hall and call a town meeting to issue a warrant before the felon could be arrested.

It is clear that, if the world organization is to have any reality at all, our representative must be endowed in advance by the people themselves, by constitutional means through their representatives in the Congress, with authority to act.

If we do not catch the international felon when we have our hands on him, if we let him get away with this loot because the Town Council has not passed an ordinance authorizing his arrest, then we are not doing our share to prevent another world war. The people of the nation want their government to act, and not merely to talk, whenever and wherever there is a threat to world peace.

We cannot attain our great objectives by ourselves. Never again, after cooperating with other nations in a world war to save our way of life, can we wash our hands of maintaining the peace for which we fought. . . .

The peace structure which we are building must depend on foundations that go deep into the soil of men's faith and men's hearts—otherwise it is worthless. Only the unflagging will of men can preserve it.

No President of the United States can make the American contribution to preserve the peace without the constant, alert, and conscious collaboration of the American people.

Only the determination of the people to use the machinery gives worth to the machinery.

We believe that the American people have already made up their minds on this great issue; and this administration has been able to press forward confidently with its plans.

The very fact that we are now at work on the organization of the peace proves that the great nations are committed to trust in each other. Put this proposition any way you will, it is bound to come out the same way; we either work with the other great nations, or we might some day have to fight them.

The kind of world order which we, the peace-loving nations, must achieve, must depend essentially on friendly human relations, on acquaintance, on tolerance, on unassailable sincerity and good will and good faith. We have achieved that relationship to a remarkable degree in our dealings with our Allies in this war—as the events of the war have proved.

It is a new thing in human history for allies to work together, as we have done—so closely, so harmoniously and effectively in the fighting of a war, and—at the same time—in the building of the peace.

If we fail to maintain that relationship in the peace—if we fail to expand it and strengthen it—then there will be no lasting peace.

Address before the Foreign Policy Association, New York City, Oct. 21, 1944

32 / All around us we see an unfinished world—a world of awakened peoples struggling to set themselves on the path of civilization—people struggling everywhere to achieve a higher cultural and material standard of living.

I say we must wage the coming battle for America and civilization on a scale worthy of the way that we have unitedly waged the battles against tyranny and reaction, and wage it through all the difficulties and disappointments that may ever clog the wheels of progress.

And I say that we must wage it in association with the United Nations with whom we have stood and fought—with that association ever growing.

Campaign address, Boston, Mass., Nov. 4, 1944

33 / In the field of foreign policy, we propose to stand together with the United Nations not for the war alone but for the victory for which the war is fought.

It is not only a common danger which unites us but a common hope. Ours is an association not of governments but of peoples—and the peoples' hope is peace.

State of the Union Message, Jan. 6, 1945

34 / The Crimean Conference [1945] was a successful effort by the three leading nations to find a common ground for peace. It spells the end of the system of unilateral action and exclusive alliances and spheres of influence and balances of power and all the other expedients which have been tried for centuries—and have failed.

Report to Congress on the Yalta (Crimea) Conference, March 1, 1945

35 / We, as Americans, do not choose to deny our responsibility.

Nor do we intend to abandon our determination that, within the lives of our children and our children's children, there will not be a third world war.

We seek peace—enduring peace. More than an end to war, we want an end to the beginnings of all wars—yes, an end to this brutal, inhuman and thoroughly impractical method of settling the differences between governments.

Final message, written April 11, 1945, for the observance of Jefferson Day, April 13, 1945
(The President died on April 12)

Appendix A

First Inaugural Address, March 4, 1933

I am certain that my fellow Americans expect that on my induction into the Presidency I will address them with a candor and a decision which the present situation of our nation impels. This is preeminently the time to speak the truth, the whole truth, frankly and boldly. Nor need we shrink from honestly facing conditions in our country today. This great nation will endure as it has endured, will revive and will prosper. So, first of all, let me assert my firm belief that the only thing we have to fear is fear itself—nameless, unreasoning, unjustified terror which paralyzes needed efforts to convert retreat into advance. In every dark hour of our national life a leadership of frankness and vigor has met with that understanding and support of the people themselves which is essential to victory. I am convinced that you will again give that support to leadership in these critical days.

In such a spirit on my part and on yours we face our common difficulties. They concern, thank God, only material things. Values have shrunken to fantastic levels; taxes have risen; our ability to pay has fallen; government of all kinds is faced by serious curtailment of income; the means of exchange are frozen in the currents of trade; the withered leaves of industrial enterprise lie on every side; farmers find no markets for their produce; the savings of many years in thousands of families are gone.

More important, a host of unemployed citizens face the grim problem of existence, and an equally great number toil with little return. Only a foolish optimist can deny the dark realities of the moment.

Yet our distress comes from no failure of substance. We are stricken by no plague of locusts. Compared with the perils which our forefathers conquered because they believed and were not afraid, we have still much to be thankful for. Nature still offers her bounty and human efforts have multiplied it. Plenty is at at our doorstep, but a generous use of it languishes in the very sight of the supply. Primarily this is because the rulers of the exchange of mankind's goods have failed, through their own stubbornness and their own incompetence, have admitted their failure, and abdicated. Practices of the unscrupulous money changers stand indicted in the court of public opinion, rejected by the hearts and minds of men.

True they have tried, but their efforts have been cast in the pattern of an outworn tradition. Faced by failure of credit they have proposed only the lending of more money. Stripped of the lure of profit by which to induce our people to follow their false leadership, they have resorted to exhortations, pleading tearfully for restored confidence. They know only the rules of a generation of self-seekers. They have no vision, and when there is no vision the people perish.

The money changers have fled from their high seats in the temple of our civilization. We may now restore that temple to the ancient truths. The measure of the restoration lies in the extent to which we apply social values more noble than mere monetary profit.

Happiness lies not in the mere possession of money; it lies in the joy of achievement, in the thrill of creative effort. The joy and moral stimulation of work no longer must be forgotten in the mad chase of evanescent profits. These dark days will be worth all they cost us if they teach us that our true destiny is not to be ministered unto but to minister to ourselves and to our fellow men.

Recognition of the falsity of material wealth as the standard of success goes hand in hand with the abandonment of the false belief that public office and high political position are to be valued only by the standards of pride of place and personal profit; and there must be an end to a conduct in banking and in business which too often has given to a sacred trust the likeness of callous and selfish wrongdoing. Small wonder that confidence languishes, for it thrives only on honesty, on honor, on the sacredness of obligations, on faithful protection, on unselfish performance; without them it cannot live.

Restoration calls, however, not for changes in ethics alone. This nation asks for action, and action now.

Our greatest primary task is to put people to work. This is no unsolvable problem if we face it wisely and courageously. It can be accomplished in part by direct recruiting by the Government itself, treating the task as we would treat the emergency of a war, but at the same time, through this employment, accomplishing greatly needed projects to stimulate and reorganize the use of our natural resources.

Hand in hand with this we must frankly recognize the overbalance of population in our industrial centers and, by engaging on a national scale in a redistribution, endeavor to provide a better use of the land for those best fitted for the land. The task can be helped by definite efforts to raise the values of agricultural products and with this the power to purchase the output of our cities. It can be helped by preventing realistically the tragedy of the growing loss through foreclosure of our small homes and our farms. It can be helped by insistence that the federal, state, and local governments act forthwith on the demand that their cost be drastically reduced. It can be helped by the unifying of relief activities which today are often scattered, uneconomical, and unequal. It can be helped by national planning for and supervision of all forms of transportation and of communications and other utilities which have a definitely public character. There are many ways in which it can be helped, but it can never be helped merely by talking about it. We must act and act quickly.

Finally, in our progress toward a resumption of work we require two safeguards against a return of the evils of the old order: there must be a strict supervision of all banking and credits and investments, so that there will be an end to speculation with other people's money; and there must be provision for an adequate but sound currency.

There are the lines of attack. I shall presently urge upon a new Congress in special session detailed measures for their fulfillment, and I shall seek the immediate assistance of the several states.

Through this program of action we address ourselves to putting our own national house in order and making income balance outgo. Our international trade relations, though vastly important, are in point of time and necessity secondary to the establishment of a sound national economy. I favor as a practical policy the putting of first things first. I shall spare no effort to restore world trade by international economic readjustment, but the emergency at home cannot wait on that accomplishment.

The basic thought that guides these specific means of national recovery is not narrowly nationalistic. It is the insistence, as a first consideration, upon the interdependence of the various elements in all parts of the United States—a recognition of the old and permanently important manifestation of the American spirit of the pioneer. It is the way to recovery. It is the immediate way. It is the strongest assurance that the recovery will endure.

In the field of world policy I would dedicate this nation to the policy of the good neighbor—the neighbor who resolutely respects himself and, because he does so, respects the rights of others—the neighbor who respects his obligations and respects the sanctity of his agreements in and with a world of neighbors.

If I read the temper of our people correctly, we now realize as we have never realized before our interdependence on each other; that we cannot merely take but we must give as well; that if we are to go forward, we must move as a trained and loyal army willing to sacrifice for the good of a common discipline, because without such discipline no progress is made, no leadership becomes effective. We are, I know, ready and willing to submit our lives and property to such discipline, because it makes possible a leadership which aims at a larger good. This I propose to offer, pledging that the larger purposes will bind upon us all as a sacred obligation with a unity of duty hitherto evoked only in time of armed strife.

With this pledge taken, I assume unhesitatingly the leadership of this great army of our people dedicated to a disciplined attack upon our common problems.

Action in this image and to this end is feasible under the form of government which we have inherited from our ancestors. Our Constitution is so simple and practical that it is possible always to meet extraordinary needs by changes in emphasis and arrangement without loss of essential form. That is why our constitutional system has proved itself the most superbly enduring political mechanism the modern world has produced. It has met every stress of vast expansion of territory, of foreign wars, of bitter internal strife, of world relations.

It is to be hoped that the normal balance of executive and legislative authority may be wholly adequate to meet the unprecedented task before us. But it may be that an unprecedented demand and need for undelayed action may call for temporary departure from that normal balance of public procedure.

I am prepared under my constitutional duty to recommend the measures that a stricken nation in the midst of a stricken world may require. These measures, or such other measures as the Congress may build out of its experience and wisdom, I shall seek, within my constitutional authority, to bring to speedy adoption.

But in the event that the Congress shall fail to take one of these two courses, and in the event that the national emergency is still critical, I shall not evade the clear course of duty that will then confront me. I shall ask the Congress for the one remaining instrument to meet the crisis—broad Executive power to wage a war against the emergency, as great as the power that would be given to me if we were in fact invaded by a foreign foe.

For the trust reposed in me I will return the courage and the devotion that befit the time. I can do no less.

We face the arduous days that lie before us in the warm courage of the national unity; with the clear consciousness of seeking old and precious moral values; with the clean satisfaction that comes from the stern performance of duty by old and young alike. We aim at the assurance of a rounded and permanent national life.

We do not distrust the future of essential democracy. The people of the United States have not failed. In their need they have registered a mandate that they want direct, vigorous action. They have asked for discipline and direction under leadership. They have made me the present instrument of their wishes. In the spirit of the gift I take it.

In this dedication of a nation we humbly ask the blessing of God. May He protect each and every one of us. May He guide me in the days to come.

Appendix B

Final Message, Written April 11, 1945, for
the Observance of Jefferson Day on April 13
[The President died on April 12, 1945]

Americans are gathered together this evening in communities all over the country to pay tribute to the living memory of Thomas Jefferson— one of the greatest of all democrats; and I want to make it clear that I am spelling that word "democrats" with a small "*d*."

I wish I had the power, just for this evening, to be present at all of these gatherings.

In this historic year, more than ever before, we do well to consider the character of Thomas Jefferson as an American citizen of the world.

As Minister to France, then as our first Secretary of State and as our third President, Jefferson was instrumental in the establishment of the United States as a vital factor in international affairs.

It was he who first sent our Navy into far-distant waters to defend our rights. And the promulgation of the Monroe Doctrine was the logical development of Jefferson's far-seeing foreign policy.

Today this nation, which Jefferson helped so greatly to build, is playing a tremendous part in the battle for the rights of man all over the world.

Today we are part of the vast Allied force—a force composed of flesh and blood and steel and spirit—which is today destroying the makers of war, the breeders of hate, in Europe and in Asia.

In Jefferson's time our Navy consisted of only a handful of frigates . . . but that tiny navy taught nations across the Atlantic that piracy in the Mediterranean—acts of aggression against peaceful commerce, and the enslavement of their crews—was one of those things which, among neighbors, simply was not done.

Today we have learned in the agony of war that great power involves great responsibility. Today we can no more escape the consequences of German and Japanese aggression than could we avoid the consequences of attacks by the Barbary corsairs a century and a half before.

We as Americans do not choose to deny our responsibility.

Nor do we intend to abandon our determination that, within the lives of our children and our children's children, there will not be a third world war.

We seek peace—enduring peace. More than an end to war, we want an end to the beginnings of all wars—yes, an end to this brutal, inhuman, and thoroughly impractical method of settling the differences between governments.

The once powerful, malignant Nazi state is crumbling, the Japanese war lords are receiving, in their own homeland, the retribution for which they asked when they attacked Pearl Harbor.

But the mere conquest of our enemies is not enough.

We must go on to do all in our power to conquer the doubts and the fears, the ignorance and the greed, which made this horror possible.

Thomas Jefferson, himself a distinguished scientist, once spoke of the "brotherly spirit of science, which unites into one family all its votaries of whatever grade, and however widely dispersed throughout the different quarters of the globe."

Today science has brought all the different quarters of the globe so close together that it is impossible to isolate them one from another.

Today we are faced with the preeminent fact that, if civilization is to survive, we must cultivate the science of human relationships—the ability of all peoples, of all kinds, to live together and work together, in the same world, at peace.

Let me assure you that my hand is the steadier for the work that is to be done, that I move more firmly into the task, knowing that you— millions and millions of you—are joined with me in the resolve to make this work endure.

The work, my friends, is peace. More than an end to this war—an end to the beginnings of all wars. Yes, an end, forever, to this impractical, unrealistic settlement of disputes between governments by the mass killing of peoples.

Today as we move against the terrible scourge of war—as we go forward toward the greatest contribution that any generation of human beings can make in this world—the contribution of lasting peace—I ask you to keep up your faith. I measure the sound, solid achievement that can be made at this time by the straight-edge of your own confidence and your resolve. And to you, and to all Americans who dedicate themselves with us to the making of an abiding peace, I say:

The only limit to our realization of tomorrow will be our doubts of today. Let us move forward with strong and active faith.

Index

NOTE: Numbers in index refer to chapter number and item number, not to page number.